Writers of Italy Series

*General Editor*
C. P. Brand
Professor of Italian
University of
Edinburgh

# 7

CASTIGLIONE

© J.R. Woodhouse 1978
Edinburgh University Press
22 George Square, Edinburgh

ISBN O 85224 346 4

Set in Monotype Bembo
by Speedspools, Edinburgh
and printed in Great Britain by
R. & R. Clark Ltd,
Edinburgh

\*

Baldesar Castiglione

Edinburgh University Press

*Baldesar*
# CASTIGLIONE

A reassessment of *The Courtier*

## J. R. WOODHOUSE

*

# Contents

To the memory of John Mathias,
a most courteous gentleman

# Preface

Generations of students have managed, by dint of studying critical accounts and précis of Castiglione's masterpiece, to avoid reading what, in franker moments, they will confess to be a ponderous tome from which they derive little pleasure. A recent straw vote among university teachers in Britain revealed a similar, if minority, prejudice against this most widely-known least-read book of the Renaissance. There is no argument about the usefulness of the *Cortegiano* as a source of background knowledge for a whole range of Renaissance custom and culture, but there has long been a strong feeling that this is drawing-room art, the exaltation of the petty and the trivial, of what Samuel Johnson called the 'minuter decencies and inferior duties'.

I first read the *Cortegiano* twenty years ago and began lecturing on the book four years later. Looking back at the yellowing sheets of those lecture notes now, I find myself staring in disbelief at the sarcastic opinions I there expressed about its author's lack of *engagement*, his uncommitted attitude towards practices, events and fashions which, I then felt, should have aroused his indignation, sorrow or scorn. It may be that the *Cortegiano* is a book intrinsically unappreciable by the young, and that one needs to experience, as its author did, more of the Aristotelean cycle of development before the awareness dawns that Castiglione's solution to the dilemma in which he and his contemporaries found themselves was the only one possible.

In one sense, then, this is a personal reassessment, which has been continuing for many years. But that is a trivial consideration; more important, I hope that the opinions expressed here may persuade colleagues and pupils alike to return to the original text and view it in a different light, less aesthetic, perhaps, but none the worse for that. At the same time the monograph, like the others in the series, is also aimed at a wider public, not necessarily expert in Italian language and literature (all quotations, for instance, are translated), and it is hoped that the central chapters (3-6) contain enough information culled from the text itself to illustrate the content of Castiglione's book without falling into the trap of allowing further generations of specialist students to treat them as substitutes for the original.

References to the *Cortegiano*, unless otherwise stated, will be made to Bruno Maier's edition as reprinted in 1964. This will be referred to as the 'final' or 'definitive' edition, and the traditionally accepted Book and chapter numbers (such as II, xxvi) will be used to pin-point such references. For quotations from Ghino Ghinassi's edition of the earlier (and previously unpublished) version, the *Seconda redazione del Cortegiano*, reference will be made to his page numbers, in order to avoid any possible confusion with the definitive edition, since the chapter numbers of the *Seconda redazione* do not, and are not meant to correspond with those of the definitive edition. Other editions are listed in the *Bibliography*.

Quotations are, for the most part, given in English translations, but difficult, potentially controversial and significantly important words have been inserted (usually in brackets) after their translation. All translations are my own.

Wherever feasible, primary sources have been used to illustrate the vicissitudes of Castiglione's life as well as the careers of other Renaissance figures, from Leonbattista Alberti to Torquato Tasso. Where possible, reasonably accessible editions of the original texts have been cited, but, in the case of Castiglione's own correspondence, the most substantial collection of letters still remains the imperfect eighteenth-century edition of P. Serassi. Unpublished letters still make seemingly casual, certainly sporadic, appearances in articles and rare editions in Italy, and it is to be hoped that an adequate edition of this most important *epistolario* may finally be coordinated and published, as promised in G. La Rocca's recent article (see *Bibliography*). Abbreviated references to Serassi, to standard editions and to other critical works are included in the body of the text in order to avoid a proliferation of footnotes. Full details of such books and articles are listed in the select bibliography.

I should like to pay tribute here to two particular critics of Castiglione and his work. The first is Vittorio Cian. Between his first edition of the *Cortegiano* (1894) and his fourth and final edition (1947) lies over half a century of painstaking research and erudition, and no one can now work on Castiglione without paying his fee to Cian's scholarship. The second critic is Julia Cartwright, whose monumental work on Castiglione, unjustly condemned by Cian as *mediocrissima*, has received little acclaim in Italy. Yet it remains true that only in *her* two volumes may one read transcriptions of some of Castiglione's most important letters, and her research in archives on the historical background and on biographical details is paralleled only by that of Cian, whose discoveries she complements. Her faults were those of her age – Edwardian value judgements on events which need viewing perhaps with greater objectivity. It might also be argued that for too long the weight of Cian's influential criticism imposed *one* set of interpretative ideas on Castiglione scholarship, until, in fact, his final monograph was reviewed in 1952. But the benefits of both outweigh any slight disadvantage and to both I am indebted.

I wish to express my thanks and gratitude to Professor C. P. Brand for his invaluable help and encouragement throughout the production of the present volume. I am also grateful to Professor T. G. Griffith for his expert advice and critical comments and to Mr D. J. B. Robey for his constructive and tasteful criticism of the first draft of the mono-graph. They are in large part to be thanked for any merit the work may have; for its defects I alone am responsible. Further thanks are due to Professor Conor Fahy who generously made available to me a personal copy of his doctorate thesis. I must also thank my wife for her moral support and practical help throughout. To the Faculty Board of Medieval and Modern Languages of Oxford University I am indebted for the sabbatical leave and the funds they have made available for me to complete this work.

J.R.W., *Oxford, June* 1978

# Introduction

To reassess a work of art on this, the fifth centenary of its author's birth, and after so many earlier volumes of critical appraisal, might seem to be either superfluous or, worse, arrogant. There has never been a consensus on Castiglione's purpose in writing the *Cortegiano*, and, fortunately, its many facets and subtleties will prevent any one assessment from ever being accepted as normative. There have been four major interpretations. The first, and most obvious, is that this is a rule-book of behaviour and practice for the creation of a Renaissance courtier, a purpose borne out by Castiglione's declared intention in Book I, chapter xii, 'to form, in words, the perfect courtier'. A second interpretation of the work is that it provides an idealised portrait, modelled on noble social gatherings at Urbino, of Renaissance court society. This, too, finds confirmation in the introductory letter which precedes the main text. A third school of criticism has described the book as a moral treatise – an unhelpfully imprecise definition, based either on the many injunctions to honest and honourable behaviour in which the work abounds, or on the rather self-evident notion that this is a book of '*mores*' or manners. Finally the *Cortegiano* has been seen as a work of art in its own right, and one with only the most tenuous connection with the practical world. That myth of non-commitment has been propagated largely through the critical authority once widely exerted in Italy by Giuseppe Prezzolini and Giuseppe Toffanin.

One further aspect of Castiglione's fortune which has undoubtedly influenced critical interpretations of the book has been its popularity outside Italy. Leonard Opdycke's translation (1901) adequately documents the many editions of the book which preceded his own and this reference to his volume may, for the moment, suffice for my purpose. Such popularity could itself have caused Castiglione's intentions to be misunderstood. Inevitably, and with justification, his name and work have been associated with the growing civility of European society in the years following the publication of his *Cortegiano*. In an essay, significantly entitled 'Italy and barbarian Europe', Denys Hay goes as far as to consider the book as the most important single contribution to the diffusion inside Europe of Italian Renaissance values, an opinion reiterated in his study *The Italian Renaissance in its Historical Back-ground*. The *Cortegiano*'s impact in England was undeniable. Sir Thomas Hoby's famous translation, which dates from 1561, was twice reprinted during the following fifty years, and has achieved several remarkable reprintings since then, including three in our own century, the latest in 1978. Many Latin versions, in use in England and throughout Europe, also followed the original publication. In Spain and France equally famous translations (noted in my *Bibliography*) preceded that of Hoby. The popularity of this kind of etiquette book is further evidenced by the acclaim given to Sir Thomas Elyot's *The Boke named the Gouernour*, which in 1531 already showed the influence of similar ideas to Castiglione's and which ran into seven editions between 1531 and 1580.

In different periods and in other countries, then, Castiglione's volume *did* provide a good answer to the ever-wealthier society which was demanding instant culture, elegance, social grace. Denys Hay says that the treatise 'exactly expressed what was most easily assimilated by the northern world' (*Italian Renaissance*, p.197). What was readily assimilable was the elegant sophistication of social be-haviour and conversation (a word first documented in the sense of *conversazione* in 1580). Unquestionably it did prove a splendid vehicle for transmitting such fashionable topics as Neoplatonism, the en-comium of wit and wisdom, the celebration of martial prowess and chivalrous accomplishments, the debate on feminism and so forth. The 'barbarian' north drank in that new knowledge and that new refinement with thirsty eagerness, and the book's importance in dis-seminating such material is clear. Such universal favour and such fashionability, however, have inevitably added to the impression that this was a precept book of superficial and cosmetic value, and may have further distracted from an accurate assessment of its author's true purpose.

Twenty years ago, Erich Loos, in the best monograph so far to appear on Castiglione, expressed regret that the demands of con-temporary criticism still remained unsatisfied by modern research on the *Cortegiano*. His hopes have been in part answered, particularly by the work of Ghino Ghinassi and Piero Floriani in Italy, and by some important items published in America, not a few of which owe their inspiration to Loos himself. Yet none have so far underlined an important consideration: survival and security in a hostile world. Observers fortunate enough to live in modern and relatively settled societies tend to lose sight of that fundamental need, which in our century has been replaced by the relative fripperies of career ambitions, social-climbing, money-grubbing, or, for the fortunate, by indulgence in pastimes and expertise in gentle hobbies. This monograph does not seek to exclude the conclusions reached by so many expert researchers, but it will have more of what Loos termed 'the very strong pragmatic interest prevalent among Anglo-Saxon critics of the *Cortegiano*'.

I believe then, that although the practicality of the work is elegantly disguised, the *Cortegiano* is functional in several senses. In the first place, Castiglione was writing a handbook for survival in the only civilised, but non-cloistered environment visible to him in that very uncertain political period. Secondly, following the illustrious precedents of great Classical pedagogues, he was offering advice to the world's leaders, particularly to the Emperor Charles v, in the way he thought that Aristotle, for instance, had offered advice to Alexander the Great – the tradition was one current since the Middle Ages and is visible in works such as the *De regimine principum* of Aquinas or Dante's *De monarchia*. In the third place, he wished in his final rewriting after 1524, to consolidate a reputation as a wise man, (not the mere preceptor of frivolity) and one worthy of an eventually high position in the Church, preferably a cardinalate but perhaps not even excluding the papacy. These three main considerations are surrounded by other minor preoccupations, but they hang together, lending added power one to the other. Practical survival was the obvious essential first step; to influence world leaders was to exert some sort of control over the environment in which one lived; and to become a cardinal was effectively to control one's destiny and achieve what was potentially the greatest tranquillity for that turbulent period of history.

To describe the work as being 'elegantly disguised' may in itself be a misleading statement; practical considerations influenced Castiglione's style and language, too. He was as aware as Ascoli was, three and a half centuries later, of the need to make his language truly national in order to reach the maximum audience. His prose is also the most elegant Italian written at this period; he knew full well the value of clothing usefulness with beauty. Beauty of style and language was as utilitarian as the message presented; the added advantage of elegance gave his prose the possibility of conveying its advice to persons who might never have opened his book had it been in an uncouth style or format, or even binding. Indeed, his instructions on the final publication include minute details on the elegance of the binding of the more important presentation copies of the work. The quality of his prose and the beauty of the book's cover helped give his work the access essential to present its information to the proper authority; the Emperor Charles v kept a copy of the *Cortegiano*, along with the Bible, at his bedside.

What follow are, in a sense, *suggerimenti per una lettura*, and the central core of this monograph will follow the course of Castiglione's own thought, superimposing upon it comments 'suggested' by the new approach. That commentary, while not distorting or ignoring the importance of major topics, which will be given their individual contextual explanations, will emphasise their relevance, artistic and practical, to the book as a whole. To put all his information across, Castiglione will use the principles of Aristotle, not the Aristotle of the *Metaphysics*, whom theological tradition, following the Scholastics, had been using in order to 'prove' supernatural theories, and whose name had become synonymous with abstraction, but the Aristotle of the *Politics* and the *Ethics*, whose empirical observations still astonish by their clarity and usefulness. Castiglione's recommended optimum will be the Golden Mean which Aristotle so favoured. His Ciceronian dialogue form, unlike the Platonic dialogue, will allow him to posit extremes from which he intends his reader to derive the *norm* of behaviour or action, either implicitly, having taught the general lesson of the Mean, or explicitly, by allowing the *via media*, in the form of a given argument, to be seen as the more reasonable alternative.

In order to demonstrate the book's practicality (perhaps the only *practical* application of the conclusions which Francesco Guicciardini was contemporaneously reaching in his researches into history and society) something must be said about the events which conditioned its composition. These events are discussed in the opening chapter, which, while dealing in the main with Castiglione's biography, also provides an opportunity to describe the very complex series of diplomatic intrigues which filled that period of history and with which Castiglione and his patrons were associated. It was a period when, as Carlo Dionisotti has said, all Italian culture was irresistibly centred on a court, and the whole of Castiglione's life was spent in a court environment. The second chapter here is concerned with placing the *Cortegiano*, which was published after over a century of important educational reform, in its pedagogical context. The rest of the monograph is concerned with specific problems raised in the *Cortegiano*, and follows the scheme laid down by Castiglione –

chapters three to six treat of his Books I–IV. The Conclusion reinforces the usefulness of the treatise for the ambitious courtier: by
following the type of precept which Castiglione enjoined, some men
had become popes; by ignoring them others had ended as cloistered
or embittered exiles from society. The Appendix contains a brief
account of his minor works.

# 1. Life and Experience

When we consider the fifty years of Castiglione's life, we may, with good reason, wonder how this sensitive, intelligent and cultured man was able to tolerate, for three decades, the petty irritations, despotic impositions and harsh injustices he had to suffer in his role as court diplomat. An analysis of his life will reveal only a few years of what is generally acknowledged as happiness. For the civilised individual of the Italian Renaissance, happiness had a range of meanings: political power, ecclesiastical preferment, acquisition of wealth or territory, artistic achievement, acclaim by fellow-scholars and so on. Probably it is impossible to speak of a general concept of happiness at that time, unless one defines it negatively as the absence of pain and suffering. But most men shared a common, and wellnigh impossible, aspiration: the desire for tranquillity. Few men would have achieved both good fortune and tranquillity during the half-century from 1478 to 1529.

Even by Renaissance standards, many of the outstanding occurrences in Castiglione's life were tragic. Three in particular dealt him severe blows. The first was, in 1499, the occupation of Milan by the French troops under Louis XII, just five years after Charles VIII's abortive expedition. The invasion coincided with the death of Castiglione's father, and marked the beginning of centuries of foreign domination or despoliation of the peninsula. The second event was the death, in 1508, of his well-loved prince and patron Guidubaldo da Montefeltro, Duke of Urbino. He was thirty-six, and his death effectively ruined the splendour and potential tranquillity of the Urbino court, which Castiglione had gone to considerable lengths to reach and which had provided him with much enjoyment of a more positive kind. He was in consequence forced out into the much fiercer world of international diplomacy, involving him particularly (and immediately) in the intrigues of Pope Julius II (whose vicious nephew, Francesco Maria della Rovere, was Guidubaldo's designated successor). The third event was the sack of Rome in 1527 by the German, and largely Lutheran, mercenaries of the Emperor, Charles V of Spain. That act of barbarity changed for ever the character of the papal Curia, and helped in the creation of new religious barriers and antagonisms throughout Europe.

Each of these tragic events came at a point in Castiglione's life when he might reasonably have been expecting a prolonged period of happiness, or at least peace of mind and tranquillity. Other tragedies marked the intervening years. Notable among them were the deaths of his great friend Falcone, of his younger brother Girolamo (for whom he had such great hopes) within the same twelvemonth, and the youthful deaths of his wife Ippolita and of his friend Raphael. And already by the age of twenty-one, Baldesar had had to undertake the responsibility of becoming head of his family on the death of his father. In the prevailing air of uncertainty about his own or the peninsula's future in those troubled times, Baldesar showed a strength of character and an ability to rise above misfortune, which his contemporaries admired and which one of the greatest courtiers of all, Torquato Tasso, was later to acknowledge and eulogise.

The impotence of the individual in such an uncertain and changing world may even have led him to aspire not simply to tranquillity, but also to an ambition to attain the highest possible offices of power, on the assumption that the one guarantee a man had of achieving tranquillity, at a period when the only constant was inconstancy, was to control the destiny of others who might otherwise control him. Castiglione had glorious precedents in this regard; Pope Pius II was one such example. As Enea Silvio Piccolomini, he had succeeded, notwithstanding the hardships and humiliations endured during years of service at several courts, and despite his initial support for a lost cause (that of the *conciliatoristi*), in attaining *the* highest office, granted that not many were born to inherit the alternative highest office of Emperor. By 1529 Castiglione's position was not so different from that of Piccolomini's in 1458. He was in a key diplomatic position, the potential reconciler of Pope and Emperor, and the future scourge of heretics (his letter attacking Alfonso de Valdés was prophetic of polemics which were to last for the next fifty years, and was itself an unusually explicit and committed document for him). He had been newly elected Bishop of Avila, and, when he died, in February that year, at fifty-one years of age, he might have expected to live on into a period of wealth, independence and power beyond the wildest dreams of his youth. That he was moving towards a deliberate end is evident from some of his letters home. One, dated 4 August 1524, states the hope that his appointment as Nuncio may bring him long-awaited tranquillity (*la quiete mia*) (Gorni, *Lettere*, p.89), a notion confirmed sixteen days later in another letter home in which there are

similar hopes expressed. Erich Loos (*Studien*, p.45) quotes Maffei's
*Annali di Mantova* to the effect that the Pope had already considered
making Castiglione a cardinal, and it will be recalled that Castiglione's
successor in Spain, concluding the alliance between Pope and
Emperor, carried out the plan long negotiated and engineered by
Baldesar, and won for himself the plaudits and honours which,
morally, belonged to his predecessor.

Castiglione was born at Casatico, near Mantua, in 1478. He came of
an ancient and noble family which had sold its original estates north
of Milan and acquired large tracts of land around Casatico. This was
Gonzaga territory, and the Castiglione family were related to the
ruling house, were favoured at court, exempt from taxes and dues,
and the possessors of a large town house in Mantua itself. Baldesar's
father, Cristoforo, was a particular favourite of the then Marchese,
Francesco Gonzaga. Although Baldesar's own experiences of
Gonzaga patronage were not always happy, Francesco's wife,
Isabella d'Este, was always willing to lend a sympathetic ear. She
seems to have been a great civilising influence on the military-minded
Francesco, and Castiglione pays her some pretty compliments in the
*Cortegiano*, sentiments with which Ariosto concurs in his epic.
   Mantua and Milan were rich and powerful centres which, by their
patronage, attracted some of the choicest spirits of the age. It was to
Milan, at its most brilliant under the aegis of Ludovico Sforza, *il Moro*,
and the influence of his wife Beatrice d'Este, that Castiglione went, as
a youth, to complete his education. Documents about this early
period in his life are lamentably few. He would have been able, while
staying with a relative, the noble Milanese jurist, Giovanni Stefano da
Castiglione, to frequent the Sforza court at a time when it was playing
host to a figure like Leonardo and to interesting men such as Bramante,
Vincenzo Calmeta, Cristoforo Romano, Jacopo di San Secondo and
Serafino Aquilano. In addition, Giovanni Stefano, who had been
ambassador of Ludovico Sforza to Naples, Florence, and Venice,
would add his own cosmopolitan culture to that present in Milan.
Perhaps through his guardian, Baldesar might have absorbed the ideas
associated with Medicean Florence. Those ideas were later to emerge
in his *Tirsi* and *Cortegiano*, as echoes of Poliziano's *Stanze*, or the
*Sylvae*, as well as reflections of Neoplatonic speculation then current.
Whatever the influences, Giovanni Stefano was able to write to the
young man's father in February 1499, describing his protégé's progress at court and saying how highly he was regarded in Milan (the

letter is published in Julia Cartwright's *The Perfect Courtier*, 1, p.431). The news came only to gladden Cristoforo's final weeks of life. He died a month after receiving the letter, and Baldesar had to return at once to Mantua to look after the family's affairs. It was a sad return for Castiglione, but the Sforza house had also been recently saddened by the death of Ludovico's twenty-two-year-old wife. For a few years he would now be able to renew old friendships and relax in the more homely or provincial environment of Mantua, after the high-powered, more cosmopolitan culture of Milan. He took over his father's role and duties as a courtier at Francesco Gonzaga's court and as diplomatic adviser on political and military matters, though he was evidently still no more than an apprentice.

It was in that new role that he accompanied Francesco to Milan in October 1499 in order to observe and assist at the triumphant entry into the city of the French under Louis XII. The military alliances ranged against him had proved too much even for Ludovico Sforza's politics of intrigue, and he had been forced to flee from Milan before the French arrived. The departure of *il Moro* meant the disappearance of the great cultural attractions of the Lombard court and the dispersal of the host of talents which Ludovico had welcomed there. Significantly, many of those courtiers were to join the Montefeltro court at Urbino, and it was a digest of their brilliant gifts and civilised discussions which later filtered through in the *Cortegiano*. In a famous letter to his brother-in-law, Jacopo Boschetto, Castiglione reflects upon the events of that October, regretting that Milan, which used to house the flower of the world's cultural genius (*già ricettacolo del fior degli uomini del mondo*), was now full of drinking booths and dung heaps (*pieno di bettole e profumato di ledame*) (Serassi, 1, p.5). He also notes in that letter the uncouthness and arrogance of the French knights and fighting-men, their discourteous attitude to the Italian women in the crowd and their violence against some of the bystanders who had been sent to pay them homage. That observation is to be confirmed later, in the *Cortegiano* (cp. below, p.86). The letter was an accurate forecast, on a small scale, of the political and military oppression which would face the peninsula during the next two hundred and fifty years. But since the Gonzaga were now allied with the French, Castiglione, like his fellows, had to grit his teeth and bear the situation, or at least give outward signs of so doing.

The broadening of Castiglione's experience by his transfer to Milan at an early age, followed by the death of Ludovico's young wife, Beatrice, the demise of Castiglione's own father, and the invasion of

Italy by the French, all within such a short span of time, no doubt
contributed to that maturity of outlook which he had achieved by the
time he was just over twenty. Tolerance, perseverance and fortitude,
those vital attributes of maturity, were by then present in Castiglione's
character in no small measure. As early as 1497 he had written to
Mario Fiera, a friend of his at Mantua and one of the Marchese's
secretaries, quoting from St Matthew's Gospel (x, 22) a verse in
support of persistence and perseverance. The solemnity and yet
naturalness of the quotation is striking in that particular letter because
of the very informality and cheerfulness of the rest of its subject-
matter. 'He that endureth to the end shall be saved,' wrote Matthew.
In the years that were to follow, it is highly probable that Christian
consolation helped Castiglione to overcome the sorrows which
affected him and the peninsula before the turn of the century.
Certainly Christian stoicism is to be praised as a necessary attribute at
court, and, indeed, after his wife's death he took Holy Orders.

Francesco Gonzaga's alliance with the French led him, in 1503, on
an abortive campaign against the Spaniards in the Kingdom of
Naples, and Baldesar, continuing to fulfil his father's role, accompanied his lord on the first of the many military campaigns he was to
experience with him and with other leaders. Carlo Dionisotti's
review of Cian's monograph has shown convincingly, against
Castiglione's detractors, that he *was* with his master during that
campaign. Dionisotti has further demonstrated, through his publication of the previously little-known sonnet *Cesare mio qui sono ove il
mar bagna*..., the telling contrast which Castiglione describes, between the ferocity of the present and the sweet memories of the past:

> Tra foco, fiamme, stridi orrendi e feri
> fame, roine e martial furore,
> meno mia vita in duri aspri sentieri;
> e pur vivon scolpiti in mezzo il core
> tutti l'antichi miei dolci pensieri,
> che Morte ha sol la scorza e 'l rest'Amore.
>
> [Amid fire, flames, horrendous, ferocious cries, famine, ruins and
> martial frenzy, I lead my life in tough, harsh paths; and yet there
> live, sculpted in the centre of my heart, all the old sweet thoughts
> of mine, for Death has only the coil, Love the rest.]

Francesco and his court retired to Rome before the final rout of the
French forces on the Garigliano. During their absence, Pius III had
died and Giuliano della Rovere had been elected Pope, with the title
of Julius II. Francesco Gonzaga left Rome for Mantua in early

December 1503, but Castiglione remained in the city, where he met his future patron, Duke Guidubaldo da Montefeltro, lord of Urbino, and his Duchess, Elisabetta Gonzaga. Guidubaldo had been called to Rome by the new Pontiff, whose kinship with him not only consolidated Guidubaldo in his Dukedom, but also ensured his appointment as Gonfalonier of the papal forces – in succession, ironically, to Cesare Borgia, son of Pope Alexander VI, and usurper of Guidubaldo's throne at Urbino until 1502.

Cesare Gonzaga, Castiglione's cousin, was already a follower of the Duke of Urbino, as was Castiglione's life-long friend Ludovico da Canossa. During his months at the papal court Castiglione was evidently captivated by the personality of the young Duke, Guidobaldo, as well as by the reputation which Urbino had as a civilised and civilising centre. After several diplomatic approaches, by Guidobaldo as well as by himself, Castiglione finally won the consent of Francesco Gonzaga to change his allegiance from the Mantuan to the Urbino court. Francesco's grudging letter of consent is dated 11 June 1504.

Castiglione's appointment under Guidubaldo was of a semi-military nature. He was nominally in charge of fifty men and was instructed to join his new patron at Forlì, where the papal troops were subduing the last remnants of Cesare Borgia's forces. The letters which Baldesar and his cousin wrote home to Mantua during this brief campaign were cheerful and hopeful, above all full of the pleasant anticipation of returning to Urbino with their lord (Serassi, I, pp.7ff.). That hope and good cheer seem evident, despite a crushed foot, the heat of the Romagna in August, and life in billets. Even his perennial lack of funds was offset by the hope of payment from the papal treasury in the near future. His later service for Francesco Maria della Rovere and for the Gonzaga dynasty was, by contrast, a chronicle of penury and poor payment for his duties.

The ascent to Urbino is difficult, steep and twisting. The city itself is unprepossessing, relatively uncomfortable, its streets narrow and windswept and with little of the picturesque character of other hill towns in the region. Yet it boasts an architectural jewel in the Ducal Palace, which, despite its modern decline and, in places, its crumbling stones, still has an ineradicable beauty, elegance and air of luxurious comfort. When Castiglione went there in 1504, Urbino had four great advantages for the aspiring courtier. It was small and unpretentious, and not under the constantly jealous (or suspicious) gaze of powerful neighbours. Its ruler, Guidubaldo, was considered by the master spirits of the time to be the most enlightened and courteous of princes. The Duchy, thanks to Guidubaldo's kinship with Pope Julius II (and his election as captain of the papal forces), enjoyed the vigorous patronage of the Roman Pontiff and a consequently strong financial and economic support. Finally, because of the foresight of Federigo da Montefeltro, that most comfortable and magnificent of palaces was endowed with the physical accoutrements of culture and learning and with a spiritual tradition which had long drawn to it men distinguished in many fields of human achievement.

Castiglione's reaction to the city may be inferred from the opening description of Urbino in *Cortegiano*, I, ii. There the interesting fact emerges that it is by no means ideal, for although that chapter is a eulogy of the surrounding countryside, the palace and its rulers, the author also inserts a concessive clause admitting that its setting, in a rugged, mountainous region, is not so agreeable as many other sites. It may seem a trivial point, but that concessive clause is a telling indication of Castiglione's acceptance of the relativity of his ideal, and will be reiterated many times during the course of his book, as indeed during his life. The genius of Guicciardini formulated that idea of 'relativity' more succinctly and realistically than any contemporary, in the aphorism from his *Del reggimento di Firenze* which declared that 'it was enough for the wise man to have the majority of things in his favour since it was impossible for them all to be favourable'.

Castiglione proceeds in that chapter to sing the praises of the old Duke Federigo da Montefeltro. His eulogy there has no reservations but it is saved from an adulatory tone by the recognisable truth of his statements. However, when Guidubaldo's merits are described, in chapter three, Castiglione takes pains to mention the two great tribulations which overshadowed his career: the first, his weak state of health, in particular the crippling gout (*podagra*) which effectively prevented his full participation in the social life at his own court; the second his remarkable lack of success in almost everything he tried to do. Whether his enterprise were military or otherwise, actions small or great always went ill with him. Castiglione's much admired prince, then, had paradoxical defects and weaknesses. And yet if we read on, we note that those deficiencies offer a lesson for Baldesar, a lesson which he followed throughout his life, which blended stoicism with Christianity; despite Guidubaldo's misfortunes, his worth shone through and everyone praised his dignified bearing: 'His virtue was never overwhelmed by fortune...he lived in highest dignity and esteem in the eyes of all' (*mai la virtù dalla fortuna non fu superata...*

*vivea con somma dignità ed estimazione appresso ognuno).*

These thoughts were composed later. The rest of that year, 1504, was spent by Castiglione in reasonable comfort, in the lodgings which he shared with his cousin Cesare Gonzaga at Urbino. A spate of letters to his mother provides evidence of the free time he had at his disposal and of the leisure which allowed him to concern himself with family affairs. (By contrast his busiest period of diplomacy, in Spain between 1524 and 1529, was to leave him little time for domestic concerns.) Nevertheless his letters also contain requests for funds or provisions – heart-cries which are to be present in all his correspondence until his eventual appointment as Papal Nuncio twenty years later.

Another major preoccupation in those letters home is with the possibility of obtaining preferment, perhaps clerical benefices, for his younger brother Girolamo, and with influencing the election to a cardinalate of Sigismondo Gonzaga, currently Bishop of Mantua. By the end of 1504 Castiglione had moved nearer to achieving those aims. Earlier that year Pope Julius had asked Guidubaldo to come to Rome, and during the months when the Urbino court was accommodated there, Castiglione carefully cultivated the acquaintance of influential men at the papal Curia. Sigismondo was created cardinal. Castiglione then busied himself to arrange for Girolamo to join the new cardinal's retinue when he should finally arrive in Rome.

In the meantime, King Henry VII of England, responding to a request for the honour by Guidubaldo, and anxious to win favour by knighting the Pope's Commander-in-Chief, had chosen to elect the papal *Gonfaloniere* to the Order of the Garter. By March 1505 it was clear that Castiglione would go as the Duke's representative ritually to accept the knighthood at Windsor. On 15 March 1505, Baldesar wrote to his mother expressing his satisfaction at the new honour and looking forward to a good summer after a depressing winter, when sickness and fever had raged among Guidubaldo's retinue. The summer was to bring little solace, however. Plague, the ever-present scourge of Italy's city-states, broke out in Urbino and in Mantua (where 'Falcone', one of his earliest acquaintances from his days in Milan, died, to the great and lasting distress of Baldesar). Guidubaldo was forced, on his return from Rome, to take refuge from the plague at his palace in Gubbio, while Castiglione went briefly to Siena to convalesce from the pain of the foot injured at Cesena the previous year. When he rejoined the court, it had moved to Fossombrone, attracting to it a great many of the talented individuals later to be immortalised on the pages of the *Cortegiano*.

In December 1505 Guidubaldo sent Castiglione as his confidential diplomatic envoy to Francesco Gonzaga at Mantua, the first time that he had been used in this capacity. But the mission was never accomplished. Francesco had long resented his former courtier's change of allegiance and, while Castiglione was in Ferrara, a rumour reached him that he would be arrested if he ventured into Mantuan territory. He was rescued from his embarrassing and dangerous situation – in hiding with a friend two miles from Ferrara – by an order from Guidubaldo recalling him, early in 1506. The episode is a good indication of the caprice and resentment of one prince and the kindness of another. Baldesar was given a friendly welcome on his return to Fossombrone. Francesco Gonzaga's resentment also held up Castiglione's plans to get Girolamo accepted into the retinue of the newly elected Cardinal Sigismondo Gonzaga (who refused to do anything which might irritate further his choleric brother).

In February 1506 Castiglione wrote to his mother in melancholic vein, seeing the world as inevitably grievous but hoping that the influence of the Duchess Elisabetta Gonzaga might succeed in softening Francesco's heart. It must have been a relief for him to return, after these experiences, to the Ducal court at Urbino. His relief and joy are perhaps visible in the dramatic eclogue, *Tirsi*, which, with some collaboration from his cousin Cesare, he wrote to celebrate Carnival. The occasion was particularly happy because this was Guidubaldo's first stay in the city since his return from Rome the year before, and, as will be seen, the *Tirsi* exalts the Urbino court with its dazzling group of courtiers and extols the tutelary deities of the place, Guidubaldo and Elisabetta.

It was not till August 1506 that Castiglione was ready to leave for England to receive the Order of the Garter. He had been knighted by Guidubaldo, as convention required for a potential recipient of the honour. Raphael had been commissioned to paint his *St. George*, an appropriate gift for Henry VII, and arrangements had been made between Guidubaldo and Francesco Gonzaga to provide Castiglione with further presents of hawks and horses when the company reached Milan. In the event, Francesco's resentment again made itself felt. The horse he provided as a royal gift was blind in one eye and half-blind in the other, and Castiglione had an embarrassing and difficult job scouring Milan to replace it. Furthermore, although Castiglione's journey took him only a few miles from his home and family, Francesco's displeasure continued to prevent him from visiting Mantua. That harsh attitude was maintained even when Baldesar's brother Girolamo died in early August, a sorrow followed that same month by the death of his nephew. There was, it seemed, no respite for the unfortunate envoy, who could now look forward to the journey through France, the Channel crossing and the unknown quantity of British hospitality. Thoughts on his own and his family's misfortunes induced him to write stoically from Lyons on 20 September, suggesting to his mother that things could surely only get better, since fortune had favoured them so little recently: 'If fortune is as fickle as she is said to be, it is time we could look for some prosperity' (Serassi, I, p.28). It must have been a pleasant surprise to receive a warm welcome at Henry's very Italophile court. The Brescian, Pietro Carmeliano, was court secretary; Polidoro Vergilio was one of the King's advisers; and Silvestro Gigli, Bishop of Worcester, his Master of Ceremonies. Probably his eulogy of the Prince of Wales, in *Cortegiano*, IV, xxxviii, and his promise to say more of the future Henry VIII 'on his return from England' are tributes to Castiglione's experiences at the English court.

By February 1507 he was once more at Urbino. On his return journey he had been granted permission by Francesco Gonzaga for a brief stay of four days at Casatico to see his mother. Three days after his return to Urbino, the court played host to Pope Julius, on his way back to Rome from Bologna (where he had put down the Bentivoglio) and fresh from his earlier triumph (in September 1506) over the Baglioni of Perugia. Castiglione used the occasion as the moment in which to set, fictionally, the events narrated in the *Cortegiano*. In chapter six of the first Book, he describes the Pope's entry into Urbino. Two days later, on 5 March, the official papal party left for Rome. Castiglione was thus able to imagine the luminaries who remained at Urbino indulging in the conversations which form the bulk of his treatise.

The arrival of Pope Julius simply added noble names from his own retinue to those already enjoying the hospitality of the Urbino court. It would be inappropriate, perhaps, to pass on without a brief mention of the courtiers whom Castiglione describes as being there at the time. Most of them are listed in *Cortegiano*, I, v. Castiglione's own name is intentionally omitted, since he had fictionally postponed his journey to England. That invention is prepared for in the dedicatory letter to Alfonso Ariosto, at the point where he writes that he 'did not take part since, when the debates were held, he was in England'.

The personages mentioned in I, v comprised two groups: the first, in semi-permanent residence at the court, included the Fregoso brothers, Ottaviano (future Doge of Genoa) and Federico (later Archbishop of Salerno); Giuliano de' Medici, youngest son of Lorenzo il Magnifico, future Cardinal and companion to his brother, Pope Leo X; Pietro (later Cardinal) Bembo, probably the most distinguished humanist and scholar of the period; Cesare Gonzaga, Castiglione's cousin; Ludovico da Canossa, one of Castiglione's intimates, who died as Bishop of Bayeux, after a distinguished career in the ecclesiastical and diplomatic worlds; Gasparo Pallavicino, a distinguished nobleman whose career as a courtier was cut short at the age of twenty-five after years of ill-health; Ludovico Pio, a friend of Bembo's with only a minor role in the *Cortegiano*; Morello da Ortona, probably the oldest of the Urbino courtiers and particularly close to Guidubaldo, a good foil for the younger members of the entourage; Pietro da Napoli, an obscure figure who makes only one intervention (Cian argues well for the theory that Pietro was one of the Pope's retinue); Roberto da Bari, a representative of the *new* courtier, with a reputation for wit and elegance as well as for prowess in music and dancing.

The second group, mentioned as adventitious members of the court who nevertheless spent much time there, included Bernardo Dovizi (*Bibbiena*), the witty cardinal who so influenced church politics during Leo X's papacy; the improviser, Bernardo Accolti (*l'Unico Aretino*), one of the more lively artistic spirits at the Renaissance courts; Giovan Cristoforo Romano, the noted sculptor, whom Castiglione had probably known at the court of Ludovico *il Moro* before the turn of the century; Pietro Monte, who seems to have been Guidubaldo's leading military expert; Anton Maria Terpandro, a great friend of both Bembo and Bibbiena, his nom de plume implying his qualities as a singer of lyrics; and finally Niccolò Frisio, a German who had spent most of his life at the Italian courts, renowned in his time for his diplomatic skills as well as for his culture. Cian's edition contains a useful *Dizionarietto biografico* which explains in greater detail who these individuals were.

We know that all these personages were actually present at Urbino during 1507. Castiglione needed to invent little of either setting or characters to create his dialogue. The subtle choice of personages allows him to exploit the many dramatic contrasts between their viewpoints and characters. And even this effect was possible without bending truth too far, since most of his contemporary readers would be personally conversant with his protagonists and Castiglione needed to produce an accurate representation of the soirées if he were aiming at verisimilitude. Jacopo Sadoleto, a man not prone to superfluous eulogy, gives a similar list of worthy courtiers in his *De laude philosophiae*, and describes the assemblage at Urbino as one of the most distinguished of all time in its genius and learning, and the court itself as the modern home and resting-place of the Muses.

In the following months, however, the blessings of Urbino were to be removed for ever, with the death of Guidubaldo. For years, any reference to the Duke in Castiglione's correspondence had invariably contained a bulletin upon his health. It may have been knowledge of Guidubaldo's ill-health which spurred Castiglione's family and friends to cultivate the goodwill of Francesco Gonzaga, hoping for a possible reconciliation between the two men, and added security for Castiglione, should his current patron at Urbino be cut down suddenly. Guidubaldo's heir was the adolescent and unpredictable Francesco Maria della Rovere, Pope Julius' nephew. Indeed, in a letter to his mother immediately following Guidubaldo's death, Castiglione reassures her that she need have no worries on his account because of his decision to remain at Urbino and serve Francesco Maria. He had earlier scotched a suggestion that Francesco Gonzaga might find him a suitable bride, and his feelings towards Francesco are expressed in a letter to his mother of 29 March 1507 – freely expressed, too, because the letter was being taken by personal messenger and he trusted its bearer 'which I would otherwise not do' (*che altramente noi farei*) (Serassi, 1, p.30). There he says that Francesco Gonzaga had always tried to oppress him, and he declares himself resigned never to set foot again in Mantua should this be necessary. Instead he proposed to exchange his own Mantuan estates (of little use and considerable trouble to him because of his continued absence) for the Bolognese estates of his friend Ercole Bentivoglio (recently dispossessed and exiled from Bologna after the triumphs of Pope Julius). This last scheme came to naught when Ercole died a few weeks after the original proposition. Castiglione had another, more pressingly practical reason for his desire to be closer to a source of revenue – the need to replenish his funds so as to allow him to live in a style worthy of the Urbino court. He seems to have been more scrupulous about the payment of debts and the repayment of loans than many of his contemporaries. Pietro Bembo, who spent six years at Urbino, boasted that he spent virtually nothing to subsist there, and advised his friends to come and enjoy the hospitality of Guidubaldo's court. Giuliano de' Medici was another who seems to have had no scruples about depending for his livelihood on the Duchess Elisabetta, despite his large income and his powerful family connections elsewhere. But, financial difficulties apart, 1507 was a good year for Castiglione. One interesting event was a diplomatic mission to Milan to pay homage, on Guidubaldo's behalf, to Louis XII. The French monarch was celebrating his recent victory over the Republic of Genoa.

The good summer of 1507 was to be followed by a grim winter and spring, rendered the grimmer by the increasing ill-health of Guidubaldo. He went into a decline and finally died in April 1508 at the palace in Fossombrone. The unsolicited tributes to Guidubaldo's merits as a prince and patron, which abound in the private correspondence of men who knew him, bear out the many eulogistic allusions in Castiglione's own writings.

Guidubaldo's funeral was a sumptuous affair and the sorrowful feelings expressed by all who had known him testify further to the regard in which he was held by his contemporaries. More explicitly, Castiglione's contributions to the funeral and its aftermath included a Latin eulogy *De vita et gestis Guidubaldi Urbini Ducis*, sent in the form of an epistle to King Henry VII (and later printed in Fossombrone). Bembo, too, commemorated the late Duke in his dialogue *De ducibus*. Guidubaldo's stoic resignation at the last, his Christian relief that he was leaving behind his physical distress must have communicated themselves to Castiglione, and no doubt later helped him tolerate the anxious years he was to spend in the next two decades.

But Castiglione's idyllic period was ended for ever. Fortunately for all concerned, Guidubaldo's will specified that the Duchess Elisabetta should be regent until his nephew should reach the age of twenty-five years. Francesco Maria was to make greater use than ever of Castiglione's diplomatic and military skills. He had taken over Guidubaldo's role as captain of the papal forces, and, a much more forceful and belligerent man by nature, he spent more time in military campaigns. In short, Castiglione returned to a life similar to that he had led under Francesco Gonzaga during the period before 1503. His letters home during the rest of the year are full of requests for money. If he was short of funds during Guidubaldo's rule, he was reduced to penury under the della Rovere aegis.

Castiglione wrote a formal eulogy of Francesco Maria at the end of *Cortegiano*, I, when he is described as newly arriving at the Urbino court to join the papal retinue. Cian portrays that eulogy and the later laudatory reference to him in *Cortegiano*, IV, ii, as exaggerated praise, but this is disputable. It is true that Castiglione praises his new patron's *virtù*, but he there implies, with an important concessive clause, that any virtues or praiseworthy habits that Francesco Maria might have, are the result of his upbringing, not least in the house of his uncle, Guidubaldo. Yet Cian's remark is understandable; Francesco Maria did not enjoy the most pleasant of reputations. It could help to explain the anxiety of Castiglione's mother, as well as to reveal further Castiglione's attitude to the courtier's role and illustrate the precariousness of the courtier's tranquillity, if we consider the character and actions of the new Duke and contrast them with those of Guidubaldo.

Francesco Maria della Rovere was eighteen years of age when he assumed the title. Pope Julius had ensured his succession to the Urbino duchy by insisting in 1504 that Guidubaldo adopt the boy. That same year the Pope conferred upon him the title *Prefetto di Roma*, and, with a diminutive similar to the nickname *Caligula*, he was known popularly as *Il Prefettino*. When he was only seventeen he had, with the aid of two henchmen, treacherously killed one of Guidubaldo's favourites, a certain Gian Andrea, who had been courting Francesco Maria's widowed sister, Maria Varana. He also arranged for the murder of Maria Varana's personal servant, who had carried letters between the two. Four years later, when the Pope's favourite, Cardinal Alidosi, cast aspersions on his military prowess as leader of the papal forces at Ravenna, he murdered him too, a crime for which he was indicted by his uncle, Pope Julius, and again, years later, by Pope Leo. A military man, he was captain of the papal forces for several years. Castiglione had to endure far more of the rigours of campaigning than he had under his old patron, leaving behind the culture and luxury of the old Urbino. After many anxious, not to say dangerous vicissitudes, Francesco Maria was removed from his Dukedom in 1516 by the nepotistic Pope Leo X, who replaced him with his own nephew, Lorenzo de' Medici. Castiglione later worked hard at the papal court for many years to get the title restored to Francesco Maria. This only happened on Leo's death in 1522, and, as we shall see, Castiglione's reward for the final tough negotiations was for Francesco Maria to deprive him of territory given to him a decade earlier.

After the death of Guidubaldo, Castiglione at first remained at Urbino, where his presence was no doubt a great comfort to the court, notably to Elisabetta Gonzaga, desolate at the death of her husband. At this time Castiglione's financial worries became more acute, and the years which follow show him preoccupied with finding a suitable marriage partner, preferably one with a large dowry. The first name to be suggested was Clarice de' Medici, and Castiglione corresponded with his mother on the subject (cp. Serassi, I, pp.39ff.). In the event, their plans were foiled when the girl married into the Strozzi household, but during the negotiations Castiglione was allowed to see his mother – for just four days. This concession was won from Francesco Gonzaga only after many overtures, despite the presence of the Urbino court at Mantua, where Francesco Maria was currently visiting his betrothed, Eleonora Gonzaga.

The spring of 1509 saw Castiglione in service with Francesco Maria against the Venetians. The summer of that year he was in Urbino again, in poor health after an inept campaign. The end of the year, however, was rather more cheerful, for Francesco Maria had decided to bring forward his own marriage (possibly to ingratiate himself with Pope Julius, displeased by Venice's more recent military successes). A contingent from Mantua, which included the Duke's future wife and Castiglione's mother, arrived at Urbino to spend Christmas there. The party later went to Rome for Carnival, and there Castiglione had the opportunity to renew acquaintance with some of the luminaries from the old days at Urbino. In fact, it may have been an advantage, in view of his future diplomatic career, for him to be forced into travelling further and meeting more international figures in the diplomatic and military field. The influence and experience thus acquired would ensure him greater freedom to choose his court and court duties in later years. (The gentility of Guidubaldo's court would have been inappropriate for the coming decade of war and strife.) The rest of the year, indeed, was spent campaigning with the papal forces against French and Ferrarese.

Despite initial successes (and the spirited leadership of the ageing Pontiff), the forces of the Church were finally beaten, and Castiglione, in a letter to his mother of 1 June 1510, sounds grateful to be alive (cp. Serassi, I, p.59). The weeks had been full of hardship and bloodshed for him, and the dramatic elegy, written before Mirandola fell to the Pope's besieging troops, the *Prosopopoeia Ludovici Pici Mirandulani*, is an indication of his hatred of the war. His troubles increased when, after one of Julius' tirades against the inept leadership of Francesco Maria, the young man murdered Cardinal Alidosi for what he considered a smirk of amusement at his predicament. Alidosi had been one of the Pope's favourites, and Francesco Maria was summoned to Rome to stand trial. Castiglione accompanied his master. During the trial the Pope fell ill and came very near to death, and, for a while,

Francesco Maria's fate and the Pope's survival hung together. There was, anyway, a good chance of disaster befalling the Duke and any who owed him allegiance. But Francesco Maria was acquitted and the Pope later absolved him from guilt and restored to him his former offices and privileges. Castiglione's relief is visible in a letter of 27 September written from Urbino to his mother (Serassi, I, p.60). His health was poor but his spirits high because of the acquittal of his master.

Fortune's wheel continued to revolve, however, and Castiglione's troubles were not yet over. His marriage negotiations had to be postponed while he concentrated his attention on allaying papal suspicions that *he* had been a go-between uniting Francesco Maria and Louis XII of France. The Pope temporarily demoted his nephew from supreme command, though after the rout of the papal forces by the French at the end of 1511 he was reinstated, and by 12 May of the following year Castiglione was able to announce the successful recovery of much of the Romagna. His letters home during the previous year indicate his activities in their frequent requests for armour, new cloth to make clothes for himself and his servants, a new tent and mules to carry it (cp. Gorni, p.10).

By mid-June 1511, the papal and pro-papal forces were victorious throughout northern Italy. Only Ferrara remained stubbornly independent and it was towards Ferrara that Francesco Maria next led his troops. Castiglione was in another dilemma, pressed by the Marchioness of Mantua, Isabella d'Este, to intercede with his master on behalf of her brother Alfonso I of Ferrara. He is unlikely to have been able to influence papal policy for such a personal motive, and delays in Francesco Maria's campaign were probably due to appalling weather conditions. But among the Duke's successes was the acquisition of Pesaro, his possession of which was later confirmed by Pope Julius. This in turn brought for Castiglione the land and revenues of the Castle of Novillara and the title of Count of Novillara. His enjoyment of the castle was to be short-lived, however, thanks in the first instance to his nomadic life and to the fact that Francesco Maria, needing it as a bargaining pawn in 1522, handed it back to Pesarese rule without consulting its 'owner'.

Yet even these triumphs were temporary, and once more joy was tempered with sadness for Castiglione. During the Romagna campaign in 1512 his cousin and life-long friend Cesare Gonzaga died of fever. *Cortegiano*, IV, i, contains a moving tribute to him, as well as to the other Urbino courtiers who had either died, moved away from

Urbino to posts of preferment or returned to their home cities from exile. But before the court at Urbino was finally disbanded, its courtiers were to enjoy the Carnival of 1513, during which Castiglione was responsible for the production there of Bibbiena's comedy, *La Calandria*. In the absence of its author, Baldesar also wrote the prologue to the play, a vernacular prose comedy, and stirringly defended its novelty, as well as giving general praise to the use of Italian as its medium, a language in which he, too, he assured his audience, was proud to write. 'I well know that my language is so dear to me that I would not exchange it for all the languages around today' (*Calandria, Prologo*). This praise for the vernacular (which was to be continued in two important sections of the *Cortegiano*) reflects a growing spirit of Italian nationalism, prophetic of nineteenth-century notions of Italy's long-standing literary and linguistic unity as asserted by men like Francesco De Sanctis and Graziadio Isaia Ascoli. 'The language which God and Nature have given us must not be held in less esteem amongst us (*appresso di noi*) nor considered less beautiful than Latin, Greek and Hebrew' (ibid.). *Eutichia*, the second of the comedies to be performed at Urbino during that carnival, also merits a mention; the play had an intermezzo, written by Castiglione, depicting Italy as a broken woman, lamenting her past glories and her present servitude, but later saved and exalted again by Francesco Maria. The production of *La Calandria* coincided with contemporary carnival pageants in Rome, held particularly to celebrate Pope Julius' recent triumphs over the French. Julius, too, regarded himself as the personification of an Italy liberating itself from the foreign yoke.

In a letter to his friend Canossa on the subject of the Urbino celebrations, Castiglione reveals some of their glamour and elaborate nature. He also implies in that same letter that he would like to spend the rest of his life in like pursuits. But his next duty was prophetically funereal: it was to attend the exequies of Pope Julius. Fortunately (or so it seemed to begin with) Giovanni de' Medici, a potential ally, was elected Pope, taking the title Leo X. Francesco Maria paid his due homage, and, initially at least, was confirmed by Leo in all his offices and titles. Bembo and Sadoleto were appointed papal secretaries, Bibbiena became papal treasurer, Canossa was made master of the papal household. Leo X also gave an audience to the traditionally anti-papal Alfonso d'Este, and a reconciliation between Ferrara and Rome seemed assured, with the possible restoration of Modena and Reggio to Alfonso. Francesco Maria left Castiglione in Rome to look after his interests and went to affirm his hold on Pesaro. Julia Cartwright lists the countless duties and favours which Castiglione was then required to carry out and beg on behalf of the Duke and of many other noble patrons and acquaintances. Requests ranged from Francesco Maria's embarrassing demand that Baldesar rebuke Canossa for failing to send him arrears of pay from the papal coffers, to an appeal from Elisabetta's sister-in-law, Chiara Malatesta, asking him to urge the Pope to reform the Order of Santa Chiara at Assisi by bringing it under the stricter control of the *Osservanti*, the reformed Franciscan Order.

The minor irritations of having to beg favours or to write diplomatically soothing replies, were offset by the brilliance of Leo's court. Castiglione found there not only old friends from Urbino days, but also other important personages closely connected with his family or with the Mantuan court, and disposed to be friendly towards him. Ariosto was one who remembered with retrospective envy the delights of the Roman court, and Bembo was another who described his exhilarating walks with Raphael and Castiglione among the ruins of Rome and the beauties of the surrounding Roman countryside. Castiglione was himself stimulated by that company to compose sonnets in a Petrarchan mould, as well as Latin poems and epigrams. During the period 1512–13 he was also able to elaborate the sketch of court life at Urbino which was to develop as the *Cortegiano*, originally dashed off in a few days immediately after the Duke's death in 1508. Indeed, so occupied was Castiglione with affairs of state and with the delights of the arts that his letters home became briefer, with the result that his mother had many occasions to complain about lack of news, as well as to regret his apparent laxness in looking after his personal and family affairs. His busy round in Rome was interrupted in August 1513 when he returned briefly to Urbino to be confirmed Count of Novillara by Francesco Maria, an honour reconfirmed in the next year in two letters from the Pope himself. One, in Bembo's hand, offered congratulations; the other, written by Sadoleto, conferred privileges, such as exemption for him and his heirs from payment of papal dues.

Leo's court, meanwhile, had developed more and more into the playground of Europe, and Leo's relatives and friends were not slow to take advantage of the pleasure-loving Pope, still only thirty-seven years of age. More seriously, murmurings against Francesco Maria began to circulate in Rome. Leo's nepotism became more and more overt and his ambiguous political manoeuvres, intriguing both with the French and with the Emperor Maximilian, created greater anxiety about his trustworthiness as an ally of Urbino. By 1515 he had deprived Francesco Maria of his powers as captain of the papal army and conferred them instead upon his own brother, Giuliano de' Medici.

Another important event for Castiglione during 1515 was the visit to Rome of Isabella d'Este. She had always thought well of her husband's ex-courtier and it could have been no coincidence that Castiglione was able, the following year, to return to the Gonzaga court and be received by Francesco Gonzaga with none of the old resentment. By contrast with this upturn in his personal fortunes, Castiglione's duties in Rome on Francesco Maria's behalf became more and more complex and less and less hopeful. Lorenzo de' Medici, now in control of Florence, had taken over from Giuliano, never very robust in health, the command of the papal forces which were to oppose the French troops of Francis I. When Francesco Maria refused to fight under Lorenzo, rumours, with or without foundation, concerning his pro-French stance began to spread, so much so that when the French defeated Lorenzo at Marignano and then made peace with the Pope, Francesco Maria's position at Urbino was considerably weakened. Notwithstanding appeals by Francis I on Francesco Maria's behalf (or perhaps because of them!), and despite an eloquent plea by Castiglione in person before both Pope and French king during their meeting at Bologna to ratify the peace, Leo was determined to make his nephew, Lorenzo, Duke of Urbino.

Castiglione was introduced to the royal court of Francis I through his intermediary Alfonso Ariosto, cousin of Ludovico. His impressions both of Alfonso and of Francis are recorded in the *Cortegiano* – notably in the dedicatory letter, where we read that Francis himself seems to have urged the publication of the treatise which Alfonso had told him so much about, and in the body of the text (I, xlii) where Francis seems to be the potential 'cultural' redeemer of the French, seen as the one individual among them who set civilised artistic achievements above the profession of arms and the glory of military conquest.

Castiglione went on to Mantua, taking advantage of his new-found favour at the Gonzaga court (and no doubt only too well aware of the precarious position of Francesco Maria and of the consequences for himself of the Duke's possible fall from grace and power). That new-found favour coincided happily with his mother's suggestion of a suitable marriage partner, Ippolita Torelli, a noblewoman whose family had its main branches in Ferrara. By January 1516, Castiglione's betrothal to the fifteen-year-old girl was announced. But if he might now hope to find a measure of happiness, his patron Francesco Maria was heading for disaster, summoned to Rome to answer charges of treason and of murder (the killing of Cardinal Alidosi in 1511). Castiglione was forced to go to Rome to plead his erstwhile master's case. His difficulties were immense. On the one hand he had to delay the Pope's promised excommunication of Francesco Maria, so that as many interventions on his behalf as possible could be made. On the other, he had, at the same time, to placate Leo in his ever more insistent demands for the Duke's presence in Rome. Castiglione's suspicions of the treacherous intentions of the Pope and his Medici advisers are clearly visible in a letter of 18 April 1516 addressed to Francesco Maria. There he declared that he had mentioned his fears for the Duke's safety to the Pontiff who, according to the letter, had uttered reassuring noises; the ultimate decision on whether to come to Rome, however, Castiglione had to leave to Francesco Maria. The situation was desperate, though Castiglione, one surmises happily, had worked himself into a position where, whatever the outcome, *he* would not suffer overmuch. No intervention, neither the politically influential pleas of the Emperor Maximilian, the request of Leo's own brother Giuliano, by now very ill (he was to die on 17 March 1516), nor the sentimental appeals of the Duchess Elisabetta, who had herself offered so much hospitality to Giuliano and the exiled Medici, was of any avail. The Pope was obdurate. By the end of May Francesco Maria, accompanied by Castiglione, had to leave Urbino, to take refuge (but only with the Pope's permission) in the territory of Francesco Gonzaga, his father-in-law. There the Urbino court was to remain for the next five years. It required little time or effort for Lorenzo's troops to impose on the Urbino populace the Medici yoke, replacing the by now more ineffectual power of the della Rovere. The usurpation was given ecclesiastical and official recognition when Leo's bull of 18 August 1516 proclaimed his nephew Duke of Urbino and Gonfalonier of the papal forces.

On 19 October 1516, Castiglione married Ippolita Torelli. Subsequently he seems to have enjoyed three of his most idyllic years, in favour with the Gonzaga court and experiencing for the first time in his existence the tranquillity of domestic life. The following year, Ippolita bore him a son, Camillo. He was able during this period to find the time necessary to complete most of the *Cortegiano*. By 20 September 1518 he could send the manuscript to Sadoleto in Rome to

ask his opinion of it ( *la prego di dargli un' occhiata*) ( cp. Serassi, I, p.160).
Next month he wrote to Bembo, asking him, too, to read the manuscript 'so that if the book has to have some errors, at least [after
Bembo's corrections] there won't be an infinity of them' (ibid.).
Unfortunately Bembo's ill-health, his convalescence in Venice and
possibly a lost letter, prevented his views on the volume from being
conveyed to Castiglione. On 15 January 1520 the latter is forced to
make another, similar request to his friend.

In February 1519, Federigo Gonzaga succeeded to the marquisate
on the death of his father Francesco. Only two months later, Leo's
nephew, Lorenzo de' Medici, died in Florence, leaving the leadership
of that city, the papal captaincy and the newly acquired duchy of
Urbino vacant. It was natural for Castiglione to be sent to Rome to
represent the youthful new Marquis. He had a regular salary for the
first time in his life and his official brief was to look after Federigo's
interests. He would also plead Francesco Maria's case for a return to
Urbino. Francesco Maria had already, in 1517, made an unsuccessful
attempt to recapture his old dukedom by force of arms, and he was
constantly alert to the possibility of offering diplomatic overtures.
But 1519 was fraught with other difficulties and there could have been
little time for Pope Leo to consider Castiglione's more parochial
interests. The death of the Emperor Maximilian in January of that
year meant that the whole of western Christendom was preoccupied
with the election of a new Emperor. In July, Charles V of Spain was
elected. Pope Leo, fearful of the already wide empire of Spain, had
favoured the election of Francis I, but he came to terms with the
situation with typical duplicity by secret diplomatic contacts with
both men. The web of intrigue became more tangled as the year wore
on, until Castiglione returned to Mantua having achieved little
concrete success for his patrons.

Castiglione was visiting Modena with his wife just after Easter
1520, when he heard from Canossa of the death of Raphael. The
sorrow which he would feel was no doubt redoubled by the memory
of his company in Rome a few months before, as well as by thoughts
of the artist's youth (he was five years Castiglione's junior) and of his
relatively unfulfilled potential. By 17 July however, Baldesar had to
return to Rome. The possible prizes for his diplomacy were the
captaincy of the papal forces for Federigo and the Bishopric of
Mantua for Federigo's young brother, Ercole. Four days after his
arrival Castiglione could write hopefully to Federigo that the first of
these objects had received the Pope's initial approval. But this triumph,

too, was blighted with sorrow a month later when Cardinal Bibbiena, informed by special messenger from Federigo, broke the news to Castiglione that his wife Ippolita had died giving birth to his third child. Federigo himself wrote a letter expressing his regret and sorrow at Ippolita's death. Even Pope Leo was so sympathetic that he awarded Castiglione a pension of two hundred crowns and, a rare honour this, insisted that he join the élite group who hunted with him. Indeed, from this point onwards Castiglione seems to have enjoyed more and more of the papal confidence.

The opening months of 1521 were full of rumours of the Lutheran apostasy, and yet the Roman court seemed concerned only with pageants, spectacles and sport. Castiglione was forced to write what amount to racing reports for Federigo, some of which, as Giannetto Bongiovanni illustrates, are doubly bizarre because of their elaborate excuses for the *failure* of the Marquis' horses to win. And yet it is probably inaccurate to suggest, as does Bongiovanni, that these were, for a man of Castiglione's mental capacity, exercises in futility and triviality. Castiglione probably welcomed the opportunity to be able to make the trivial sound important, aware all the time of the harrowing nature of his tougher negotiations. In May, however, Federigo was confirmed in his command of the papal forces and Leo, at last, seemed to have given his support decisively for the Emperor Charles, who promised to defend the Church, particularly in its growing need for support against Lutheranism. The Pope also invited Baldesar to spend the summer in the Belvedere palace, another mark of esteem. Indeed, when Federigo offered him the command of fifty lancers, Castiglione's arguments in favour of his remaining at Rome were not entirely altruistically intended. His appointment as Mantuan envoy at the Roman court was reconfirmed at a higher salary (though in effect this was not paid regularly!). He would, no doubt, count himself fortunate, during the summer of 1521, to be in Rome and not campaigning with the allied forces of Pope and Emperor against the French in northern Italy. Leo appears to have consulted him assiduously about the campaign, and Castiglione's letters to the Mantuan court reflect the anxiety which the Pope felt, his continual changes of mood, his expectations of a sudden victory.

In early November Federigo was able to tell the Pope that the papal forces were victorious. The Mantuan star seemed in the ascendant and it seemed a propitious moment to ask Leo for a further favour – the elevation of Federigo's brother Ercole to a cardinalate. A week after Federigo's victorious despatch and the consequent celebrations Leo was dead. When Castiglione sent the news to Federigo, he contrasted the gloom of mourning Rome with the festivities of a week previously and, as he meditates there upon the fickleness of Fortune and God's ability to shatter the plans of poor mortals, his words, though referring to the late Pope, reflect his own state of mind.

Without doubt those mournful words were also appropriate to the tragedies which affected his personal life in this period and as prognostications for the hard task ahead, of ingratiating himself with a new Pontiff. The gloomy atmosphere was deepened by suspicions that the Pope had been poisoned. There were many who hated Leo. Barely a month after his funeral, Francesco Maria, allied with the French and the Ferrarese, had recovered his Duchy and was even making inroads into Medici territory in Tuscany.

The long conclave to elect a new pope reached a compromise with the election of Adrian, Bishop of Tortosa, formerly tutor to Charles V. During the conclave, and during the following months which it took to bring Adrian from Spain to Rome, Castiglione had somehow to persuade the cardinals 'caretaking' in Rome that Federigo's formal appointment as papal commander should be renewed, and that funds be made available to pay his troops, this last an impossible request. And while he was attending to his public duties, Castiglione suffered one more private blow when Francesco Maria, as a condition of his acceptance by the city of Pesaro (where he intended to hold court in future) had to hand over to the Pesarese the castle of Novillara. Despite this action by his former patron, Castiglione worked hard to obtain from the College of Cardinals ratification for Francesco Maria's newly recovered titles and territories. His difficulties may be appreciated in view of the recurrent divisions, national and internally parochial, among the cardinals, aggravated particularly by the fact that Federigo Gonzaga was still fighting the French in the north, relying, theoretically, on the papal treasury for funds.

During the whole of that early summer of 1522 Castiglione was under pressure from these old problems, to which were added a spate of requests from various patrons and high-ranking friends, and, more deadly, an outbreak of plague which raged at Rome for months to come, particularly among the lower classes. And still the new Pope had not arrived to give a lead to the cardinals or to restore some order to the chaotic uncertainty. When he did arrive, in August, Adrian VI's ascetic and scholarly attitudes were in complete contrast with the profligacy and merry-making of Pope Leo. Castiglione seems to have kept his head and his sanity by thinking of his young family. His letters home are full of domestic references, which tone down the grimmer descriptions of the streets and the gloom of his diplomatic missions. On broader horizons, the Turks had laid siege to Rhodes (and indeed would capture the island by Christmas) and perhaps now an idea, already formed in Castiglione's mind, was confirmed: that by uniting against the common foe, the Turk, Christendom could reduce its internal problems and so possibly create, at least for the innocents at home, a period of tranquillity. This would give some rationale to the apparently anti-historical, some have said fatuous, suggestion made in *Cortegiano*, IV, xxxviii, that a new Crusade would be a worthy enterprise for the West. The notion was one favoured by Adrian himself, though perhaps for more dogmatic reasons. Castiglione eventually obtained the Pope's assent to Federigo Gonzaga's appointment as papal commander, but there was little else he could achieve diplomatically with a pope intent upon maintaining peace between France and Spain, keeping his own independence from either and building up again the papal finances.

Meanwhile the plague was worsening. The brief for Federigo had still not been officially given and Castiglione had to stay on in Rome, seeing people dying around him, the city becoming more and more deserted of his friends and fellow-diplomats, his funds rapidly disappearing and no money available from banks closed because of the plague. But by the end of October he had received the official agreement to Federigo's appointment. He also had success with his plea for Francesco Maria's recognition and confirmation in the recovered Duchy, and by the spring of the following year, Francesco Maria had received his investiture from Adrian. Baldesar could now make his way back to Mantua, by a roundabout route, delaying at Casatico to make sure that the plague, which had killed two of his servants, was not being carried with him. He arrived at Mantua for Christmas 1522.

Life at Mantua was not entirely domestic and tranquil for Castiglione, however. The conspiracy of Cardinal Soderini, in April 1523, the object of which was to instigate an insurrection in Sicily and to hand over Milan to the French, provoked the Pope into an alliance with the Emperor. Castiglione had, during the whole of this time, been in correspondence with the Holy See. His contact there, Andrea Piperario, was a trustworthy fellow-Mantuan and a secretary in the papal court, whose help was to prove even more invaluable when Baldesar was sent as Papal Nuncio to Madrid. The Soderini plot involved Federigo in an armed campaign at the head of the papal forces. Accompanied by Castiglione he engaged in hostilities with the French around Lodi during September 1523. Adrian died the same month. In October Giulio de' Medici was elected Pope, with the title of Clement VII, and a month later Castiglione again left for Rome.

In view of Castiglione's later experiences with Clement VII, it is worth noting here the names of two men who exerted an enormous influence over the Pope from the outset: Matteo Giberti, Bishop of Verona, and Nicholas von Schönberg, Archbishop of Capua, the former a partisan of the French cause, the latter a supporter of the Emperor. It was their conflicting advice which helped to contribute to the vacillating policies which Clement adopted almost from the first, particularly vis-à-vis Charles V. From the beginning of his rule, too, several contemporary ambassadors noted Clement's indecisive attitude and the unreliability of his friendly utterances. Nonetheless the first months of his papacy were tranquil, disturbed only by another outbreak of plague in Rome. Castiglione was able to attend adequately to small requests from Mantua, and, although skirmishes continued in northern Italy between French and Imperial forces, he was by now out of reach of those minor storms and growing in favour at the Roman court. On 19 July Clement offered Castiglione the post of Nuncio to the Imperial court in Spain. Federigo soon consented to his envoy's request to be relieved of his Mantuan commitments, backed as his petition had been by a letter from Clement himself.

Castiglione's immediate task was to settle several outstanding financial matters. Federigo had a large sum owing to the Marquis of Pescara, and Castiglione's first job before leaving Rome was to obtain funds from the papal treasury to pay this debt. A further debt, incurred by Castiglione on behalf of Francesco Maria, remained undischarged in spite of Baldesar's appeals to the Duke and to the Duchess Eleonora. The Sauli bankers, who had made the original loan in 1513, were still unpaid when Castiglione departed for Spain. Before he finally left for Mantua, he was also able to obtain arrears of salary for Federigo. His services on behalf of his patrons and his financial successes in obtaining funds for them contrast strongly with his own domestic situation, where the estates, according to letters from his mother, were unprofitable. Indeed he had to pawn family plate to equip himself for Spain, and Julia Cartwright underlines Luigia Gonzaga's bitter comment that, with so many of his own debts, Castiglione should have to pay those of Francesco Maria, too. It was also clear to her that her son would receive no salary as Papal Nuncio. Indeed in September 1524 Castiglione wrote to her denying a rumour that he would be paid a salary, though the perquisites (as well as the unpleasant and trying task) of collecting papal revenue in Spain were to be his. But when he tried to avail himself of his tithe, the Pope protested. In fact, he had requested five, not ten, per cent (a thousand ducats), specifically to pay off his debts in Rome, incurred for the most part on behalf of his superiors. The Pope regretted that he should have kept back even that *half* of his entitlement from the twenty thousand ducats he had raised.

The new Nuncio left for Spain in late December, 1524, after a brief last spell in Mantua. In the meantime Francis I seemed to the Pope and his advisers to be gaining the upper hand militarily and, unknown to his own envoy, on 12 December the Pope had signed a secret treaty with France and Venice. Castiglione gleaned hints of the agreement as he made his way westwards, calling on regional rulers as he went, and meeting Francis I at Pavia on 26 December 1524. By the time he reached Lyons on 9 January, news of Clement's treaty with Francis had been made public, the Pope was seen more and more to be openly favouring the French, and former Imperial minions in Italy began to secede to them. It must have been difficult and embarrassing for Castiglione continually to have to defend the Pope on the grounds that he was compelled by the military weakness of his own forces to mollify Francis. One can imagine his bewilderment and further embarrassment when he finally arrived in Madrid, on 11 March 1525, to hear that the French had been wiped out by the Emperor's forces at Pavia and that Francis himself was the Emperor's prisoner! From the beginning of his time at the Imperial court, however, Castiglione was impressed, it must be said, by the Emperor's modesty, his Christian attitude and his devotion to the papacy. The rich correspondence with Andrea Piperario in March 1525, published by Serassi, particularly emphasises those favourable opinions. And from the beginning Castiglione was unequivocal in urging Clement to declare himself in favour of the Emperor. But the pro-French Giberti was in Rome..., and Clement was never a man to make decisive moves.

In June 1525 Francis was brought to Spain as an honoured prisoner, treated with great hospitality by Charles until the Treaty of Madrid was signed in January of the following year. There was an evident danger that Charles V would now move in to dominate Italy, and both Castiglione and his fellow-Mantuan, Federigo's envoy Soardino, feared this possibility. Similar apprehension must have been felt in Italy. Francesco Sforza had been crowned Duke of Milan in 1521 on the expulsion of the French, and now his secretary, Girolamo Morone, tried to form a secret alliance of Italian states in order to ensure the continued independence of the individual city-state. The Pope lent his support to Morone's idea. By now, Castiglione and the newly-arrived papal legate, Cardinal Salviati, were baffled by the Pope's policies and found it impossible to know his wishes and increasingly difficult to understand the Emperor's intentions.

On 10 December, a month before the Treaty of Madrid, Castiglione openly expressed his fears that hostilities would break out between Francis and Charles, since no peace treaty between them could last more than six months (Serassi, I, p.9). Other letters reveal his fears that his own attempts to bring Pope and Emperor together might be undermined by the courtiers at Rome. Charles V seemed, anyway, to be increasingly (and probably justifiably) distrustful of papal policies. So worried, indeed, did Castiglione become at the dangers of a break between Empire and Papacy that he took the unprecedented step of writing directly to the Pope, urging a more open alliance with Charles. His advice went unheeded. No sooner had Francis I returned to his own territory than he proceeded to ignore all the terms of the Treaty of Madrid. On 22 May 1526, the League of Cognac was formed, allying Pope, France, Venice and Milan, with England's Henry VIII as its 'Protector'. The Emperor was required to release the French king's hostage sons and to recognise Francesco Sforza as the Duke of Milan. The first hint that Castiglione and Salviati had of these machinations was when rumours began to circulate at the Granada court. Charles decided to send an expeditionary force to Italy led by his Viceroy, Count Charles Lannoy, ostensibly to oppose the French.

No communications were forthcoming from Rome, and Castiglione must have been at his wits' end looking for excuses for both Pope and Emperor. Charles at one point seemed ready to make concessions to Clement, who, ill-advisedly perhaps, viewed his overtures as marks of weakness and accused him, through Castiglione, of breaking the peace by his recent actions. Charles' reply was an angry one, and, by mid-September, Spanish troops under the command of Don Ugo Moncada had marched through Rome, vandalised the Vatican and driven the Pope and his cardinals to seek refuge in the Castel Sant' Angelo. The attack was to be a foretaste of the disaster to come. Simultaneously the Turks had swept into Hungary and had killed the Hungarian king, Louis, at Mohacz. The news of the pillaging of Rome filled Charles with remorse, the death of his brother-in-law,

Louis, with sorrow and anger; for a while there seemed a slight chance (given a new-found contrition, or apprehension, on Clement's part) of a united front against the Turks. The Pope, indeed, volunteered to come to Spain to discuss a lasting peace, and Charles sent Cesare Fieramosca to Rome to treat with Clement, while the papal Chamberlain, Paolo d'Arezzo, was sent from Rome with a message for the Emperor. Both envoys were delayed and their respective missions achieved nothing. Meanwhile, in Italy, affairs were becoming increasingly complicated and Castiglione was kept almost completely in the dark, receiving no despatches from Rome and being given no information by Charles v. The situation was not helped for the Papal Nuncio by the Pope's temperament. In September, Francesco Maria took Cremona for the League, and Clement immediately repudiated his earlier overtures to Moncada and sent troops to destroy the strongholds of his traditional enemies, and the allies of the Emperor, the Colonna family. Then news of large Imperial forces gathering in northern Italy made him negotiate with Charles v's Viceroy in Naples. When Charles' forces suffered a defeat at Frosinone, Clement once again renegued.

Events now succeeded each other quickly and inexorably. A message from Charles Lannoy to the Imperial army under George von Frundsberg in the north of Italy, failed to prevent the troops from beginning their march south. His message had intimated a truce with the Pope. The troops had not received their pay, and a treaty would have meant no hope of either wages or plunder for them. By 5 May, the army, 40,000 strong, was preparing an assault on Rome itself. For eight days the rebellious troops ran riot. The Pope was once more driven to take refuge in the Castel Sant' Angelo, the papal apartments were ransacked, cavalry was stabled in Raphael's *stanze*, churches were desecrated, relics destroyed and the populace, both lay and clerical, outraged. The artists and littérateurs, the patrons of art and learning were robbed and tortured and driven from the city. The Emperor was given the news on 17 June. He expressed regret that his troops had taken affairs into their own hands, but put the blame firmly on the soldiery.

Amid the anxieties of his office and the dangers of chronic bouts of fever, Castiglione had had time for friendly recreation at the Spanish court, notably with Gaspare Contarini, the Venetian envoy, whom he had known in Rome and who was soon to be replaced by an even greater friend, Andrea Navagero. There were fellow-Mantuans there, too, including Soardino, the Mantuan ambassador to the Imperial court, and Ferrante Gonzaga, youngest son of the Marquis. The Imperial Chancellor, Arborio di Gattinara, an Italian by birth, always seemed favourably inclined towards the individual Italian city-states and had a temperament congenial to Castiglione. Furthermore, the excitement of recent discoveries in the New World would also serve as consolatory interests during the more routine tedium of court life, along with the novelty and proximity of the Arab civilisation (particularly the Arab quarter in Granada). Intellectual pabulum was also provided by the latest books from Italy. Letters home requested current publications. One such letter, of 14 March 1525, written to Piperario, requested Trissino's *Grammatica*, Bembo's *Prose* and Leone Ebreo's *Dialoghi d'amore*. There, too, he mentions having read a reply to Trissino's *Epistola*. And then there were pageants and tournaments and the marriage celebrations of 1526, when Castiglione was present in Seville at the wedding of the Emperor to Isabel, the Infanta of Portugal. And there was Castiglione's *capolavoro*.

A combination of events now precipitated publication of the *Cortegiano*. Nostalgic recollection, no doubt, had some part in influencing its author. The recent tragedy had destroyed the Rome once frequented by the choicest spirits of the sixteenth century, now shattered by the barbarity of Spanish and German mercenaries. In January 1526 Duchess Elisabetta Gonzaga, patroness of so many pleasant soirées, had died in Urbino. The epoch of the city-state with a ruling court seemed to be more and more a thing of the past. It had been shown that the survival of individual courts depended upon the whim of the current Emperor or Pontiff. The deposition of Guidubaldo by the Borgias and the replacement of Francesco Maria by Lorenzo de' Medici, as well as the Morone conspiracy, had all been a foretaste of that development. But perhaps more importantly, the Marchioness of Pescara, Vittoria Colonna, who, as early as 1524, had taken the manuscript of the *Cortegiano* to read for her own enjoyment, seems to have had parts of it transcribed, and those copies, Castiglione learnt, were circulating in Naples. Confirmation of this last is to be found in the most elegant and diplomatic of letters, addressed to Vittoria Colonna on 21 September 1527 (Serassi, I, pp.171–2). He had earlier written to Piperario, on 6 April 1525, indicating that he was 'more than ever stimulated to let it go to the printers' (Gorni, p.96). He was seeking some tranquillity from the distress of the sack of Rome, and literary studies had always provided him with this kind of consolation. The death of the Duchess (very poignantly commemorated in the *Cortegiano*'s dedicatory letter) recalled the pleasant life at Urbino. The disappearance of that life for ever would persuade him to record it with nostalgia, particularly in a time of stress, and this, too, is one of Baldesar's declared objects. Finally, fears that his manuscript had been pirated and might be more widely publicised in garbled forms which he couldn't check, convinced him that it was time to set in train its official publication. On 8 April 1527 Castiglione wrote to his steward, Cristoforo Tirabosco, with instructions about the expenses of publication. Contemporaneously he sent the manuscript to Giovanni Battista Ramusio in Venice. He was to help supervise its printing on the Aldine presses. The work finally came out in April 1528, its final proofs revised by Bembo and Ramusio, and to Tirabosco went another careful letter to tell him of the complimentary copies that he wanted to send, as well as detailing their paper and bindings.

For another year after the sack of Rome the city was to be under the heel of the Imperial soldiery. The organisation of the city collapsed, food was reserved for the Emperor's troops, and the citizens of Rome starved to death in their hundreds. The plague struck again and even made its way into the Castel Sant' Angelo, where the Pope had to spend the next ten months. Castiglione's major task now was to secure from the Emperor guarantees of Clement's freedom and safety. Charles v's offer was delayed until December 1527, and his terms were crushing – a ransom of 360,000 ducats, 145,000 payable at once and the rest guaranteed by the handing over of papal fortresses and five cardinals as hostages. The agreement was signed on 6 December and the Pope was allowed to leave the Vatican, secretly and in disguise, to seek refuge in Orvieto. There he was to remain for six months. Contemporaneously Castiglione received a terrible letter of rebuke from him, written on 20 August 1527, but delayed in transit. The letter put responsibility for the sack of Rome on Castiglione. It implied that Charles had duped the Nuncio, causing him to rely overmuch on Imperial goodwill and wrongly to reassure the Pope that the Emperor was trustworthy. The reply which Castiglione wrote to Clement more than vindicated his position, but the rebuke must have been a bitter blow to him (cp. Serassi, II, pp.147–52). His reply seems to have been well received by the Pope in the calmer atmosphere of Orvieto and with the sack of Rome almost a year behind him. But many contemporaries, even in Italian clerical circles, believed that the sack of Rome was a visitation from God on the

corruption of the papal court. The Emperor's secretary, Alfonso
Valdés, gave coherent expression to these beliefs in his pamphlet on
'the events in Rome', an attack on the decadence of the Roman clergy
and particularly of the Pope, using words and ideas not far removed
from those of Martin Luther. The pamphlet vindicates the position of
Charles and sees him as a potential saviour and restorer of the true
Church. Castiglione's brilliantly argued reply was based on the
proposition that the evils wrought by the Emperor's soldiers did not
correct the evils of the corruption in the Church. His condemnation
of Valdés as a heretic showed his loyalty to his master and to the
Christian ideal as he saw it, as well as revealing a deep knowledge of
theology and church history. (The polemics are published in Bruno
Maier's edition.)

Nevertheless Charles kept on Valdés as his secretary. Indeed he
went further, rejecting peaceful overtures from the League, determined to pursue the war against France more vigorously than before.
At the beginning of 1528 he arrested the envoys of the major powers
opposing him, including Andrea Navagero, and held them as
hostages for the safe return of Spanish ambassadors still abroad. By the
autumn of 1528 his troops, despite an initial lack of success, had
broken the French, and by October he was willing to make an
approach to the Pope. Thanks in large part to the diplomatic activity
of Castiglione, whom Charles seemed to favour above any of the
other foreign envoys, Clement was allowed to return to Rome in
October with many guarantees and concessions from the Emperor,
anxious now to regularise his position in Italy. In December, Castiglione wrote to Rome to say that the Emperor would probably sail
for Italy for a meeting with the Pontiff. He now seems to have felt
able to accept the Emperor's offer of the Bishopric of Avila and a
yearly income of 12,000 ducats. All the evidence points to his being
Bishop elect when, after one of his periodic bouts of fever, he died, on
7 February 1529, on the threshold of a security and a tranquillity
which had evaded him since Urbino.

Castiglione was buried with great, even royal, ceremony in Toledo
Cathedral, and his funeral was attended by the most distinguished
noblemen of Spain. Charles v described him as one of the finest
gentlemen in the world, and sent a letter in his own hand to Clement
with condolences at the Nuncio's death. Clement, too, seems to have
realised for the first time what a reliable servant he had lost, and the
concessions he made to Castiglione's mother and family, indicate a
new degree of esteem and regret at his loss. In 1530, Castiglione's

remains were brought home, to be buried as he himself had desired, alongside his wife Ippolita. His mother, Luigia Gonzaga, commissioned a tomb and founded a chapel for her son in the church of Santa Maria delle Grazie.

Three months after Castiglione's death, Girolamo da Schio left Rome, on 7 May 1529, to take the late Nuncio's place. He had instructions from Pope Clement to conclude a treaty of alliance with the Emperor. The Treaty of Barcelona of June 1529, followed by the friendly meeting between Pope and Emperor at Bologna in the autumn of the same year, would have been the realisation of his dream had Castiglione lived. Francis I had withdrawn his claims after the Peace of Cambrai (1529), and the way seemed clear for a stabilisation of the political situation in Italy. Even Baldesar's old patron, Federigo Gonzaga, obtained the long-hoped-for title of Duke after the agreement reached at Bologna. On 24 February 1530, Charles was crowned Emperor at Bologna by the Pope. His actions thereafter seemed those of an Emperor ready to act in the cause of a stable peace in Italy, in spite of Clement's further intrigues with the French before his death in 1534.

The Emperor had honoured Castiglione before he died, with the grant of the diocese of Avila. Pope Clement was rumoured to have considered his late Nuncio for a cardinalate, a notion for which Erich Loos argues, adducing Maffei's *Annali di Mantova* (of 1675), to the effect that 'the Pope had already deliberated to make Castiglione a cardinal'. There is little doubt that had he lived on for a further three years Castiglione's position would have been very powerful indeed, and so, virtually by his own efforts, he would have achieved his two main objects: peace and order for the peninsula, and an inner tranquillity (and prosperity) for himself, thanks to new ecclesiastical benefices. His life had followed, *mutatis mutandis*, the perfect curve of Aristotle's 'political animal' – in youth, schooled in the best traditions of the best society, in his physical prime, a soldier, in middle years, an adviser-statesman, and, at the end, a priest. His masterpiece, in its final form will follow the same pattern, recast according to the ethical and political schemata of Aristotle in order to give it an added seriousness and a worthwhile purpose.

## 2. The Educational Ideal

One of the glories of Castiglione's native city was the tradition of humanist education instituted by Vittorino Rambaldino da Feltre (1378–1446) under the patronage of Gianfrancesco Gonzaga, first marquis of Mantua. Vittorino had studied at Padua under Giovanni di Conversino da Ravenna (1343–1408); among his fellow-students had been Pier Paolo Vergerio (1370–1444), whose treatise on education, the *De ingenuis moribus*, was to prove one of the most popular handbooks of the Renaissance. In his youth Castiglione had not been immune to that educational revolution and his letters home on the subject of his son's education, as well as the variety of training and accomplishments of his courtier, reflect the influence of that great tradition. At this point then, it would seem fitting to consider more fully to what extent Castiglione's opinions coincided with the educational aspirations of the Renaissance humanists. Such a survey might appropriately begin with one of the most important discoveries of the early Renaissance – the twelve Books of Quintilian's *De institutione oratoria* (*On the education of the Orator*), which formed the theoretic basis for many of the reforms of Vergerio and his successors.

Marcus Fabius Quintilianus (c. A.D. 35–c. 95) had been renowned among his contemporaries as something more than a guide to oratory, and though modern Classical scholarship tends to value highly his literary critical opinions, the Renaissance, rather like his own contemporary and fellow-Spaniard, Martial, regarded him as the 'supreme guide of wayward youth'. The breadth and wisdom of the views he expressed (particularly in Books I, II and XII of the *Institutio*) were especially influential for the humanist educational ideal. They find an echo throughout the *Cortegiano*, either as the result of Castiglione's personal acquaintance with Quintilian or as the filtered product of a century of educational theory based in large part on his work.

Petrarch (1304–74) had possessed a copy of Quintilian's treatise, but it was Poggio Bracciolini (1380–1459) who discovered a complete version of the work in the monastery of St Gall, where he managed to carry out his magical discoveries during the intervals in the tedious routine of following in the papal retinue over the period of the Council of Constance (1414-18). Poggio, famed for his penmanship as for his erudition, copied the *Institutio* in 1417, and, from that date, the influence of the book became enormous. Quintilian's concept of education accorded well with the aspirations of the early humanists and his treatise (and, five years later, Cicero's newly discovered *De oratore*) fulfilled one of their fundamental needs. Both Quintilian and Cicero had been imbued with a sense of Rome's ancient traditions, the continuity of Roman civilisation, and it was inevitable that Quintilian's system of education, in particular, would produce pupils conditioned by Roman values. The fifteenth century was seeking to steep itself in those very traditions, keen to imitate their outstanding aspects. Furthermore Quintilian's Latin style (although he was writing a century after Cicero) was usually as elegant as that of his illustrious precursor, and so more acceptable to the Renaissance humanists, in a way that Scholastic Latin was not. His treatise illuminated many details of Roman life (particularly the traditions of the Forum), previously only dimly known, and so helped to add to the store of knowledge and information being avidly collected by those students of antiquity. And, while doing these things, he was also describing a system of education which was thought-provoking in that historical situation where the process of teaching the young was only just being freed from the hands of the Church. Details of his system were intrinsically stimulating, too: the question, for instance, of whether pupils should be educated at home or away from home; in classes or by private tutors. Perhaps no one ancient authority could have satisfied so well the fifteenth century's thirst for information and stimulation.

Quintilian had used Cicero's *Orator* and the *De oratore* as sources for some of his comments; indeed, his debt to Cicero is acknowledged at many points. The rediscovery of the *De oratore*, therefore, in 1422, reinforced humanist appreciation of Quintilian's great precepts, and the humanists even more readily seized upon his purpose – to provide an all-round education which was designed to produce not pedants but men of high moral character and general culture. That need is stressed particularly in Book II of the *Institutio*, which also discusses the qualifications of the good teacher and the proper treatment of pupils. The early education of the future 'orator' is dealt with in Book I, which contains a discussion of the home environment, the influence on the pupil of those persons most likely to come into contact with him, such as nurse, parents, and the slave, who would be, in a very literal sense, his 'pedagogue' or παιδαγωγός. There, too, is underlined the importance of a thorough study of Latin and the need for a knowledge of Greek. The same preoccupations are later to be displayed in Castiglione's correspondence with his mother on the education of his son, Camillo.

Perhaps here it might be relevant to stress briefly the importance of oratory for the ancient world. In Athens, for instance, a man's life or property often depended upon his ability to persuade judges of the validity of his case, while on a less fundamentally practical level, if he wished for almost any sort of professional career, he had to prove himself in the *Ecclesia*. In Rome, by Cicero's time, the orator combined in himself all the attributes of top civil-servant, university professor, army commander, provincial governor-general, philosopher and lawyer. Hence, for centuries, under both Republic and Empire, higher education meant rhetorical training, with all the subsidiary qualities which that implied, and Chairs of Rhetoric were founded in every important city of the Roman Empire. Significantly enough, Vittorino da Feltre, as Professor of Rhetoric at Padua, continued that tradition, long after the need for the Ciceronian orator had passed, and he, like his contemporaries, imitated the educational advice of the ancients as unquestioningly and as dynamically as Alberti would imitate their architecture or Raphael their painting.

Some idea of Quintilian's broader aims may be seen in his definition of the perfect orator as the perfect man, who has never existed, but to whose ideals all should aspire: 'Thus the orator should be such a man as may be called truly wise (*sapiens*) and in all his rhetorical faculties such a man, perhaps, as has never yet existed' (*Institutio*, XII, xi, 11). That idea, too, may be classified as Platonic, as Castiglione's 'ideal' courtier has been, and Quintilian's notion of emulation may be compared with Castiglione's archers, competing to hit the bull's-eye. Yet the Romans (and, one suspects, Castiglione, too) always had a practical approach to learning, and usually tried to combine cultural diversion with career qualifications (whereas the Greeks, by contrast, were much more ready to pursue knowledge for its own ends). For the Romans, literature was read as a potential aid to oratory, and oratory, in turn, was the stepping stone to a career in public service. It was the Elder Pliny who once asked, rhetorically, 'What man is so patient that he is willing to learn what he'll never make use of?' (*Epistolae*, VIII, xiv). If perfection as an orator is also perfection as a human being, then it follows that the perfect rhetorical training is also the perfect education. Further, if that perfect education may assure a good career, in a practical Roman sense, then it has a perfect practical application, too.

There are striking similarities of tone between Quintilian and Castiglione. Just as Castiglione's final book rises to a pitch of enthusiasm which approaches Christian gospelling, so Quintilian's paean of praise to his *orator perfectus* becomes almost religious. And both men recall in their words the Aristotelean type of eulogy to the very human ideal which all should emulate (below, p.182). 'Let us strive to this end with all our mental powers and let us work at this task. We may even attain to our ideal. For, if Nature does not prohibit the combination of moral and rhetorical perfection, why may one single man not achieve both ideals?' (*Institutio*, XII, i, 31). But, although this seems an idealistic conclusion, the practicality of Quintilian's purpose for the tormented Renaissance (and for the uncertainties of life at court) is borne out by his stoic and contemplative, and more personal conclusion: 'Now secluded and venerated, free from envy, far from controversy, his fame will be safe, and he will receive, in his own lifetime, that reverence which is usually reserved for his posthumous reputation, and he will see how his own posterity will assess him' (ibid.). The words have an uncanny relevance for Castiglione.

The early humanists had defended their love of the new learning with all the subtlety they knew. Coluccio Salutati (1331–1406), for example, justified the study of poetry on the grounds that the whole of the Bible was a great poem. More specifically, in a letter of 1401, he tells Giovanni Dominici (1357–1419) how a deeper knowledge of the Classics aids towards more accurate interpretations of the Bible and Church Fathers, and how an acquaintance with allegory and symbolism is almost a prerequisite for scholars hoping to understand, for instance, the secrets of the Apocalypse. The debate on the usefulness or morality of Classical studies, as opposed to the revealed truth of Christianity often finds echoes in the early humanist educators. Thus Leonardo Bruni (1369–1444) in his *De studiis et litteris*, pays lip-service to the need for the educated woman to study the Scriptures, but emphasises above all the moral benefits which may be simultaneously derived from reading the Classics. And, conversely, San Bernardino (1380–1444), while he stresses the need for Christian faith in whatever training a person undergoes, and while he enjoins upon his flock the avoidance of blatantly 'immoral' texts (such as Ovid or the Boccaccio visible in the *Corbaccio*), nevertheless has an attitude to the past not dissimilar to Machiavelli's, and suggests that by reading the Apostles and Church Fathers, one can communicate directly with them. 'Wouldn't you find immense pleasure in seeing or hearing Jesus Christ preaching? Immense indeed! Does the same apply for St Paul, St Augustine, St Gregory, St Jerome and St Ambrose, and the other holy doctors? Of course! Then go and read their books... and you will speak with them and they with you; they will hear you and you them, and you will derive great delight from it' (San Bernardino, *Prediche*, III). And in Bernardino's eulogy of education and learning we see a hint of the universal man, qualified to do anything, go anywhere, able to overcome the blows of fortune. Education or study for Bernardino was useful to the individual for benefiting his family, his city and his friends. Through study he would then be able to show his face in every country in the world and before every and any lord, and become a Man (while without study he would be a nonentity) (ibid.). Significantly the same Sermon preaches, as a necessary precondition for the attainment of such freedom-through-study, the need for tranquillity – freedom, that is, from fear and from presumption, the avoidance of dissipating one's energies in frivolity or in melancholy, the avoidance of excessive love of anything except study, and the avoidance of hatred of all things. The catalogue begins to sound like a plea for the Aristotelean Golden Mean, an impression confirmed by the physical Means adduced – eat and sleep in moderation, etc., all extremes are vicious.

Those ideas are to recur throughout the history of educational theory and practice, both among Bernardino's contemporaries and during the following decades, notably in the *De educatione liberorum clarisque eorum moribus* of Maffeo Vegio (1407–58). Indeed, so closely are educational and humanistic ideals bound up during the fifteenth century that it would be an artificial distinction to separate out those treatises, such as the *De ingenuis moribus* of Pier Paolo Vergerio, from the more general political, economic or social preoccupations of his time.

Vergerio's treatise enjoyed enormous popularity for the two hundred years following its composition, not only because of its erudite good sense, but also because of its practical nature and its concise and quickly assimilated pieces of advice. The work is readily available in Eugenio Garin's very readable Italian edition and in W. H. Woodward's translation, and attention will here be drawn only to those aspects most significant for a further understanding of the tradition which led to Castiglione's advice in the *Cortegiano*. Thus Castiglione will make much, in Book IV, of the virtues of an active as well as a contemplative life. Vergerio, perhaps concerned more with his diplomatic ambitions, certainly concerned more with being diplomatic, dwells upon this aspect. The 'liberal' life-style and education require, for Vergerio, contemplative and active life, study and meditation and action and social commitment. Later in his book he condemns the purely speculative and contemplative individual, who, he says, will be of little use to himself or to his city. The sentiment echoes that expressed by Bruni in his *Vita di Dante*, where there is to be found harsh criticism of the pure contemplative – 'Such scholars don't know more than three letters,' remarks Bruni. Commenting on this point of the active life, Garin concludes that the new criterion for nobility is not dependent upon aristocratic birth, but is obtainable through the exercise of a man's virtue in action. He quotes San Bernardino as a contemporary witness of both Bruni and Vergerio: 'Nobility (*gentilezza*) does not consist in lack of action (*oziosità*) but in the exercise of yourself, your family and your city' and the study of letters goes hand in hand with such action in order to reinforce such nobility (cp. Garin, l'*Educazione*, p.9). We shall see that Castiglione is willing to concede, to the well-qualified but non-noble man, equal status with his courtier, but he is only too well aware that the non-noble needs to work much harder at his qualifications than the noble, whose simple accident of birth gives him automatic advantages in the eyes of the world, however mediocre his true character. Castiglione has an eye, as ever, to the practicalities of court life, while Vergerio (and his contemporaries) could still permit themselves the luxury of allowing such potential to every virtuous man.

Giovanni Della Casa (1503 – 56) was to urge his youthful pupil 'not only to do things well, but to take care to make them elegant also;... without such elegant proportion (*misura*) even the Good is not beautiful' (*Galateo*, XXVIII). From a practical point of view again, such elegance, in learned writings, might ensure their survival, as well as their popularity. Vergerio suggests that 'ugly writings', on the contrary, 'do not acquire faith, and soon die, while if books are written in an elegant style, their memory lives on, especially if the style is worthy of the material contained in the book' (*De ingenuis moribus*, p.77). The fate of the Schoolmen's philosophical writings during the final quarter of the fifteenth century may serve as an object lesson here. More will be heard of the blend of elegance and practicality which Bruni was to emphasise in his *De studiis*, a piece of advice followed by Castiglione in his deliberate search for elegant prose and in the practicality of his own suggestions.

Vergerio saw, in the death of rhetorical training, the death of truth. More precisely, he regretted the demise of the rhetorical ideal, not for any nostalgia, it would seem, for the Ciceronian ideal *per se*, but rather because no other training seemed so clearly to posit distinctions between Truth and Falsehood. He regretted the passing of the clarity of rhetorical argument, and he tried to compensate for it by an oft-stated preference for the debating method. It 'sharpened the mind, made for eloquence, reinforced the memory and added self-confidence'. The dialogue form which enjoyed such enormous popularity during the rest of the Renaissance, reaching its apogee with Castiglione, is an example of Vergerio's preference at work, as well as being a straight imitation of the Classical dialogue. Almost every educational writer seemed to emphasise the need for clear discernment and truth (the need for 'truthful' readings of the Classics was to lead to such brilliant textual criticism as has hardly been surpassed since). I shall consider Alberti's thought on the matter in a moment, but more particularly, Vergerio devotes a special section to the need to condition the young against the habit of lying, which if it becomes ingrained, he fears, is the worst habit that the adult can have. At the end of Book I of his treatise, he regrets that there are few who have the courage to tell their masters the truth, and even fewer potentates who have the desire to listen to it. It will be a contention of this monograph that one of Castiglione's major theoretic ambitions was to show his potential audience the dangers of an inability to discern truth from falsehood.

Vergerio devotes some space in his treatise to less profound considerations, such as his cautions against paying overmuch attention to personal appearance. Too much care of this kind carries with it, he suggests, the danger of appearing foppish, of being accused of vanity and of having an effeminate mind. Proper attention to such details is covered by a general admonition, stated early in the book, that the Golden Mean should be a key ambition. In this context he quotes from Terence's *Andria* (I, i, 60), advocating moderate actions and avoidance of excesses. He particularises in various instances, such as in social relationships, which should not be rudely austere, nor yet ridiculously frivolous. That commonplace is to be repeated throughout the Renaissance and will surface again in the *Cortegiano*. But, continuing in now less serious vein, Vergerio concedes the pleasure which may be obtained through the playing of musical instruments (though preferably not wind instruments!) and through dancing. Indeed, he sees a certain utilitarian value in dancing, in encouraging exercise and in enabling the body to acquire greater agility. On the whole, however, he is against the potential dangers of corruption and vanity which he fears that dancing may bring. Music may also have a practical use in moderating excited passions and 'tempering' the mind, another possible example of the Mean, imitated from many Classical sources, and repeated *inter alios* by Castiglione. Vergerio also quotes Aristotle (*Politics*, VIII, 3, 2, and VIII, 2, 6) on the need to know about the techniques of figurative art, and his motives for that advice combine aesthetics (such knowledge teaches men to distinguish the beautiful from the ugly) with economics (with such expertise men are less likely to be cheated over the price of a work of art!).

In the field of civic education, Vergerio, following Aristotle again, states clearly that it is in the interests of the state to provide an education, since the usefulness of such an education will redound to the benefit of the state or the city as a whole, as well as upon the individual who is thus trained. Parents (and the home environment) tended, according to Vergerio, to spoil children – hence they were best educated by friends, or away from home. Castiglione, it may be recalled, was educated in Milan, away from his close family, though his suggestions for the education of his son, Camillo, seem to indicate that he preferred the boy to remain with his mother and grandmother, and be taught by a pedagogue in Mantua. And, Vergerio insists, the richest gift a parent can give to his son is to ensure that he is taught '*bonae artes, honestae artes, liberales disciplinae, honestae disciplinae*'. Such training, says Vergerio, would provide fame for an obscure house, and a glory for one's place of origin if it were humble. The idea is one which Alberti will amplify in his *Della famiglia* and the personal nature of Vergerio's advice, which here seems directed at the betterment of the individual and his household, rather than at any ideals of perfection in behaviour, may be a glimpse between the lines of something less universal than the civically beneficent education which he is normally considered as advocating. Despite that personal note, Vergerio pays a very subtle compliment to his possible masters. Dante had urged that his monarch should possess all and so desire nothing; Vergerio confessed himself frankly astonished that potentates could be decent men (*bonus et sapiens*), since their positions of power, surrounded by everything they could possibly desire and besieged by parasitic acolytes, 'who make fools into madmen', seemed to leave little room for reason and right judgement; and the end of the first Book echoes Plato's *Gorgias* (526a): 'Surrounded by so many opportunities for sinning, it is doubly praiseworthy for a prince to live as a just man.'

There are other general hints which Vergerio offers. He is not slow, for instance, to urge his pupil to keep his own counsel, an attitude visible in Castiglione's restriction of friendship to one well-trusted man, and brought to a peak in the way Niccolò Strozzi (1590–1655) cautions against trusting anyone at all. Vergerio also points to the value of ethics to teach men moral goodness, a lesson that goes hand in hand with the study of history, which teaches men the proper behaviour on given occasions. The use of historical exemplars to bolster moral precepts (often Aristotelean precepts) is to be a feature of the Renaissance humanistic treatise, and Castiglione's *Cortegiano* is no exception to that rule. Among Vergerio's general remarks about moral (and good) exemplars, particularly significant in view of what Castiglione will have to say about the moral examples of both courtier and prince in Book IV, is his argument that the best way to arouse love of virtue and honest moral conduct in a person, is to provide him with a living example of a good, honest man. On his part, too, the pupil should make a positive effort to select someone worthy of his veneration, in order to imitate his behaviour. The idea was not new, and Vergerio probably took it over from Quintilian, but his words help keep alive the tradition which is still visible in Castiglione.

If Vergerio's treatise was the theoretic basis for most educational institutions during the Renaissance, the practical basis was provided by the two great pedagogues, Vittorino da Feltre and Guarino da Verona (1374–1460), whose names we may briefly join here in considering their methods. Not that those methods seemed wholly to Castiglione's taste, but their two schools (at Mantua and Ferrara) kept alive and passed on, through a whole series of fine teachers, the precepts of Quintilian and other great educators. Both men began their careers as university lecturers. At a time when the glories of the Latin Classics were first being discovered, when manuscripts and documents were rare (and printing yet to be invented), the exegetic method of a man like Giovanni di Conversino da Ravenna, who taught both Vittorino and Guarino, was appropriate and economical, travelling around Italy as he did, and spreading the new gospel. Parallels with the publicity given by St Paul to the message of Christianity are extraordinarily close, and Manuel Chrysoloras (c. 1350–1415) and Francesco Filelfo (1398–1481) were among similar publicising disciples of the new learning. It was Giovanni di Conversino's Chair at Padua which Vittorino eventually inherited for a brief period. The peripatetic teacher, then, usually attracted by a rich patron (or municipality) to a temporary position as public lecturer, had been one feature of the system by which the noble and bourgeois public were educated during the fifteenth century.

Another major element which here requires mention was the patronage of great dynasties, such as the Medici in Florence, who encouraged select groups of intelligent and cultured individuals to join together in informal groups, sometimes referred to as academies, where the new learning might be discussed, commented upon and perhaps adapted to meet the contemporary situation. A very informal group of this kind is the one imagined as gathering at the Urbino court in the *Cortegiano*, where social graces and conversation impose an added informality upon the academic discussion. The smaller size of such gatherings would inevitably lead to less formal exegesis and to a friendlier social atmosphere, such as that which characterised the Platonic Academy, for instance, centred around Marsilio Ficino (1433–99). The academicians saw their own activities as reflections of their Classical precursors in the Athenian agora, and celebrated, in the case of the Florentine academy, the 'anniversary' of Plato's birth (and death) with almost mystic rituals which implied for them direct continuation of the ancient traditions.

Similar groups sprang up at all the major courts and centres of learning in Italy. An early portrait of the kind of group which came together and a description of the discussions which they held is given in the *Disputationes Camaldulenses* of Cristoforo Landino (1424–92), composed in 1475 in the form of a dialogue in which the author imagines a group of Florentines, including Leonbattista Alberti (1404–72) and Lorenzo de' Medici (1449–92), who have withdrawn from the heat of the city to a Camaldolite monastery in the Apennines. There they discuss, over a four-day period, the relative merits of the contemplative and active life. That theme is one which Castiglione himself will treat, and the discussions described by Landino, themselves based on Classical dialogues, such as those of Cicero's *Tusculanae disputationes*, are similar to the conversations which form the body of the *Cortegiano*. The advantages of the cut and thrust of dialectic argument, which Vergerio admired in the Classical authors and imitation of which he advocated, are seen there to great advantage. In Castiglione's treatise a leading figure, not necessarily an expert, in a particular field, starts off a discussion (on wit – Canossa and Bibbiena; on the role of women – Giuliano de' Medici; on politics – Federico Fregoso; on Platonic love – Bembo, etc). The company then join in to discuss, contradict or confirm the views expressed, leaving the resolution of the problem under discussion clearly indicated by the dominance of one speaker (often underwritten by the approval of the ladies present) or by the positing of the Golden Mean. The elements of earlier educational dialogues are easily discernible in Castiglione's work.

To complete the picture we need to consider briefly those unwritten precepts which characterised the teaching of Vittorino and Guarino. Although Castiglione seemed to want his son educated at home in Mantua (aware perhaps of the benefits he himself had missed by spending so much of his life among strangers, and remembering perhaps with nostalgia the two happiest years of his life, spent with his wife during their first years of marriage in Mantua) the appropriateness of their methods is nonetheless implicitly recognised in the advice offered in parts of the *Cortegiano*.

Guarino's teaching method seems to have consisted essentially in the graduated reading of Classical authors, with critical comments of a linguistic and historical nature upon the texts. He appears to have encouraged physical exercise in order to maintain an equilibrium of physical health similar to that advocated by Aristotle. Similar methods were being practised by Vittorino in Mantua at the *ca' zoiosa* ('house of joy', the name given to his school). Guarino, it should also be noted was unusual among the earliest pedagogues for his ability as a Greek scholar. He had spent five years (1403–8) in Constantinople learning the language, and for several years Vittorino and he exchanged lessons of Latin and Greek. In middle life, Guarino spent his years as a lecturer, in Florence, Venice and Verona, before transferring his talents to Ferrara in 1429, where he was, first of all, like Vittorino, the head of his own school, and then private tutor to Lionello d'Este. Vittorino was more of the dedicated schoolmaster, though his attention to readings of the original texts of the Classics, and the regime he devised for his pupils was, more or less, the same as Guarino's. We can glean such information from contemporary witnesses, such as Vespasiano da Bisticci (1421–98).

Aristotle's explanation of the distinction between body and soul, and between instinct and reason had led him to advocate in the *Politics* a discipline which trained the mind in a way not dissimilar from that adopted and perpetuated by the two great pedagogues. The kind of physical exercise which seems to have formed an integral part of Vittorino's system, trained the body (and by maintaining its fitness kept the humours in equilibrium and ensured tranquillity.)

The moral edification of Vittorino's pupils would be inculcated by habit and personal example (and Vespasiano makes much of this last in his biography of Vittorino), while intellectual rigour is obtained from the study of Classical authors. The similarities between the practice of Vittorino and Guarino and the theories put forward by Vergerio are clear. The custom of using pupil-teachers, who taught the material they were learning, was an amalgam closer still to Vergerio's idea that the pupil should model himself upon virtuous exemplars. Garin has suggested that one of the most significant influences exerted by the two schools was to help create in the young a personality untrammelled by previous conditioning, an individual able to think for himself. The old compendia of learning gave way under the new schoolmasters to a study of the original texts of the Classics, and an imitation not only of their style, but also of their way of thinking. By growing up with an appreciation of the 'pagan' texts, a series of new generations arose, to whom a defence of the Classics, such as the apology of Salutati, would seem utterly super-fluous. The removal of education from the hands of the Church was complete, and the possibility of the free-thinking, autonomous individual, able to develop himself as highly as he was humanly capable, was now no longer a concept visible only in the historical past.

Although the wheel had turned full circle by the time Castiglione's career reached its peak, and although, under totalitarian regimes, that old individualism and freedom no longer had the dynamic potential which they had had a century before, nevertheless Castiglione had the advantage of the store of experience and knowledge laid up by the previous century. By drawing upon that inheritance he was better able to formulate for his own times a solution which, within the limits imposed, could ensure some approximation to the *uomo universale* of the previous century. For the next two hundred years or more of Italian history after the publication of the *Cortegiano*, every outstanding individual had to pay a price for being allowed to practise, even in a limited way, his art or profession. Some paid with their liberty, some with their lives, others by prostituting their artistic or professional offspring. But if a line were drawn between the more successful survivors and the more unfortunate (if often 'greater') failures, then the former would be seen as coming closer to Casti-glione's norm. The teacher had himself been a pupil, learning in a harsh school the material he now promulgated to others.

It is a curious reflection on the development of educational practice that the earliest movements towards the laicising of education had as their object the creation of what Garin calls 'a quality (*virtù*) capable of being of service everywhere and in any situation, a benefit which lasted for the whole of life, resisting all adversity, a preparation for citizenship, not only of one's own city, but also to fit men to meet citizens of all cities. It was an education of Man as such for the world' (*Pedagogia*, p.xiii). In the fourteenth and early fifteenth centuries, that movement was breaking away from the totalitarian hold of the Church. As the equally totalitarian hold of worldly rulers began to tighten during the fifteenth century, until the French invasion of 1499 brought with it colonialism, writers grew increasingly pre-occupied with using education in a broad sense to find solutions to new problems. And, naturally, they relied upon past experience and particularly upon Classical precept to prove their case, cramming their works with increasingly numerous Classical quotations, as for example, in the *Della famiglia* of Leonbattista Alberti or the *Della vita civile* of Matteo Palmieri (1406–75), a fictional dialogue imagined to have taken place in 1430, in which Palmieri paraphrases or translates large selections from Cicero, Quintilian and Plutarch and includes many echoes of Vergerio and Vegio. But the objectives of these men are now changing, and when San Bernardino emphasises the useful-ness of study in benefiting the individual, his family, his city and his friends, he seems to be stating the priorities which the Renaissance observed in its educational practices. As the importance of city-states diminished after 1500, and as friendship between more than two persons became too unreliable a source of comfort, the benefits of the educational precepts to the individual and to his family became more relevant. Alberti, perhaps more independent and hence more realistic in his appraisal of circumstances and events, has a practical approach to education (and to friendship) as appropriate to Casti-glione's time as it was to his own. But before considering Alberti's treatise in slightly more detail, a word needs to be said about Leonardo Bruni's important *De studiis et litteris liber*, composed some years before the *Della famiglia*, between 1422–9.

Bruni's volume emphasises the necessary harmony between 'things and letters' (*scientia rerum et peritia litterarum*)–between, that is, academic knowledge and its expression in language or literature. The blend of the two is enhanced by his plea for beauty and elegance, which will find an echo for the next century and a half, and one which Castiglione, as is evident from his declared appreciation of those qualities and from the enduring beauty of his own literary style in the

*Cortegiano*, could easily take to heart. Continuing his advice, Bruni adds, to a personal experience of the world and its ways, a thorough knowledge of all types of literary writings, 'For if [we say that] letters, without a knowledge of reality, are sterile and empty [then] even the knowledge of their contents, however vast, if beauty is lacking in the literary form, seems obscure and impervious. Of what avail is it to know many things, beautiful things, if they cannot be spoken of with dignity and written of without provoking laughter?' (*De studiis*, pp.37–8). And Bruni's conclusion that a blend of elegance and utility is essential for the man ambitious for excellence, is one which Della Casa, among many, was to underwrite a century later. One further piece of advice from the treatise may be usefully adduced here in view of its essential practicality: 'One should always bear in mind the times in which one lives and always attend to the most important and advantageous (*giovevoli*) things, and not pre-occupy oneself with what is too obscure or too unhelpful for future events' (ibid.). Bruni's civic humanism is undeniable – an Aretine exile, later honoured by Florence with her highest office, he saw, in the city which flattered him, a potential new Athens or Rome, and he exalted her as such, dedicating his most fruitful years to her aggrandisement and praise. With the demise of the city-states (or at least the utter reduction in their importance) after the end of the century, it would be the more practical side of Bruni's advice which was of greater avail (though Florentine 'purists' and patriots continued to remember Bruni's other advice, perhaps anachronistically, for the rest of the sixteenth century). By contrast with Bruni, Alberti was ideally concerned, in his *Della famiglia*, not with state, but with individual and family.

One of the declared purposes of Alberti's influential dialogue (written between 1433 and 1434 but having a fourth part added in 1440) was to demonstrate the superiority of *virtù* over *fortuna*. *Virtù*, according to Alberti's definition, consists mainly in a combination of foresight and determination, and his clan, the *famiglia alberta*, is an example of the success of that particular blend of qualities. Exaltation of man's potential fills the prologue to his masterpiece: '*Solo è sanza virtù chi nolla vuole*' (He alone is without virtue who does not want it) (*Della famiglia*, p.9), and it is man's reason, rather than fortune or chance which is of greater importance in human life and civilisation (ibid.). Only rarely do families fall into decay for reasons other than lack of prudence and diligence (ibid., p.10). Alberti's object, then, is 'to give advice to fathers and to the whole family, which will be of use in achieving full and supreme felicity and in preventing at any time submission to untoward and wicked fortune' (ibid.). The family under consideration was predominantly a unit of organised self-defence, willing, it is true, to help in the aggrandisement and the preservation of the state or the society in which it existed, but never willing to put at risk its own prosperity or safety. The advice was the result of Alberti's realistic appraisal of the circumstances of his age, and has close parallels with Castiglione's own awareness of his contemporary situation, and of his attitude to the self-preservation of the courtier and his family. The first Book of the *Della famiglia* is more strictly relevant to the theme of educational treatises because of the pedagogic advice given. He there treats of the duties of fathers, the need to stimulate a child's natural aptitude, the avoidance of a wholly ascetic, contemplative ideal, the advisability of physical exercise, the training of the memory, the potentially more dangerous defects of youth, religion, punishment, the need for a literary education, amusements, and (briefly) physical and military training. Of some interest for Castiglione, all of this, and significantly perhaps, the strictures against lying, a theme which recurs in the *Della famiglia*, particularly in Book IV. The boy who gets into that habit ends by being distrusted and hated by his fellows (and possibly unable to discern truth from falsehood).

When one considers the wealth of miscellaneous qualifications which Alberti packs into such concentrated paragraphs, similar advice from Castiglione, for instance on the need to be a good horse-rider and cavalryman, does not seem so extraordinary, and perhaps not even so superfluous. Castiglione even counsels *against* tumbler's tricks on horseback, while Alberti hints to his potential pupil that one test of skill would be to ride a horse, as Caesar was able to, galloping hard with both hands tied behind his back. But of major relevance to Castiglione's *Cortegiano* is the advice offered in Book IV of Alberti's treatise, where the discussion of friendship (and the avoidance of enmity) is most significant.

The whole of that discussion is relevant, but here let it suffice to make two allusions, the first, and more important, to the friendship between prince and courtier which may best yield fruitful results for the courtier and his family: 'And friendships with princes are most important to acquire and use in order to increase and enlarge for himself and his family, fame and good reputation, and dignified authority and praise' (ibid., p.275). And, interestingly enough, Alberti's spokesman there, Lionardo Alberti, confesses that his friendship with King Ladislao of Naples was sealed when riding to hounds with him. The second allusion is to friendship of a more general kind, the need for someone trustworthy in a deceitful world: 'A friend in need is a friend indeed' (*L'amico certo si possa conoscere ne' casi incerti*) (ibid., p.287). Earlier, Adovardo Alberti had pleaded for a practical discussion of friendship (as opposed to the abstractions found in text-books of philosophy). His reasons are equally down-to-earth: 'Against fraud, falsehoods and perfidy one has to be prepared, alert, cautious; against the temerity, audacity and rapaciousness of the wicked one must oppose constancy, moderation and mental virtue. For all these things I need some practical man who will teach me to create and make use of friendship, rather than to describe and design friendships as a learned philosopher' (ibid., pp.285–6). If any more proof of Alberti's practical approach is needed, let the example of Catiline suffice, adduced by Adovardo as a man who knew how to make good and practical use of gifts in order to obtain friendships! 'certainly a most prudent man and the best of workers in this particular art' (*uomo in questo certo prudentissimo e ottimo artefice*) (ibid., p.298). And though Castiglione published *his* work under vastly changed historical circumstances and had to colour his admonitions with more altruistic and universal exhortation to personal virtue and fidelity, a basis for his advice is visible in Alberti.

It would be wrong to pass on from Alberti's treatise without mentioning the revival of Italian as a cultural vehicle, helped in its resurgence by Alberti's stimulation and example. This, too, was a major educational innovation, replacing the traditional Latin with a dignified language that implicitly exalted and vindicated the rights of contemporary men, providing, at the same time, the potential for widening learning and, more important, giving a new creative impetus, through a growing and vigorous new medium, to all fields of human culture. The language of Alberti's treatise testifies to his faith in the vernacular as a vehicle to express dignified and elevated thought. That belief had further been confirmed in his single-handed organisation of a *Certame coronario* at Florence, in 1441, the vernacular poetry competition (significantly, perhaps, on the theme of friendship!) which might help to demonstrate the beauty and the usefulness of the vernacular.

Alberti was Florentine in origin, but much of his development had been away from Florence, and his language, far from being exclusively Florentine, approaches in its vocabulary and syntax a noble and Latinising norm, which enhanced the reputation of Italian as opposed to Latin. It will be seen that Castiglione, in his introductory remarks to the *Cortegiano* and again in Book II, affirms a norm of language not unlike the practical example visible in the noble prose of Alberti's work (cp. below, p.82). This is not to say that their language was identical, but the linguistic aims of each writer were very similar.

Castiglione's faith in the future of his own elegant new vernacular was as prophetic in its way as Dante's statements about his new Italian *sole novo* had been two centuries earlier. He did not set his sights on the past elegance of classical Tuscan, nor on the contemporary fluency of the modern Florentine dialect. In that preoccupation with his own variety of Italian may be seen, too, his concern with the very people his treatise is meant to help: 'one must not despise the speech habits of other noble Italian cities where wise, ingenious and eloquent men come together and discuss important matters of state, cultural matters (*lettere*) and business affairs of all kinds' (I, xxxv). Linguistically and 'educationally' he, like Alberti, set a fashion.

By the end of the fifteenth century the heroic possibilities of grasping Fortune's forelock and achieving the heights of power, as the great *condottieri* and military leaders had done, were rapidly diminishing. Exhortations on the subject, such as those of Machiavelli (1469–1527), were already out of date by 1512. When subtle diplomacy and ingratiation were the main avenues to success, it was of little avail to urge men, as he did in *Il principe*, to crush fortune as a young man might dominate a woman. For the vast majority of men of his status, a much more passive attitude was called for if success was to be gained. In addition to the old concept of fortune as an unknown quantity in human affairs, men now had, more than ever before, to contend with the capricious whims of unworthy masters whom an accident of birth had placed above them, and whose caprices might be influenced by others intriguing for their own personal interests. To devise a system of overcoming such novel obstacles meant a complete reappraisal of the cultivated man's position in society. Political and religious repression removed for ever not only the chance of the advent of a new Federigo da Montefeltro but also the possibility of throwing up a man of the moral independence and stature of Alberti, Leonardo or Michelangelo, and the few who were thus thrown up (men like Ariosto, Cellini, Tasso) had to dissipate their efforts in order to survive and stay sane enough to practise their art.

The noun *cortegiana*, with its undertones of 'prostitute', was studiously avoided by Castiglione, who stated that, instead, he would call his court-lady a *donna di palazzo*, but the prejudice there shown against the feminine equivalent of *cortegiano* was just that – male prejudice which preferred to ignore the moral servility of the male courtier's own situation. V. Borghini (1515–80) had to argue, against the Inquisitor during the 1560s, for the inclusion in the 1573 edition of Boccaccio's *Decameron* of potentially heretical or blasphemous terms such as *cielo* (heaven), *eziandio* (also!), or *pietà* (compassion). Amongst the other nonsensical accusations of immorality against which he had to fight was the excision of *uomo di corte*. He had to counter the suggestion that *uomo di corte* in the sense of 'buffoon' (*buffone*) or 'herald' (*araldo*) was the equivalent of *cortigiano* (and so in context an insult, among others, to the papal court). But the thought remains that the fourteenth-century *court-jester* could be mistaken in 1527 and again just before 1570 for the *courtier* of the high Renaissance by court officials (admittedly some of them Spanish) unwilling perhaps to admit the debasement of the courtier's status to something little more than a Boccaccesque *uomo di corte*. And when one reflects upon the countless attacks by reasonable men upon the corruption of the courts, and considers, by contrast, the stature of the *uomini universali* whose presence characterised the courts and city-states of the fifteenth century, then the Inquisitor's linguistic mistake may seem a Freudian error which reveals the true status of the courtier as it declines throughout the century.

Castiglione's supreme achievement was to grasp the new situation. He was young enough in 1499, when he realised change was coming, and that, for instance, a court like that of Ludovico *il Moro*, the pearl of Europe, could never be the same again, to condition himself to the new circumstances. He was still young enough in 1508 to be able to adapt himself to what he saw would be an inevitably changed regime of life, after the removal of that decent man, his protector, Guidubaldo da Montefeltro. *Virtù* for him no longer implied simply the heroic qualities which had characterised earlier writers on the subject. His strategy was that of the waiting game. The complexity of new political alignments and the internal problems of court diplomacy, required the subtlety of chess rather than the brusqueness of a duel or a tourney (now reduced largely to a ceremonial role). Castiglione's experience showed him that the acquisition, in some measure, of all possible virtues (qualifications or qualities) was more important for survival than the injunction of the early educationists: the acquisition of as many excellences as possible with a special qualification in one's *forte*. Francesco Guicciardini (1483–1540) had mused in his *Ricordi* on the 'trifles' (*leggiadrie*) which he had 'mocked as a young man' because they seemed unnecessary social trivia. Later he came to recognise that 'to have an abundance of all accomplishments (*tutti gli intrattenimenti*) opens the way to the favour of princes, and the man who has this abundance sometimes finds it the prelude to great profit and exaltation, for the world and its princes are no longer formed as they should be, but as they are' (ibid., CLXXIX). Guicciardini's remarks are lent greater point by his personal situation – out of favour with the Medici and in exile from his beloved Florence. Being prepared to take fortune's offerings now meant advocating something closer to Guicciardini's reflections than to Machiavelli's heroic exhortations on dominating destiny. This was Castiglione's new course and new message.

The advantages of what Castiglione considers his particular educational suggestions are shown in the 'list of successes' which precedes the main business of Book IV. The catalogue is impressive – two Dukes, a Cardinal, a Doge of Genoa, a Papal Secretary, an Archbishop and a Bishop, all of whom 'graduated', so to speak, from his school in the course of ten years or so (IV, ii). The other noble spirits (who had died before attaining such high honours) would, Castiglione suggests, have reached similar heights and 'would thus have provided for all who knew them a clear proof (*argomento*) of the praiseworthy qualities of the Urbino court and of its adornment by so many noble gentlemen. Such proof has been provided by almost all the other gentlemen who have been *created* in that court (*che in essa creati si sono*)' (ibid.). The theme is taken up in the eulogy of Francesco Maria della Rovere, for whose elevation 'greater praise is to be accorded to the [Montefeltro] household in which he was brought up (*la casa ove nutrito fu*)...than to his accession to the Duchy of Urbino' (ibid.). And between the two important statements is an aside which may seem awkward to us today, but which would have been very familiar to his contemporaries, namely that, 'truly so many lords and captains, so outstanding for their virtues and held in such universally high esteem, never came out of the Trojan Horse'. The allusion is to a simile in the *De oratore* of Cicero, referring to the school of Isocrates (436–338 B.C.): 'From his school, as from the Trojan Horse, came out innumerable men of the first rank.' Isocrates was well known to the Renaissance educationists: Vergerio quoted from him, Guarino translated his works, Vittorino included him as set reading for his pupils and Chrysoloras transcribed his writings. Castiglione evidently regarded the court (and particularly the Urbino court) as his *school*,

an institution with a record of practical successes proved by its distinguished 'graduates'.

The reputation which Urbino had for producing great men (and
great rulers) allows Castiglione to 'hope that good fortune should
continue to so favour these virtuous works (*queste opere virtuose*)...
that house and state...continue to prosper'. Eleonora Gonzaga, wife
of Francesco Maria, is praised for her qualities of 'learning, grace,
beauty, intelligence, good breeding, humanity and other polite
attributes, qualities which would ensure a continuation of the prosperity of the Duchy'. And yet Castiglione *knew* that the Duchy, particularly after the depredations of Pope Leo in 1517, was destined for
anything but prosperity. But he left the pre-1517 version of that
eulogy as it stood. Educationally, if not historically, his injunctions
were valid, and they and his auguries were meant for all time. He
believed, in other words, that such a school of behaviour trained the
best elements in society and that fortune usually favoured such high
qualifications. On a more personal level, the man who is willing to
train and qualify himself so 'universally', even though he may not
necessarily be inclined or destined for high office (though that was
where maximum self-determination lay), nevertheless affords himself far more possibilities of finding freedom in society by making his
many talents desirable. And such freedom – for instance to move from
court to court – was the best that most men could expect, the best way
most men had of controlling their fortune, during the 1520s.

The notion of the *Cortegiano* as an educational handbook does not
stop here. One of the most significant changes between the *Seconda
redazione* and the final edition of 1528 is the relinquishing, in the new
Book IV, of the title *cortegiano* in favour of *institutor del principe*: 'If you
do not want to call him *courtier*, I am unconcerned,' says Ottaviano
Fregoso (IV, xlvii). The importance of that change will be stressed
again in this study, particularly when Castiglione's full purpose is
discussed in chapter six. But to the epithet *institutor* at that point in the
book are added other qualifications. The courtier, for instance,
should instruct his prince as Aristotle and Plato had done. To this
Cesare Gonzaga adds the interjection, 'You would deserve, rather,
the name of a good schoolmaster (*maestro di scola*) than good courtier
[if that be true]' (IV, xxxvi). As becomes clear from that fourth Book,
Castiglione regards it as part of the courtier's duties, to society as
much as to his prince, to instruct his lord as best he can, and this is his
principal role and purpose. At the same time, such a powerful and
intimate counsellor, by definition, would be in his master's good

graces and secure in his court employment – as tranquil and as
fulfilled a situation as an individual could hope for. Further, he could
use his influence to help create a more tranquil environment for his
fellow men. All these conclusions may be applied to Castiglione's own
position at the court of Charles v. Aristotle and Plato had been, in
addition to their function as tutors to princes, preceptors to other
'courtiers' (and citizens). It is probable that, as author of the *Cortegiano* and as Papal Nuncio to the Imperial court, Castiglione viewed
his own role in the same dual fashion – effectively and potentially
adviser to princes, and, in the final version of his treatise, educational
adviser to others who might hold similar positions. The idea would
not seem unfamiliar to a society used to the schools, like Vittorino's,
which turned out both princely rulers, such as Federigo da Montefeltro, alongside great scholars and lecturers – Lorenzo Valla (1407–
1457) was a pupil of Vittorino's – and great pedagogues – Vittorino
himself was a pupil of another great pedagogue, Gasparino Barzizza
(1360?–1421) – who were often regarded as official or supernumerary
court advisers.

## 3. Book One of *The Courtier*

The Italian Renaissance witnessed a peak of human culture unknown since the great days of Athens. When Castiglione died in 1529, he was just over fifty years of age. During those fifty years Michelangelo and Leonardo had done their greatest work; cities like Florence and Rome had changed from conglomerations of timbered houses, with occasional gems of medieval architecture, to the glorious streets which still delight our eyes; Ariosto had written Europe's greatest poem since the *Divine Comedy*, and his achievement, in turn, was simply the high point of a pyramid of lesser poets. In the field of thought, Greek philosophy was given a renewed lease of life in academies whose atmosphere Aristotle himself would have recognised. Columbus sailed to the New World and confirmed opinions which those philosophical and literary academies had long been discussing. Machiavelli and later Guicciardini reflected and theorised, with unsurpassed originality, on politics and history. In medicine, the unappreciated polymath, Girolamo Fracastoro, anticipated the discoveries of Lister on contagion (in 1977 a medical monograph on rabies still cited him as an authority) and Falloppio would soon revolutionise anatomy. In literary theory, the work of Pietro Bembo and vernacular commentaries on Aristotle's *Poetics* were to influence Europe for centuries. All these achievements could be disseminated on a vast scale through the relatively new medium of printing.

The worlds of political diplomacy and social etiquette were proportionately as highly developed in Renaissance Italy as were the more obvious fields of cultural excellence. Perhaps the example of Lorenzo de' Medici (1449–92) is the most significant. Without any formal position of power in a republican Florence, he not only gained recognition as the city's ruler, but, with a blend of guile, poetry and hard cash, also kept in harmony the fragmented and often fiercely antagonistic Italian city-states. And Lorenzo's example was to provide future diplomats, particularly in Florence, with an expertise which became legendary. To these new developments in diplomacy Castiglione contributed perhaps no less significantly than did Michelangelo to the new flowering of sculpture. Such was Castiglione's world. It was also the world of the court, and the best courtiers were invariably used by their patrons as diplomatic representatives.

In a private sense, the court was an environment where a man needed all the diplomatic guile he could muster, just to survive and keep his patron's favour. The subtlety of the diplomat has always been legendary; it is a truism that without that quality he ceases to be a diplomat. During the present century increasingly intricate mechanical devices have been able to tell the diplomatic corps almost everything they need to know about the *pros* and *cons* of a given situation, the strengths and inclinations of opponents. At the highest and most sophisticated diplomatic levels only at the final moment, when all information is collected and the problem virtually resolved, are negotiations conducted between individuals whose decisions will be binding. How much more subtle a diplomat had to be in the Renaissance, often with no supporting information, poor communications, treating with allies whose allegiances could change at a moment's notice and with capricious patrons at home surrounded by lying adulators. For Castiglione and his fellows, then, it was much more necessary to use some kind of personal judgement. But since human judgement had to depend upon so many imponderables, and since it was not certain that information received would not be false anyway, or that advice given would be carried out in practice, the only reliable factor upon which courtier or diplomat could count was his own talent, and, Castiglione will tell us, one friend. In the world of Renaissance diplomacy all truth was relative, and an exclusive piece of information (exclusive to oneself and one friend) was, in a sense, an inalienable truth, uncontaminated by the deceptive interpretations of others, and uncontaminable by the use which they might make of it if it were to be shared. Under these circumstances the old Greek adage 'Know thyself' will take on a new meaning. On a utilitarian level, to know something which your opponents do not know, can give you practical advantages in a social or diplomatic relationship (Guicciardini called it the greatest single advantage for an administrator); and, on a personal, private level, it is a comfort to have a world of one's own in which to withdraw from the gold-fish bowl of the court, or of public life.

Castiglione's main preoccupation was survival – for himself and for his family, and if, to achieve that end, he had to serve a master, then he would serve the best patron he could find (and there was no great choice of good patrons). He would serve him to the best of his ability until something preferable turned up. Now, one of the principal aims of the diplomat through the centuries has been to hold back his secrets, to veil the truth from potential opponents, and at the same time, to seek to probe to the truth which lies beneath the façade which others are simultaneously creating to mask their own secrets. Castiglione's major problem as a diplomat and as a courtier was to conceal his own secrets, to dissemble his own feelings, and to perceive the reality which lay beneath the polite or inscrutable exterior of possible rivals or enemies. One ever-present message in the *Cortegiano* will be the greatest lesson learned from thirty years of work as a diplomat: to discern truth from falsehood, to differentiate between appearance and reality. Yet, paradoxically, his book must simultaneously impart the crucial diplomatic lesson of dissimulation. Little wonder, then, that his precepts are presented in such a subtle guise that the *Cortegiano* has been the subject of such simple individual explanations: a portrait of the Urbino court; the dreamed-of Ideal Court; the Ideal Courtier (but only in his externals); a handbook of high moral behaviour; a collection of contemporary topics for discussion under headings like *Platonic love*, the *Querelle des dames*, the *Questione della lingua*, *Wit and Wisdom of the Renaissance*, *Renaissance Man at play*, and so forth. All these ideas are accurate as far as they go, but individually they are bric-à-brac, the trivia of court life, and we should take heed of the author's own warning, put into the mouth of Ottaviano Fregoso, incredibly near the end of the book, that up to that point, that is, after discussing everything which *seems* to contribute essentially to the ideal courtier, *the company had not talked about his purpose.*

After all the lessons derived from a lifetime of diplomatic activity, it would have been unlikely for Castiglione to speak out with forthrightness; such bluntness would have defeated the whole object of his treatise. He also has, as one of his aims, to sweeten the rim of the glass, so that his didactic medicine may slip down the easier. To the subtlety of the diplomatic veil, which at times approaches allegory, is added the stylistic ambition, visible in Cicero and other Classical authors, to gild the pill. Further, he has the Renaissance awareness of the lasting value of a work of elegance and the unreadable (and short-lived) quality of stylistically bad writing. Hence the 'practical' aspect is further disguised by his most elegant prose. Many of his important statements will be introduced with the casualness which he extols in Book I (chapters xxvi and following), and I believe it necessary, if we are fully to appreciate Castiglione's meaning, to consider not only the significant and self-evident statements which he makes, but also, and perhaps more importantly, to read between the lines and listen to the diplomat's whisper.

From the outset, in the letter to Bishop De Silva, which prefaces the whole, Castiglione gives enough clues that his aims are more oblique than have been generally thought. Vittorio Cian's authoritative monograph (*Un illustre nunzio pontificio...*) expresses the traditional interpretation of the dedicatory letter, that its author had five main objects in placing it as preface to his book: firstly it provided him with an opportunity for name-dropping in mentioning the Bishop, 'paying homage towards a spirited and intelligent humanist' (ibid., p.244) and offering what Cian calls this 'testimony of his esteem' for a potential ally in any disputes between Pope and Emperor; secondly he wished to popularise his work, explain why its final version was put together and printed so hurriedly and at that particular time, and mention Vittoria Colonna's name 'to arouse the curiosity of the public' (ibid.); thirdly, Cian says that he wished 'to exalt the glories of the Urbino court' and to eulogise nostalgically and pay a debt of gratitude to the 'memory of Urbino's illustrious dead' (Duke Guidubaldo and others); fourthly, he wished to justify the linguistic medium he used; fifthly, he wished briefly to reply to adverse criticism by allowing time to judge his work. That broad summary is accurate and I would not want to detract from Cian's interpretation. His views on the dedicatory letter colour the rest of his critical approach, and, over the half-century or so which he spent working on Castiglione before publishing his monograph (c. 1894–1951), his theories, particularly his idealist views, influenced others to take similar directions, until, in fact, Carlo Dionisotti's review of the monograph itself in 1952.

But there is another side to the dedicatory letter. There is no deny-ing that the opening pages of the *Cortegiano* have many references to the creation of an ideal courtier: 'to choose the most perfect form and the flower, as it were, of this courtliness (*cortegiania*)' (i, i). Castiglione also states that if he fails in his object, he will have been simply following the examples of Plato, Xenophon and Cicero in their respective attempts to formulate the perfect republic, king and orator (Dedicatory letter, iii). Yet he also says that his picture of the Renaissance court of Urbino 'will not adorn the truth with pretty colours or make things seem what they are not by using the art of perspective' (ibid., i). New colours and the *trompe l'oeil* effect of perspective had revolutionised the artist's technique in the previous fifty years. Castiglione's modest disclaimer, that he is unable to portray the court as the great Michelangelo or Raphael would have done, conceals a deliberate reference to that most deceptively beguiling of artistic tricks and may not have been so unintentional as appears on the surface.

If we then take a different approach to the normally idealist attitude, read between the lines and listen to the voice of the diplomat, we may get a rather different view. Thus it is true that he eulogises the Urbino court, but he qualifies his eulogy almost immediately (1, ii), stating that its surroundings are 'not so pleasant (*ameni*) as many other places'. Its glory, we shall see, will consist in what its lords and courtiers had done to improve the place and to introduce culture and social joy. The site of the court itself, then, is not the most ideal he could have chosen. Secondly we are told that the greatest achievement of Federigo da Montefeltro, founder of the dynasty, was to have generated such a son as Guidubaldo, whom Castiglione evidently idolised for his humanity and culture and to whom he devotes the greatest of his eulogies. Yet poor Guidubaldo, though evidently Castiglione's 'ideal prince' was a chronically sick invalid whose every enterprise seemed to be attended by bad luck. Although Castiglione gives the impression of portraying an ideal court and an ideal prince, the flaws are quite clearly stated. If we now consider the more direct statements on his *ideal*, we shall find that these too, are qualified very subtly. Thus, although he implies that he may be 'choosing, from a variety of customs practised in the courts of Christendom, the most perfect form of courtliness', he has prefaced that remark by saying 'what a difficult thing it would be to do so' (1, i). His disclaimer is again implicit, qualifying the ideal by the difficulty anyone would have in depicting it. The other references to what seems a Platonic ideal, that is to the perfection of oratory, monarchy or republican government, which he says he will 'rest content to have erred in imitating' (the convoluted language of diplomacy is there at its most notable) are also given further qualifications. This will be, paradoxically, a 'relative' ideal, a practical proposition for potential courtiers, who may never attain the heights of *cortegiania*, but who, 'like archers aiming at a target' may attain relative degrees of excellence the nearer they come to the bull's-eye.

The opening of Book One follows the pattern laid down in Cicero's *Orator ad M. Brutum*. The address to Alfonso Ariosto parallels Cicero's remarks to Brutus in its explanation of the purpose of the book: to teach the kind of courtly behaviour most appropriate at the courts of princes, so that the courtier may acquire his master's grace and favour and his fellows' praise. As in Cicero's treatise, the task of cataloguing the indispensable qualities is recognised to be fraught with difficulties, not least of which is the inevitably changing fashion in courtly virtues. Nevertheless, Castiglione presses on with his purpose and here, for the first time, is to be found a subtle but important change between the *Seconda redazione* and the final edition. In the earlier version, he had said: 'let us form such a courtier that the prince whom he serves, however small his state/status (*stato*), may be called a very great lord' (p.4). In the edited version, Castiglione adds to the notion of service to the prince the qualification that the prince must be worthy of the courtier's service. Hence 'that prince who shall be served by him' (*quello principe che da lui serà servito*) becomes 'that prince who shall be worthy of being served by him' (*quel principe che sarà degno d'esser da lui servito*) (I, i). The onus of 'worthiness' has now been transferred from courtier to prince, and, as will be seen below, the possibilities of leaving the service of an *unworthy* master are discussed at greater length. It may be an early indication of the more practical nature of Castiglione's handbook for survival.

The opening address concludes with a further comparison with the Classical authors of dialogues, whose methods the author preferred to imitate, rather than to write a didactically formalised book of rules. He also explains that, since he was away in England when the events in the dialogue took place, he relies on trustworthy eyewitnesses. And here there occurs a further modification from the *Seconda redazione*, which requires our attention. In the earlier draft, and in the even earlier *Proemio*, published by Serassi (op. cit., I, p.91) he had stated that the dialogues would renew a personal happy memory 'Recalling the grateful memory of a happy time' (*rinovando la grata memoria d'un felice tempo*), the implication being that these were memoirs of his happy sojourn in Urbino; whereas in the final version, the personal and individual aspect is universalised by the omission of *felice tempo*, a deliberate move confirmed below, as will be seen.

Castiglione goes to some lengths to set his dialogue in the recognisable geographical location of Urbino. And his account proceeds with a eulogy of the Montefeltro dynasty and particularly of the achievements of Duke Federigo and the personal qualities of his son, the invalid Guidubaldo, whose life, in the eyes of the world, must have seemed one of wretchedness and failure: 'in all matters military and in every other detail, small or important, things went badly for him'

(*e nell' arme e in ogni altra cosa o piccola o grande, sempre male gli succedesse*)
(I, iii). Guidubaldo's most painful affliction was gout (or arthritis)
which reduced him to immobility and which eventually helped to
kill him at the age of thirty-six. But it is Guidubaldo's spiritual and
cultural achievements, and his stoic disposition in the face of terrible
tribulation (*atrocissimi dolori*) which occupy the major part of the
chapter devoted to him (I, iii). In particular there is an extended paragraph (not in the *Seconda redazione*) which emphasises the Duke's
inability to participate in the physical activities of the court, but which
stresses his good taste and judgement and his ready encouragement
of others who did take part. It is as though Castiglione wished, at the
very outset of his treatise, to hold up as an example to his readers a
contemplative of an Aristotelean and stoic kind. It is the qualities of
mind and soul which are stressed – Guidubaldo's 'most wise counsel
and indomitable soul' (*consiglio sapientissimo e l' animo invittissimo*). His
strength of mind (*vigor d' animo*) prevented his natural virtue from
being overcome by fortune's blows. His life was the perfect example
of mind overcoming matter: 'In his infirmity he lived like a whole
man, and in his adversity like a favourite of fortune (*fortunatissimo*)
dignified and esteemed by everyone' (I, iii). Castiglione's earlier use
of *invittissimo* to refer to Guidubaldo's moral fibre is doubly interesting when one reflects that the Duke had hardly any military success
and that other writers, notably Vespasiano da Bisticci and Angelo
Poliziano (1454–94), refer to Guidubaldo's more successful *father*
as *invittissimo* (ἀνικήτοιο πάτρος γόνον – Poliziano, *Epigrammatica
Graeca*, p.207) because of his physical, military victories. Guidubaldo
is further praised for his learning and hospitality and for his sociability and encouragement of those noble physical activities in which
he could no longer participate.

But Guidubaldo's ill-health also meant that he could no longer
share in the evening conversations. Instead, his wife Elisabetta
Gonzaga presided over the soirées, aided by her good friend (and
sister-in-law), Emilia Pia. The pleasant and civilised atmosphere of
the Urbino court is underlined again and again, an atmosphere due in
no small part, we are told, to the presence of the Duchess and her
lively companion. And apart from her obvious social virtues, misfortune had brought out Elisabetta's hidden qualities of prudence and
strength of mind. One final point must be made about the atmosphere.
In the *Seconda redazione*, Castiglione states that he considered his
period at the Urbino court 'to be truly the flower of his life' (*reputo
veramente che fosse il fior della vita mia*). This allusion, like the earlier

reference to his *tempo felice*, is deleted in the edited version.

The treatise proceeds with a list of the participants at the various soirées (noted above, p.16), and with a brief allusion to the earlier arrival there of Pope Julius, on his return from subduing the rebellious Bentivoglio of Bologna. Some of the Pope's distinguished retinue had remained behind when he returned to Rome, thus increasing the noble talents already present at the Urbino court. After this aside, Elisabetta asks Emilia Pia to begin the evening's entertainment and she, in turn, suggests that each of the company propose a type of entertainment (*gioco*) and that a vote be taken on the most appropriate or amusing course to pursue. Emilia asks the misogynist, Gasparo Pallavicino, to start, and when he demurs, countering that Emilia herself should begin, the Duchess grants her friend her own authority, and Gasparo is thus forced into initiating the evening's discussion.

With typical economy of rhetorical devices and casualness of style, Castiglione has, as we shall now see, very subtly told his readers his purpose and set out the main moral and philosophical themes of the remainder of the book. The prelude should be a hint on how to read the rest of the volume, for Baldesar's counsel will be delivered with the *sprezzatura* (casualness) which he so strongly advises later (cp. below, pp.78ff.) and his major precepts will be introduced with the deceptively casual suggestion rather than the 'fixed order or rule of distinct precepts' (*certo ordine o regula di precetti distinti*) (I, i), which he says at the outset he intends deliberately to avoid.

At the present, initial stage of the book, it may be useful to see what precepts he may have intended his readers to assimilate already. The naturalistic setting of the palace, which, as we have noted, was not necessarily idealised, allows him to give a precise location and also to hint at the civilising centre which such a court should be. Casually we are given a precise date for the dialogues by the fact of Castiglione's absence (at Windsor) and the presence of Julius II's retinue at Urbino (beginning of March 1507). The universality of the topics to be discussed is emphasised by what we know of the modifications from the *Seconda redazione*, the deletion of specifically personal references to the author's own happy time at the Urbino court. The eulogies of the Montefeltro family conceal a host of precepts which will be elaborated in the body of the treatise: the prince must be a firm ruler, beneficent to his people and helpful in the task of civilisation (Federigo); concord and peace are necessary for human fulfilment (the peace and harmony of the Urbino court); virtue can overcome the adversity of fortune, and the contemplative man may find happiness whatever his physical condition (Guidubaldo); indeed misfortune often brings out the best in humanity (Elisabetta); women have a harmonising and civilising influence (Elisabetta and Emilia Pia).

Forced, then, to continue, Gasparo Pallavicino (after a typical aside on Woman's ability to avoid work!) gives the theme which I hope to show underlies most of the rest of the treatise. Here, perhaps, one should add that these opening proposals are usually skated over quickly by critics, in order to arrive at the more obvious suggestion of Federico Fregoso in chapter xii, that they discuss the perfect courtier. Only one critic, Lawrence V. Ryan, has hinted at the importance of the preliminary proposal concerning *love*, in order to support his excellent theories on the unity of Book IV. Toffanin goes as far as to dismiss no less than five of the opening propositions as 'inept, empty or obscene' (*Il Cortegiano nella trattatistica*, p.12). Here we will deal with *all* of the propositions in some detail; their relevance to the whole will then be made clear. Pallavicino states the truism that men, despite their different tastes and judgements, 'agree on one thing: that each individual holds most dear a beloved object' (I, vii). The statement is akin to Aristotle's definition of The Good, and the changed text, from the '*quella persona che essi amano*' of the *Seconda redazione* (p.12) to the edited version's '*cosa amata*', may imply a closer adherence to the Aristotelian neuter pronoun (τἀγαθὸν οὗ πάχτ'ἐφίεται) in the *Nicomachean Ethics* (I, i), though it is true that later in the chapter *persona* is also used. But here the important notion is that our natural affection for object or person may deceive our judgement: 'one cannot deny that such people deceive themselves and that the lover becomes blind about the beloved object' (*non si po dire che questi tali non s'ingannino e che lo amante non divenga cieco circa la cosa amata*) (I, vii). Hence Pallavicino proposes a discussion of the merits and (inevitable) defects of a loved person. That theme is to be taken up several times in the course of the book, and will reach its most important point of discussion with Bembo's eulogy of love in Book IV, but there are other noteworthy echoes of Pallavicino's proposition. Thus in Book III Giuliano will call for some sort of protection for his *donna di palazzo*, against the inherent dangers in believing in love's illusions, as well as the perils which the guiles of the cunning (and perhaps unscrupulous) lover may bring to bear upon an ingenuous woman. They must be taught, he will advise his audience, how to distinguish the false from the true (*quelli che simulan d'amare e quelli che amano veramente*) (III, liv). This theme will be treated in chapter six, but our thesis, that these preliminary statements contain casual references to the more important themes of the book, requires its mention here.

A similar motive lies behind the next proposal, that of Cesare Gonzaga, which seems at first glance to be frivolous, if not inept: 'If one had to show madness in public what sort of madness would one exhibit?' (I, viii). The suggestion is apparently further removed from reality by Cesare's next analogy, that of those victims of the bite of the tarantula who dance in public to get rid of the poison. Yet the idea of true and objective discernment is present in the technique of the musician who varies the rhythm of his tune as he sees the victim affected well or adversely at varying stages in the dance. In other words, by casting aside inhibitions and allowing one's audience to judge one's merits and defects, vices may be criticised and virtues revealed. Cesare's initial premise is that it is impossible for the individual to judge himself with complete objectivity, and such a failure to achieve self-knowledge produces 'various defects in all our actions' (I, viii). The theme of the discernment of truth is put into higher relief by Castiglione's evident lack of interest in the aspect of public madness, for the chapter concludes with the indifferent anti-climax, 'etcetera' (*e tal cose*), not found elsewhere in the edition, an indifference confirmed by the swiftness with which Cesare, much later, passes over a similar proposal (III, lxxii). It is the discernment of truth which is here, as so often in the rest of the book, the most important thing, and Cian and other critics are probably bringing in irrelevances when they adduce long notes on madness, as treated by Renaissance writers and philosophers, alluding to Erasmus' *Moriae encomium* (*In Praise of Folly*), Ariosto's *Furioso* (and Astolfo in the moon valley) as well as to Classical precedents (Plato's *Phaedrus* and Horace's *Satires*, I, III). Castiglione's purpose is consistent with the rest of his treatise and in the present case it seems unlikely that this is a fashionable reflection of current trends.

A typical device for changing the mood of the discussion (though not the topic of distinguishing truth from falsehood) is the casual introduction of Serafino Aquilano's attempt to tell an obscene story (on the preference of women for snakes rather than mice). The story is rapidly cut short by Elisabetta, who passes the word to L'Unico Aretino. Without breaking the new humorous mood and although *seeming* to propose a different kind of *gioco*, he says that he would like to investigate methods of extorting truth from the wicked, 'and this in order to uncover the deceits of an ungrateful lady' (I, ix). He is referring, with amusing gallantry, to the Duchess and proposes that the company suggest a meaning for the monogrammed [s] (probably the zodiacal sign for Scorpio) which she wore around her neck. Emilia suggests that he give his own explanation, and he 'improvises' a sonnet on the bauble, in a manner typical of the sixteenth-century occasional poet. (The sonnet, *Consenti o mar di bellezza e virtute*, was printed in some sixteenth-century editions of the *Cortegiano*, by editors wishing to be helpful to their readers and Cian reproduces it in his footnotes (ed. cit., p.31)). Possibly the most interesting feature of Accolti's intervention is a personal judgement by Castiglione himself, a type of comment not usually made in the *Cortegiano*. He suggests that the subtlety and ingeniousness of the sonnet indicated that it had been premeditated. The fashionable practice of the improviser is here shown in its proper light, anything but spontaneous, and another myth is revealed for what it truly is.

The next proposal, made by Ottaviano Fregoso, contains in germ the questions on love which had occupied Italians for two centuries past, and which were to degenerate, during the remainder of the sixteenth century, into the formalised pedantry of the Academies, as exemplified by the many lectures of Benedetto Varchi (1503–65) delivered in the Florentine Academy. These included the *Sopra sette dubbi d'amore*, and the four lectures, subdivided into twenty *quistioni*, *Sopra alcune quistioni d'amore*, which formed only a small part of his production in this vein. Ottaviano's apparent misogyny, he implies, requires a clear appraisal of what true love is. His aversion to women derives, he says, from the evident emotional conflicts which he sees in people in love, conflicts which cause him personally to stifle any such feelings of love in himself, not out of misogyny, but for reasons of health. On the other hand, others do seem to find bitter-sweet delight in the disdain which their loved ones may feel for them. The *dolci sdegni* and the conflict of emotions which Ottaviano adduces echo such Petrarchan paradoxes as '*Dolci ire, dolci sdegni e dolci paci*'. His rather contorted proposition, then, is that the company should state for what motive they would like their beloved to feel disdain towards them. The question is typical of those topics for discussion which during the century hesitated between psychology and art and found their supreme interpreters in the poets of Petrarchism. Ottaviano Fregoso's aim and purpose, he says, are to clarify for himself other aspects of love, perhaps find such sweet consolation himself, and so prove to his audience that he was not inherently misogynist. The idea, of clarifying his psychological state vis-à-vis women, may have Petrarchist undertones, but it is stated here in terms worthy of a Pirandellian investigation and explanation of the truth which lies behind our public reputation (in Ottaviano's case, for misogyny) so often misjudged by our fellows.

Bembo, the next interlocutor, had already written on the very subject which Fregoso had touched upon. In particular the words of his creation, Perottino, in Book I of the *Asolani*, discuss the oxymoronic delights of love, and play upon the concept of *amore* and *amaro* in a pun which is timeless (it may have begun with Plautus' *Trinummus* (II, i), it continues in the modern advertising slogan, referring to a well-known bitter aperitif with the epithet *amarevole*). Castiglione's own language here is almost that of the *dolce stil novo* as he repeats the words *amorevole, amarissimi, amorosi, amaritudine* and the like, much as Bembo had done in the *Asolani*. Yet the precepts of that book are *not* forthcoming and Bembo's next remarks tie in his proposed topic with the overall theme of true discernment. He goes on, then, to say that his own experience of 'love's disdains' (*sdegni d'amore*) had always been bitter. On occasions, for instance, his lady may have been led into *falsa opinione* about him by malicious gossip, or some unnoticed fault of his own may have caused her anger. In the first instance he was innocent; in the second, the pain felt at being, himself, the cause of disdain was redoubled. He proposes, then, to examine the relative pain suffered either in causing grief to one's beloved or in receiving grief from him (or her).

It is at this point that Federico Fregoso proposes that, since the company is composed of such excellent courtiers, and in order to 'repress the many fools who believe that through presumption and ineptitude they can acquire the name of courtier', they choose 'someone from their number to form with words the perfect courtier' (I, xii). All applaud the idea, and Emilia imposes upon Ludovico da Canossa the task of expatiating on the subject. The antagonistic attitude shown here to the 'presumptuous and inept' courtier is a further example of Castiglione's new professionalism (cp. below, p.189).

The proposed themes are now ended, but two further points need here to be made which will provide all those disparate proposals with a measure of internal consistency. Castiglione was too clever an artist to use these preliminary remarks as a mere incidental introduction to the main stuff of his treatise. This may be the impression conveyed by his casual style, but, firstly, the propositions of Gasparo, Cesare,

Aretino, Fregoso and Bembo, and even the symbolic novella begun by Serafino, all contain hints that man's judgement and discernment may be deceived and may often need to be clarified. The truth is often disguised by personal bias (Gasparo), ignorance or lack of objectivity (Cesare), subtle symbolism which covers one's real intent (Aretino), the ambiguity of the passions (Fregoso and Bembo). In the second place, if one studies the *Seconda redazione*, five significant proposals there are omitted from the later edition. Two of the proposals may be dismissed rapidly: which is the greater grief, for a man to love a married woman unrequitedly, or for a married woman to be forced to submit to a hated husband instead of offering herself to her beloved? And, in semi-humorous vein: how can one best undo one's rival in love? These find a minor mention in Book III (see below). But three topics which are omitted at this point find greater expression in the edited version's Book IV, namely: which is preferable, a woman of impeccable morals and manners who may not be beautiful, or a great beauty lacking in morals and manners? (p.17); next: 'which are the most certain and positive signs to discern true love from false?' (*Quali sono gli più certi e sicuri segni per discernere l'amor vero dal falso*) (p.18); finally: which extreme is most likely, that a man constantly courting women be despised or that a man constantly despising women be loved by one of them? 'Because,' says Bibbiena, 'I'm firmly decided to settle for one of these two extremes' (p.19).

The final dilemma, posed by Bibbiena, may perhaps have been too obviously an Aristotelean positing of two extremes in order to suggest a Golden Mean, and Castiglione later omits it because he shies away from obvious statements. The other questions, on the true nature of love and the sometimes specious nature of beauty are treated at great length in the important Book IV. It is significant, however, that nearly all these topics, loosely connected with love, are fundamentally concerned with the discernment of truth and clear understanding, and were originally intended as further topics prefacing the formulation of the courtier. From chapter xii onwards, the questions discussed are almost exclusively concerned with fashionable façades, social behaviour, the very activities which help conceal and dissimulate true feelings and frank investigation. There is a paradox in this 'handbook for survival at court', which in its subtlety and complexity has a beauty all its own. Survival itself was not enough. To create a civilised environment for himself and his fellows, the courtier will need to ingratiate himself (by using social graces, social *disguises*, if need be) to the point of influencing his master's decisions, but, to be able to influence such decisions, his advice must be based on a true assessment of circumstances, and a true discernment of character and actions. Hence all these casual hints at the need to recognise truth from falsehood, to know oneself and one's true qualities, hints which reach their apogee in Bembo's eulogy of love in Book IV, are here, at the very outset, placed before his reader.

Emilia Pia chooses Ludovico da Canossa because of his provocative and controversial style of speaking, which guarantees contradictory responses from his audience, and so ensures a more lively conversation. But Canossa is, by his own admission, no expert in the subject, and can only give a middle-of-the-road view of courtly behaviour, based on his own experience and preference, and subject, as necessary, to modification by the views of others. Despite the 'variety of judgements' which will see the same loquacious man, for instance, as a lively companion or as a boring chatterer, everything has a norm of perfection, however hidden it may be, and it is the expert's task to judge that norm. With a further self-effacing remark or two, Canossa ends his introduction, but not before Castiglione has allowed him to emphasise that 'truth often lies hidden' (I, xiii). There is no denying that Canossa's statements contain quite clear Platonic notions of an Ideal and of a Truth which need to be teased out by a Socratic investigation and discussion, but attention must also be drawn to the Aristotelean character of these prefatory remarks and their 'mediocre' proponent. Misjudgements (or biased judgements) are often made by those who 'disguise a vice with the name of its closest virtue, or a virtue with the name of its nearest vice; as in calling a presumptuous man "free" or a moderate man "arid"...' (ibid.). Much of Castiglione's efforts henceforth will be devoted to positing the norm of the Golden Mean, in this case the *via media* between extremes of vice and virtue, and, elsewhere, the norm of good taste in dress, language, food and so forth.

The Aristotelean Golden Mean had long been a tenet of many Classical authors, notably of Cicero, as well as of such sects as the Stoics, and Castiglione's familiarity with the idea becomes more and more obvious as the treatise proceeds. Indeed, in the very next chapter the Mean is openly advocated. But first, Canossa insists that, all other things being equal, a man born of noble blood will have advantages over his non-noble fellows in attaining to a perfection of courtly virtues, and that merit is usually, though not always, transmitted in the noble blood-line. Sometimes, too, an individual may be born of humble stock endowed almost divinely with all the gifts of mind and body, while others may be so inept and graceless that no amount of training can ameliorate them. Between the peak of gracious excellence and clumsy ineptitude is a Mean (*il mezzo*) to which the less gifted may, with studious application, attain, by correcting in large part their natural defects. Cian has indicated how close to a paragraph in Aristotle's *Politics* (I, ii, 19) is Canossa's idea of nobility and its hereditary transmission. Certainly the mood is more Aristotelean than Platonic, for what sort of ideal is this? It has more of the pragmatic approach of Aristotle than the idealistic mysticism of Plato. Canossa's advice is aimed at raising the standard of 'those who are not so perfectly gifted by nature' (I, xiv), to a point below 'gracious excellence', but above 'senseless folly'. Further, Canossa concludes the chapter with a desire that the courtier, apart from nobility, needs an amiable disposition and appearance, which will create 'a good first impression' and 'guarantee that he will be worthy of the society and the grace of any great lord'.

The idea of creating a good first impression is taken up again after Gasparo Pallavicino's very well-reasoned objections to Canossa's thesis; he has known vicious men of noble birth and illustrious men of humble origin, and, as for hereditary 'seeds of virtue', these must, logically speaking, be present in us all, since we have a common origin (I, xv). It is the fickleness of fortune, Pallavicino suggests, which is seen most often to exalt those who have no particular merit and to bring low the most worthy. Ludovico Canossa counters these objections with words which show Castiglione's own recognition of the superficial way men conceive of nobility. Critics who have sneered at Castiglione's alleged snobbishness seem to have ignored the practical way he here applies his observation of his fellows' attitude to hereditary and honorary titles and pomp. Canossa repeats that, all other things being equal, a nobleman will at once make a favourable first impression upon public opinion, an impression the like of which the non-noble would have to work hard to achieve. It was another means of portraying the courtier '*cumulato d'ogni laude*' (laden with every praise) (I, xvi). The opinion is the subject of other treatises during the Renaissance, notably the work of Poggio Bracciolini, *De nobilitate*, at the opening of the period and the spate of tomes at the end of the sixteenth century. Castiglione wants to take advantage of common prejudices in favour of nobility.

The popular notion of nobility certainly seemed important in the way Canossa implies. By mid-sixteenth century, titles were being handed out with scant regard for the nobility or otherwise of their recipients. Vincenzio Borghini regretted this 'squandering' of titles and worked for a long time trying to define what nobility was, and who the truly noble families were: 'Our forefathers handed out titles with good cause and not, as nowadays, at random, for now they're squandered (*si scialacquano*), not distributed' (*Storia della nobiltà*, p.48). The ancient nobility struggled to find an identity for themselves when the major dynasties threatened to smother their former glory. Two of Borghini's most arduous commissions were to help draw up family trees for the Benivieni and the Valori families, in about 1570, at a time when the Medici were coming to a peak of their power. The second of those tasks led him on to a general discussion on 'How to retrace and distinguish families' (ibid., p.94). The *nouveaux riches* had always been able to buy their way into the nobility, through rich marriages or public works, and very often a superficial indication of their 'venerable' origins was sufficient to satisfy their ambitions. Earlier Giovanni Boccaccio (1313–75) and Franco Sacchetti (1330?–1400) had both mocked the falsification of 'ancient' coats of arms or the compilation of new escutcheons. And the families thus satirised were acting as they did precisely in order to obtain that instant respect which Castiglione realised was one of the inherent perquisites of nobility. As social gaps widened after 1500, the mystique of being part of the noble caste increased, and while Castiglione recognised that the *omini bassi* (non-noble classes) may possess the same qualities as the noble, it was inevitable that the popular mind saw the nobility in a favourable, and, no doubt, enviable light. The pragmatist Castiglione wanted to make use of what might be a popular myth in order to give his courtier more apparent influence. Spanish *puntillo* and French obsequiousness were growingly more important fashions than Albertian ideals of the self-made man of a century before.

The discussion next turns to a topic which Castiglione might well have played down had he had more time for revision, a topic which is slightly satirised anyway, namely that the courtier's first and foremost profession should be that of soldier. It was a piece of advice picked up by Torquato Tasso (1544–95) in his own courtly dialogue, *Il Malpiglio*. Courage is necessary, but not boastful or pretentious vainglory. Military virtues should be kept for appropriate occasions, unlike the courtier who refused a lady's invitation to dance because 'his profession was fighting', thus earning the witty riposte: 'Well, since you're not at war now, or about to fight at all, you'd better get yourself well greased and put away in a cupboard along with the rest of your accoutrements' (I, xvii). Here, for the first time, the bystanders are given a glimpse of the wit, which, even at most solemn moments, is introduced by Castiglione in order to re-establish a connection with his audience, and perhaps warn them that life is not to be taken too seriously. The best example of this clever debunking will be seen at the peak of the book's solemnity, when Bembo has completed his discourse on love. The witty stories continue, in order to illustrate the virtues of moderate self-praise, and provide warnings against presumptuous arrogance or pride.

It is a natural step for the company now to discuss the physical attributes of the courtier, and Castiglione allows Bibbiena to lead in the subject by suggesting, with a mixture of self-praise and self-denigration, that he thinks he has a pleasing face, but he is doubtful about the shape of his body, especially his legs! Canossa, then, after harshly criticising those effeminate courtiers 'who curl their hair and pluck their eyebrows and plaster themselves in make-up like the most lascivious and dishonest of prostitutes' (I, xix) (echoes there of Vergerio), suggests this time a physical mean between extremes of size and stature. The courtier should also be urged to cultivate physical fitness and litheness and a training in the use of arms (for duelling as well as for more practical campaigning). The ability to wrestle, too, has practical usefulness for a man who is fighting on foot. The courtier should also be familiar with questions of etiquette, so as to know when the demands of chivalry may require him to defend his good name, but this, only in the last resort, by force of arms. That opinion contrasts strongly with the need to fly to arms to defend a woman's honour, and, significantly, to defend truth, against calumny (see below, p.127). Horsemanship and knightly exercises (jousting, dressage etc.) associated with horses, are noted as Italian specialities, and in these the courtier should achieve the highest degree of excellence, while in French and Spanish specialities (which include the mass tourney and the *corrida*), he should be among the best exponents of those activities. Even Cian draws the line at this praise of bull-fighting as an accomplishment saying that it is too much to expect the courtier to become a toreador! However, the chivalric tradition of horsemanship and jousting was still a fashionable pursuit. Its fashionable quality is reflected in the 'popularity' of contemporary chivalric romances, as well as of specific poems such as Poliziano's verses on Giuliano de' Medici's tournament or the poem of Luigi Pulci (1432–84) on Lorenzo's joust, or even, at the end of the century,

Tasso's attention to technical details in describing duels and battles in his *Gerusalemme*.

The purpose of all these accomplishments, which should be accompanied by 'grace and good judgement' is to ensure for the courtier 'that universal favour which is so highly prized' (I, xxi). Practical considerations for creating good first impressions, maintaining a public image (as well as acquiring practical skills which may be useful in war) lie at the basis of the other physical exercises and recreations which Canossa continues to enumerate: hunting, playing ball (tennis?), vaulting on horse-back (he draws the line at tumbling tricks and tight-rope walking!). Hunting is particularly recommended, praised not only by Castiglione, for the practice it gives for military purposes, but also by Alberti (*Della famiglia*, Books III and IV) and by Machiavelli (*Discorsi*, III, 35) and, it will be recalled, a hunting party was a good occasion for obtaining an intimate audience with one's master. There is here an almost long-suffering note in the allusion to acquiring a good public reputation 'especially in the eyes of the multitude, with whom one must also (*pur*) arrive at an accommodation' (I, xxii). And all these actions should be accompanied by grace.

The word grace (*grazia*) and its derivatives recur again and again in Canossa's discourse, and it is natural for one of the company (Cesare Gonzaga) to break the rule of the evening (that one should argue and contradict and not simply *ask* direct questions to obtain information), by wondering what Canossa means by grace and whether, in the case of those unendowed with this quality, it may be acquired by art and artifice. Canossa suggests that by beginning to learn at an early age a pupil may be taught to be graceful. Philip of Macedon entrusted his son Alexander to Aristotle at a very early age (and the example is almost a literal translation of Quintilian's advice in the *Institutio*, I, 1). The reader is reminded, too, at this point, of Castiglione's own plans for his son's education and the letters home which reflect closely Canossa's admonitions here. The opening of chapter xxvi has a deep significance for what is later to be said in Book IV about the role of the courtier as political adviser: 'the good pupil must always do his best to become like his teacher, and, if possible, to transform himself into him'. Having thus profited from his training, the pupil can study and select the better qualities from other experts. As for grace itself, a universal rule is 'to avoid affectation and, adopting what may be a neologism, to use in everything a certain casual attitude (*sprezzatura*), which disguises artifice (*arte*) and gives the impression that what one does and says is done without trouble and almost without thought' (I, xxvi). Castiglione's awareness of the importance of his concept of grace has been prepared by Cesare's remark in I, xxiv, that: 'without the quality of grace, all the other properties and good conditions are of little value'.

The concept of *grazia* (and later *sprezzatura*) was adapted to his purpose from a long tradition of 'artless' embellishment which probably has its origins in the Greek notion of τὸ πρέπον (that which is seemly). There is a curious and, for our purposes, important example of its use in Plato's *Politicus*, 243e: 'πρὸς τὸ μέτριον καὶ τὸ πρέπον', where the concept of 'seemliness' is linked to an idea of 'equilibrium' or 'just measure' (in much the same way as Della Casa was to use *misura* in his *Galateo*). Cicero translated this πρέπον into Latin in three important places, the *De officiis*, i, 27 and l, 35, and, notably, in the *Orator*, 21, 70: 'As in life, so in oratory (*in oratione*) there is nothing more difficult than to discern what is seemly (*quid deceat*). The Greeks call this πρέπον; we shall, of course, call it *decorum*.' Quintilian used its Silver Latin successor *decor* in precisely the same way and the word, indeed, occurs with great frequency in his *Institutio*. That these usages were generally well-known during the Renaissance is easily demonstrable and here we may content ourselves with Della Casa's almost literal translation of Cicero's *De officiis*, l, 35: 'Polite (*costumate*) persons should have regard to the quality of decorum (*misura*) in walking, standing, sitting, in actions, comportment (*portamento*), in their dress, in their words and in their silences, their moments both of repose and of activity.' Della Casa further develops the idea in chapters XXVIII and XXX of his *Galateo*. These precedents were as well-known to Castiglione as they were to Della Casa; indeed, he quotes that sentence of Cicero in his eulogy of Guidubaldo (see below, p. 201). And he reiterates the importance of the concept when he shows that he is deliberately coining a new meaning for *sprezzatura* (in the sense of 'casualness').

That chapter (xxvi) is full of allusions to and direct quotations from the Classics, including Quintilian, who discouraged affectation, Ovid, who regarded Art as the skill of concealing art, and above all, Cicero, who advised his orator to dissimulate and hide his learning and academic study. And Castiglione sees that Cicero's motive for that dissimulation is to obtain his audience's confidence. Therein lies the subtlety. The orator's audience might have suspected they were being deceived if he had seemed *too* sophisticated. The orator, then, must use Art to conceal the sophistication of his own art in order that the people thus deceived or persuaded may not realise that they are being deceived. This important notion of *sprezzatura* is itself 'casually' placed between two trivial examples: the courtier (known to the assembled company) who imitated Ferdinand II's unfortunate physical deformity of twisting the corner of his mouth, and Pierpaolo (another well-known courtier, we are told) whose wooden dancing is affected in the extreme, unlike the *sprezzata disinvoltura* of the present company.

The discussion draws to an end with the admonition that the Golden Mean should be observed in one's *sprezzatura* as in anything else, and to dance as casually as Roberto da Bari (who affects not to notice the loss of a shoe or a cloak!) is as mistaken as to dance like a wooden doll. The same norm is applied to personal appearance: 'such over-attention to smartness or casualness in our appearance tends too much to extremes, which are always vicious' (I, xxvii). The conclusion of that chapter generalises from what seem trivial instances, just as is done elsewhere: 'The same happens in every practice and in everything in the world which one may do or say.' Examples taken from the arts reinforce what has just been said. Music which is wholly harmonious produces satiety, while many discords offend the ear. Good music is a blend of both. Apelles criticised Protogenes for over-elaborating his paintings.

Della Casa's notions of *leggiadria* and *avvenentezza* seem, by contrast with Castiglione's wider purpose, superficial (cp. *Galateo*, XXVIII and XXX) though continuing the sort of general admonition to elegance in style which we noted earlier in the advice offered by Leonardo Bruni. That artistic 'artlessness', as Vittorio Cian rightly claims, is splendidly exemplified in the *Orlando furioso* of Ludovico Ariosto (1474-1533) and less splendidly if more explicitly in Tasso's *Gerusalemme*: 'E quel che il bello e il caso accresce all'opre |, l'arte, che tutto fa, nulla si scopre' (*Gerusalemme liberata*, XVI, 9) (And what increases the beauty of the task, artistry, accomplishes all without revealing itself). Castiglione's contemporary (and friend) Mario Equicola (c. 1470-1525) had noted in his volume on the nature of love that 'the art of speaking well is true art when it is not visibly art' (Book V). But all these examples are applications of the old Classical concept; Castiglione's adaptation of the idea is much more subtle than the traditional usage.

Earlier we saw how Castiglione used Cicero to show the point of his use of *sprezzatura*, namely to conceal one's erudition and so avert

public suspicion that one was attempting to deceive one's audience!
One further advantage he sees in casualness is that it seems to conceal
greater potentialities: 'it often makes him thought to be much greater
than he actually is' (*spesso lo fa estimar molto maggior di quello che è in
effetto*) (I, xxviii). The concept is repeated several times in the next
three sentences: '…gives the public the impression that anyone
acting with such ease knows much more than his action shows and
that if he were to work at it studiously could do it much better…'.
The singer who achieves a difficult note-grouping with apparent ease
'makes it known by that single fact that he knows more than his
actions show' (ibid.). The unusual stress given to the concept of
*sprezzatura*, and the fact that, in the edited version, Castiglione
devotes to the subject a further three hundred or so words not found
in the *Seconda redazione* (cp. ibid., pp.42–3) indicates his interest in
its importance. The concept seems to have a significant application for
Castiglione which is not merely fashionable as would be the case with
Della Casa, or as had been the case even with Alberti (whose *De
iciarchia* insists upon physical activities being carried out without
apparent effort, artistically studied so as to appear casual). In the
elaborate poker-game which diplomatic and courtly behaviour had
become, such casualness could serve the courtier as well as inscrut-
ability served the card-player. We know that the history of western
Europe, since Camillus' starving Romans threw bread from the
besieged Capitol to deceive their Gaulish attackers, has been studded
with daring diplomatic or military bluffs. Our author is here crystal-
lising for the courtier a precept which, far from advocating languor
and useless grace, teaches him one of the tougher rules of diplomacy
and has a practical application to the only civilised life available to
men like Castiglione. A century later Niccolò Strozzi adapts the
notion of artlessness to the duplicity which he thought was essential
for survival at court: 'Take no thought to being considered clever
and wise, but rather simple and ingenuous (*bonario*) and make use of
this precept so artfully (*artatamente*) that no one becomes aware of
your subtlety, for that would ruin the whole stratagem (*tutta la
macchina*)' (*Avvertimenti*, p.24v).

    The critical picture of this 'casual attitude' would not be complete
without mentioning a more traditional view of the linked concepts
of *grazia, leggiadria, sprezzatura* and *disinvoltura*. Joseph Mazzeo
expresses that view succinctly in his *Renaissance and Revolution*:
'*Grazia* is a quality actualized, if at all, only in a self which like a great
work of art, is truly a harmony of parts' (ibid., p.146). Hence Mazzeo

insists upon the importance for Castiglione of avoiding any *déforma-tion professionnelle* through the cultivation of certain specialities, developing instead a multitude of talents without searching, as the earlier Renaissance had done, for supremacy in one or more fields of human culture. I have preferred a less aesthetic and more practical explanation for Castiglione's cultivation of a multiplicity of talents and a casualness in their display.

The discussion of casual attitudes in duelling, dancing, singing and painting leads naturally on to the next major topic. The opposite of *sprezzatura* is *affettazione*, and Canossa goes on to deplore those affected people (especially Castiglione's fellow-Lombards!), whose desire to show off their exotic knowledge and experiences, causes them, on their return home after a year away, to pepper their speech with Hispanisms, Gallicisms or Roman dialectisms. Canossa says that it would be an affectation (and would cause him no little trouble) if he used those ancient Tuscan words of the literary tradition which were being rejected even by contemporary Tuscans. The topic, the *Questione della lingua*, was one which would be very familiar to Castiglione's readers, and one of its major aspects was the subject, mentioned here in passing by Canossa, of the priority of 'classical' Tuscan as written by the great Trecento writers, notably Petrarch and Boccaccio. In the dedicatory letter Castiglione had defended his style against several charges, including the criticism that he had not imitated Boccaccio. The discussion now broadens to comprehend the types of issue which fill the pages of Bembo's *Prose della volgar lingua*, effectively the first influential grammar of the vernacular, a work probably begun in 1502 and publicised in 1512, but known to the world in its published version of 1525.

    The great language in which Dante, Petrarch and Boccaccio had written their masterpieces had entered a period of decline during the fifteenth century, when Latin humanistic studies dominated culture and the vernacular was reduced to a secondary form of expression. So bad had the situation already become by 1441 that Leonbattista Alberti failed that year to stimulate any competition for his *Certame coronario*, the contest for vernacular poets announced by him in Florence. By the end of the fifteenth century, Latin humanists, educated, like Pietro Bembo (1470–1547), in the tradition of the Greek and Latin Classics, brought their training to bear upon verna-cular studies, partly for nationalistic cultural reasons. From that point on, Italian gradually extended its scope during the sixteenth century to include most fields of civilised activity, barring university teaching and scientific and juridical usage. Thus the problem of Latin versus Italian was virtually solved by the time of Castiglione's *Seconda redazione*, and need concern us no longer. But the problem of the *type* of vernacular was to persist, and despite its effective solution by Bembo, was to recur until our own times.

It is difficult to simplify the complex debate: the first areas of contention were temporal (should the language be that established by literary tradition over the previous two hundred years, or should it be contemporary?) and geographical (should the language be restricted to the language spoken in Florence and/or Tuscany, or should it be a language common to all Italy?). Giangiorgio Trissino (1478–1550), a Vicentine, proposed a language made up from all the Italian dialects, and he adduced Dante's *De vulgari eloquentia* to support the thesis of a *lingua comune* propounded in his *Castellano* of 1529. Machiavelli was a fierce protagonist of Florentine hegemony. The *Discorso* attributed to him by some, linked the linguistic tradition of the fourteenth century to his own day (and it adduces the *De vulgari eloquentia* to show how mistaken the Florentine, Dante, was!). The idea of a highly cultured, possibly courtly language (commonly called the *lingua cortigiana*) was proposed by such scholars as Vincenzo Colli (c. 1460–1508) nicknamed *il Calmeta*, and Mario Equicola and, later it was said, by Castiglione himself, though he never used the term. Such a language would be a 'common' Italian language based on the cultured speech used at Italian courts. It would, fundamentally, comprise learned Tuscan, enriched with elegant, noble and possibly regional forms, and would include Latinisms where appropriate.

The solution which ultimately triumphed was that initiated by Pietro Bembo, who was largely concerned with the artistic aspect of writing, and whose *Prose della volgar lingua* (1525) recognised the pre-eminence of the Tuscan tradition (as seen, in prose, in the work of Boccaccio, and, in poetry, in that of Petrarch). His proposition was to imitate, in such a dynamic way as eventually to supersede his models, the language of Petrarch in poetry and Boccaccio in prose, just as, in his youth, he had imitated Virgil and Cicero in order to perfect his Latin. That cultured Florentine tradition was lent authority by the conversion of the Ferrarese Ariosto, whose third edition of the *Orlando furioso* (1532) largely conformed to Bembo's theories. At the close of the century, Tasso's *Gerusalemme liberata* (1585), which again inclined to the Bembist norm, excluded living Florentine from the, by now, national cultural vehicle, and so, incidentally, provoked a most hostile reaction from the Florentine purists who began publication of the authoritative (and continuing yet) *Vocabolario della Crusca* (1612). These were the main battle-lines; other minor aspects, such as the question of Florentine versus Tuscan need not concern us here.

Castiglione's position on the language question is that of the reasonable liberal, and it could well be argued that his solution to the problem is an individual one, as successful in its own way as Bembo's more formal and stylised grammar. Like Bembo, he is keen that the written language should be more beautiful than any spoken language, but, since he is dealing with language as a social as well as a literary vehicle, the best spoken language should, he believes, come as near as possible to the standard of carefully written language. Indeed Gasparo Pallavicino later says that elegance in the spoken tongue is more important for the courtier than the ability to write stylishly (I, xxxiv). Canossa begins the topic by briefly reviewing the development of vernacular Italian from the intermingling of Latin with the tongues of the barbarian invaders (I, xxxii). Italian is seen, thus, to be still a relatively youthful language. The arguments for and against classical Tuscan are adduced, and Petrarch and Boccaccio are extolled as the best linguistic exemplars. This last viewpoint is qualified by the Florentine, Giuliano de' Medici, who, while agreeing that Tuscan is the most beautiful language, wishes to cut out archaisms from any proposed imitation of the Trecento writers. (Florence, incidentally, is urged at this point to take greater pride in her neglected linguistic and literary inheritance.) Bibbiena is able to point out that those so-called archaisms still live in country dialects of Tuscany.

From the outset of the debate, the company is presented with Castiglione's own solution that one's vocabulary should be made up of 'words in contemporary use, not only from Tuscany, but from all Italy, provided that they are not ungracious to the ear' (I, xxix). And, in spite of the lip-service paid to the traditional arguments, the notion of a cultivated language common to the whole peninsula is kept before the reader. After Petrarch, culture had broadened – and not only in Tuscany, 'but in the whole of Italy, among noble men experienced at courts, in arms and in letters' (I, xxxii), and while it is a touchstone of one's general culture to know the classical Tuscan authors, the antiquity of words is in itself no recommendation to imitate them in modern communication, certainly not if clarity is thus sacrificed, since clarity in writing is essential (for the author is not usually present to be cross-examined on an unclear statement).

The idea of a common language made up of elements from the usage of cultivated men from all over the peninsula is firmly asserted, though Castiglione, in common with many of his contemporaries, mistakenly adduces the Greek *koiné* as if it were a mixture of four dialects (rather than the result of the domination of Attic) to support his notion of Italian. Latin precedents, from Horace to Cicero, from Cato to Virgil are adduced in traditional ways to back up the argument for language as a cultural vehicle. Critics have chosen to call this solution to the language problem a *lingua cortigiana* and the name has been associated with the book's title, but Castiglione's avoidance of the term *lingua cortigiana* may indicate his desire to avoid the precise solution which Calmeta had proposed. He seems to have had far more of a national linguistic aspiration than would be allowed for in the rather restrictive epithet *courtly*. In chapter xxxv he goes on to describe it as 'an Italian language, a common language, copious and varied, like a garden, full, as it were, of different flowers and fruits'. That harmonious miscellany implies more than the mere linguistic aristocracy suggested by 'courtly language'.

The issues of the *Questione della lingua* are trite and seem, many of them, futile and empty to us nowadays, but, apart from the valuable creation of a unified national language in a peninsula divided politically, the debate produced other incidental results with fascinating implications. Castiglione's speakers also offer many interesting 'by-products' of the *querelle*. For instance, the good sense of Horace is imitated in the suggestion that the first requirement for a writer is to have something worthwhile to say; he must then be able to arrange his thoughts and sentiments elegantly, and finally express them clearly in words. And the suggestion that the language might be restricted to the idiom of Petrarch and Boccaccio, prompts the reaction that it would be unjust to omit the names of Poliziano, Lorenzo il Magnifico and Diacceto – probably, Castiglione suggests, the equals of the great *trecentisti* in judgement and learning. The name of Francesco Cattani da Diacceto (1466–1522) is an interesting addition here, not found in the *Seconda redazione*. Castiglione's obvious admiration for the Florentine Platonist probably indicates that Diacceto's *I tre libri d'amore* had impressed him with its learning and, we may assume, had been helpful to him in sketching out his own discourse on Love in Book IV.

To return to the *querelle*; broadly Castiglione urges his charges to have the nerve to write and speak the language they have learned at their mother's knee, and not to be overawed by writers with a reputation for Tuscanising. The Italians, he suggests are more severe on themselves than ancient grammarians would be (I, xxxv). Conclusions are drawn of a more modern-sounding nature, such as Canossa's statement that, to obtain a beautiful effect, form and content must be considered indivisible: 'to divide what is expressed from the words which express it is dividing soul from body' (*il divider le sentenzie dalle parole è un divider l'anima dal corpo*) (I, xxxiii). Finally, with an injection of his usual good sense, Canossa says that frivolous and trivial details do not make or break a language, and when Demosthenes was accused by Aeschines of using neologisms, he retorted that the fortunes of Greece did not depend upon such trivialities (I, xxxix). Perhaps a little more common sense and a little less chauvinism might have curtailed the vast literature on the subject which was subsequently to occupy some of Italy's leading thinkers in the centuries to come.

The language discussion seems to have gone on for too long, and after several attempts to interrupt the speakers, Emilia Pia finally succeeds in channelling the discussion back to the less abstract details of courtly behaviour. Canossa casts his mind back to the original discussion of grace and its opposite, affectation, and rounds off his statements in chapters xl and xli. His first examples (of women who plaster on their faces too much make-up, or who pluck their eyebrows exaggeratedly) seem almost like one of Pallavicino's anti-feminist statements, though they are common to writers who, like Angelo Poliziano (*Rispetti*), Agnolo Firenzuola (1493–1543) (*Dialogo delle bellezze delle donne*) or Alessandro Piccolomini (1508–78) (*La Raffaella*), touched on the subject of women's cosmetics. Canossa is urged 'rather to speak of courtly behaviour than to wish to uncover the defects of women in this purposeless way (*senza proposito*)' (I, xl). Yet Canossa emphasises that this argument 'has much purpose' (*Anzi molto a proposito*), since such defects are, by definition, affectations which spoil gracefulness. The best cosmetic treatment is the lightest possible: 'This is that casual purity (*sprezzata purità*) so dear to men's eyes and minds, ever fearful as they are of being deceived by artifice (*dall'arte ingannati*)' (I, xl). And so, rather like Cicero's orators noted above, women are most pleasing when they conceal their cosmetic arts with as much subtlety and grace as possible.

The discussion, then, is brought back to the issue of deception (*inganno*). And if the argument still seems confined on a trivial level, Castiglione adds a brief hint of the spiritual discussion ('of which we have so far (*per ancora*) spoken little'), which will fill Book IV. The relative superiority of soul to body implies that the soul should be proportionately 'more cultivated and embellished' and, 'to put it briefly, the courtier should be a man of honesty and integrity, a definition which comprehends prudence, goodness, fortitude and temperance and all the other conditions which attach to such honourable titles' (I, xli). The brief chapter ends with a complex and apparently over-abstract statement culled from Socratic philosophy to the effect that 'the only true moral philosopher is the man who wishes to be good', and to obtain that end, he needs few other precepts beyond the *will* to be good. Hence, Canossa says, Socrates was gratified that his teachings had borne good fruit when through them men could come to know and learn virtue. 'When men simply *want* to be virtuous, they easily acquire the knowledge necessary for such an aim.' This unusual abstraction ends when Canossa says that that particular topic will detain them no longer, since he is 'attending to our [original] purpose'.

And yet it is interesting to speculate why Castiglione inserts such a complex metaphysical (or ethical) notion, however briefly, between a discussion of trivial beauty-treatment, and the more important topic of a literary education (chapters xlii and following). Castiglione's tone is apologetic: 'Leaving aside the precepts of so many wise philosophers... we will say briefly, attending to our original purpose, that it is enough for the courtier to be a man of honesty and integrity ... Yet we will talk no more of this.' The chapter, li, is the shortest so far in the *Cortegiano*, made shorter since the *Seconda redazione* by the omission of an embarrassing aside by Ottaviano Fregoso (ibid., p.56) on women who are willing to show more leg than the elegant ankle which Canossa had earlier said could be gracefully shown.

Although Cian implies that it is natural for Castiglione, having treated of physical beauty, to treat, too, of spiritual merits, yet the allusions to the 'true moral philosopher' and the 'good man' seem intrusive in context, and, one suspects, would be lost upon any audience interested only in the triviality of cosmetics. But we know that Castiglione's decision to retain the small paragraph is conscious and deliberate (since he has equally deliberately excised from his final version the neighbouring remarks of Ottaviano).

There are, I believe, three good reasons for its retention. First, Castiglione is preoccupied here, as he is throughout his treatise, with Platonic and Aristotelean philosophy, and to *him* the relevance of the remarks to his overall theme would be clear. At the same time, he was aware that his audience might not have been so *au fait* with the philosophy or with the train of thought which he was following, and so he abbreviates his remarks to a minimum. Yet his words do harmonise naturally with what had just been said on the subject of deception (*sempre temono essere dall'arte ingannati* – I, xl). Socrates always insisted that depravity was simply a perversion of truth, equated, in other words, with ignorance, and to show the way to virtue one simply had to uncover the truth, to disperse the deceiving clouds of ignorance. Talk of the 'true moral philosopher', then, is almost a Freudian glimpse of Castiglione's main preoccupation, which will reach its climax in Book IV. The importance of the opinion here expressed by Canossa will be underlined at that point (IV, xiii), when Castiglione openly declares that 'Men never choose evil under the impression that it is evil, but deceive themselves because of a certain similarity to good'. The second purpose stems from this last. For those who *were* able to comprehend his deeper message, the remarks here help make even the trivia of cosmetics and beauty-treatment relevant to his major theme of training the courtier to see through deceptive exteriors. Thirdly and finally, the added depth and complexity of the thought here helps to add to the seriousness of tone which Castiglione wished to impart to the final version of his book, so that he, as a future potential cardinal might avoid possible accusations of triviality or fatuity.

After Canossa's brief aside, he takes up again his theme of the courtier's accomplishments, and adds that the 'true and principal spiritual embellishment is, in my opinion, the study of letters' (I, xlii). The topic allows a polemical reference to the barbarity of the French, who consider littérateurs as inferior beings, and who use the word *clerc* as an insult. The remarks seem to be confirmed by Castiglione's famous description of the entry of Louis XII and his French troops into the Milan of Ludovico *il Moro*. Yet he is also able, with hindsight, to pay a pretty compliment to Francis I, whom he regarded as a potential cultural saviour of the French nation, and whose influence he thought would bring his subjects to appreciate literary studies. Illustrious precedents are here adduced: Alexander's love of the Homeric epics (influenced by Aristotle) or Alcibiades' love of letters (taught by Socrates), not to mention many Roman leaders. Immortality and glory are conferred by great literature, and reading about great heroes stimulates a man to glory, even centuries after their death. The lamentable state of Italy, reduced to servility, despite her supremacy in the arts, seems paradoxical, but is due, Canossa says, to the ineptitude of Italy's leaders. The tone here, as Castiglione, albeit briefly, describes the abject state of Italy, in subjection to her foreign dominators, is again similar to his youthful letter of 1499 in which he described the despoliation of the fairest court in Europe by the French soldiery: 'yet it is better to pass over in silence what one cannot recall without sorrow'. And the glimpse of national tragedy is again skated over with a tone not dissimilar to the final chapter of Machiavelli's *Principe*, which, like the *Cortegiano* here, blamed Italy's military humiliation on the weakness of the country's leaders.

The study of the Greek and Latin Classics, and a knowledge of composing both in verse and prose are next considered, and seen to be almost indispensable requisites for the courtier, not only for their intrinsic value, but also because they allow him to judge the work of others. Castiglione's letters home on the subject of his own son's education bear out that he practised what he preached in this regard. It is significant that he again uses the newly acquired skill in literature to whet his courtier's judgement. Good judgement, indeed, should prevent the courtier from false persuasion that he knows more than he actually does know, since there are always adulators ready with their praises to help such self-deception. Canossa alludes again to Plutarch (with a prophetic allusion to the importance of the advice in Book IV) in his warning on 'how to tell the true friend from the adulator', since many prefer such flattery and 'hate those who tell them the truth' (I, xliv). Such people are 'blind in their self-deception', and the courtier should cultivate good judgement to prevent him from 'taking black for white', or 'from persuading himself falsely that he knows what in fact he's ignorant of!' (I, xliv), for his own assumptions must be based on truth.

The recurrence of the word *vero* and of opposite concepts (*blindness, delusion*, etc.) is surprising in the academic context of the typically humanist preoccupation with the *litterae humaniores*, and may be a further indication of Castiglione's overall preoccupation that the courtier *must* be able to penetrate the veil of deception. Knowledge of this kind also gives the courtier the self-confidence to approach and talk with anyone (echoes of San Bernardino's views on education). The company is next led on to discuss the relative importance of skill in arms (said to be the principal occupation of the courtier) and of letters (which Bembo insists are superior to arms as the spirit is to the body). Alexander envied Achilles, not for his feats of arms, but for the fact that Homer sang his exploits in the *Iliad*. Canossa shows the fallacy in Bembo's argument, and the discussion drifts into amusing banter on the capacity of the courtier to assimilate all the qualifications being desired of him.

The arguments for and against qualities of military, as opposed to literary, excellence were hotly debated during the Renaissance. Cian (ed. cit., pp.112–13) has a list of minor treatises where the debate flourished, as well as quotations from the Classics and from Castiglione's contemporaries, to show the importance of the topic. It is perhaps, then, extraordinary that Castiglione devotes only two brief chapters to the subject. There are more qualifications, asserts Canossa! He should have knowledge of music. Plato and Aristotle urged their 'pupils' to learn music. Here again Castiglione puts emphasis on the *true* value of music, 'not so much for that superficial melody which one hears, but because it is sufficient to induce in us a fresh and good disposition (*un novo abito bono*) and tendencies towards virtue' (I, xlvii). It is also interesting to see his chivalric *courtoisie* evidenced by the desire to please the ladies, who were particularly receptive of musical delights. The harmonising power of music is legendary, and its consolatory effect on all types and classes of people is undeniable. Here, too, one might emphasise Aristotle's attitude to music in the *Politics* (VIII, 5) which suggests that music is a perfect medium for achieving a Golden Mean of emotional stability. The chapter ends on an elegiac note – children are sent to sleep by the sound of a lullaby, and forget their tears, a symbolic foretaste of the rest of their adult life (which may, implicitly, be equally well comforted by music).

The virtues of the painter's art as a training for the courtier are also stressed by Canossa (against the current opinion that the artist was, with few exceptions, little more than an interior decorator). And 'not only is the discipline most noble and worthy in itself' (I, xlix) but it is said to have a *practical* value in time of war as an aid to map-making, the designing of fortresses and bridges and the like. On a more mystic level, the man who can imitate God's handiwork, visible in the beauty of nature, 'would seem deserving of the highest praise'. And while sculpture and painting have their fountain-head in the art of design, painting is superior because of its greater capacity for artistic variation.

The ideas put forward are typical of those current during Castiglione's life and after. The notion that 'design' was the creative fount of both painting and sculpture is still visible in the *Accademia del disegno* in Florence, and the dispute over the relative superiority of both aspects finds a mention in many artists and art critics of the Renaissance, from Alberti, who gave priority to painting, as did

Leonardo, to Michelangelo, who shrewdly suggested that both were of equal artistic dignity. Cian (ed. cit., p.124) has a useful documentation of the current essays on the subject, but the topic, as Michelangelo wisely observed, 'uses up more time itself than the actual sculpting or painting of figures!' The dispute here is evidently also an idle one, and Castiglione pays lip-service to the current conversational topic, allowing Cristoforo Romano to advance a defence of his own particular art of sculpture, while Canossa is granted a much longer discourse to justify the supremacy of painting.

From the argument several interesting and important asides may be gleaned: that the major disadvantage of paint is its lack of durability; that the Classical epoch, judging by the few paintings which had survived, and by the opinions of Classical contemporaries, perhaps had finer artistic skills than the Renaissance; that a knowledge of how to paint beauty enhances our ability to appreciate beauty itself; and, perhaps most important of all, that painting is a closer imitation of the truth than is sculpture. Sculptors cannot match the painter's ability to capture the subtlety of nature's phenomena, the grace of a pair of blue eyes, the colour of golden hair, the drama of a thunderstorm, the rosy fingers of dawn. Yet this *truthful* imitation of nature relies on artifice, and on devices, such as perspective, to 'deceive the eyes' (i, l) into believing that a scene has depth or realism.

As if to remind his reader that one of his purposes in writing the *Cortegiano* is to teach him how to discern the truth beneath the surface of reality (or, as here, the surface of the paint), the concluding chapter of the discussion turns upon the appreciation which Cesare Gonzaga says he would have for a beautiful woman. He considers that he would have a fuller pleasure of a woman than that of Apelles (who took such a delight in painting Alexander's mistress Pancaspes that Alexander gave the girl to the painter because he evidently appreciated her more than his master did!). Canossa explains that Cesare's 'enjoyment' would be caused primarily by an emotional reaction to the woman's beauty, and, while beauty itself may provide such emotional reaction, 'there are many other factors apart from beauty, which cause our souls to be kindled – manners, wisdom, speech, gestures and a thousand other things…but, above all, the feeling that one is loved (*il sentirsi essere amato*)' (i, liii). Nevertheless, those feelings of love which arise from 'superficially visible and physical aspects of beauty' (*che superficialmente vedemo nei corpi*) may be heightened by the trained appreciation of beauty (which the painter in particular possesses in greater measure).

The debate is interrupted by the sudden arrival of Francesco Maria della Rovere, who had returned to Urbino, having escorted his uncle, Pope Julius, on the first stage of his homeward journey, bringing in his retinue 'Marchese Febo da Ceva, and his brother, Gherardino, Ettore Romano, Vincenzo Calmeta, Orazio Florido and many others'. The interruption gives Giuliano de' Medici the opportunity to reiterate an earlier request that Canossa typify the occasions on which the courtier ought to use the qualities which have so far been conferred upon him. Federico Fregoso is asked to carry out that task on the following evening. The entertainment concludes with two dances performed by Margherita Gonzaga and Costanza Fregoso, and accompanied by Barletta, a musician favoured at the Urbino court. The hour is late, and the company disperses.

## 4. Book Two of *The Courtier*

The second Book is unusually long – half as long again as the next longest Book (111). Yet its subject-matter seems at first glance less important than that of the rest of the treatise, and the discussion, even of such items as skill in arms, seems trivialised by petty admonitions. The courtier is advised, for instance, to do nothing to minimise his prowess, such as participating in minor skirmishes (with little hope of increasing his reputation in the eyes of those whose opinions count). Further, the second half of the Book is concerned with various kinds of wit and humour, which most Italian critics dismiss briefly, often with literally only two epithets, 'lively' or 'amusing' or the like. Thus Cian, though he calls this the 'liveliest part of the *Cortegiano*', thinks that it creates 'a vivacious and almost thoughtless festive atmosphere (*vivacità e quasi festosa spensieratezza*) which is the opposite of pedantic precepts' (ed. cit., p.236), and Maier qualifies his brief praise for the comic stories with accusations of 'prolixity and padding-out' (ed. cit., p.33). The length of the section is generally regarded as disproportionate to its importance. It is, in fact, almost as long as Book iv, the most important Book of all. Mazzeo ingeniously considers that the significance of the Book lies in its non-verbal means of communication (not fully appreciated, that is, by modern man bombarded by newsprint and deluged by voices on radio waves) and, though Mazzeo is less explicit here, by 'its non-referential uses of language' (alluding to the humorous stories?) (op. cit., p.147). These last remarks may be incidentally true, but there are probably more subtle reasons for Castiglione's treatment of his new themes, particularly when we bear in mind the casualness (*sprezzatura*) with which important lessons are introduced into the book.

*O tempora, o mores!* The second evening opens with a statement by the author on the general dilemma of those who praise the past and condemn the present. Castiglione proposes physical and psychological explanations for the phenomenon: that as men grow older their minds recall only brighter days, while physically they are surrounded by pleasures which failing vitality prevents them from enjoying to the full. The subject, if not the explanation, is one which has been familiar in literature since the Romans. Horace criticised ironically the *laudator temporis acti* (*Epistolae*, II, iii) though the relaxation of the moral code during the last phases of the Republic also made both him and Cicero genuinely regret the degeneracy of their fellows. Among Castiglione's own contemporaries similar sentiments were expressed by Jacopo Sannazaro (c. 1455–1530) in the *Arcadia* (VI) and, significantly, *his* poetry (see below, p.101) later replaces that of Giovanni Pontano (1426–1505) as a literary exemplar. Cian has shown, in an article in the *Giornale Storico* (XXXIV) and through a letter noted by him in his edition (cit., p.190), that, as a young man, Castiglione transcribed some of the Neapolitan poet's work and possibly corresponded with him.

And yet what might have become a trite repetition of past arguments is turned by Castiglione to his own purposes, not only by applying it to courts of the past and present, but also by using it to highlight the uncertainty of man's discernment, since the failing vitality, mentioned earlier, indicates that: 'So fallacious (*fallaci*) are our bodily senses that often they deceive (*spesso ingannano*) the judgement of the mind' (II, i). Body and mind are contrasted, and the opening chapter introduces convincing analogies from life to support the argument. As if in confirmation, it is interesting to see Leopardi quoting extensively from this section of the book (*Pensieri*, XXXIX), and adding to Castiglione's analogies amusing parallels from his own time. In the idylls, too, Leopardi makes use of Castiglione's notion of the *fallibility* of memory in order to evoke some of his more beautiful, less defined, less finite images (cp. *Le ricordanze* etc.).

The relevance of the author's abstractions becomes obvious when the theory is applied to his contemporary courts and courtiers in the next chapter. There Castiglione, blending Platonic philosophy with his own good sense, suggests that extremes of vice and virtue invariably co-exist in any society. Thus, if courtiers, for instance, were less vicious in the fifteenth century (a doubtful premiss, anyway) they were also less virtuous. Socrates had suggested, in the *Phaedo*, that Aesop should have written a fable to illustrate the inevitable connection between pain and pleasure, vice and virtue, and Castiglione quotes that sentiment with relish in order to bolster his own theory. In apophthegms which recall what Leopardi was later to derive from him for poems like *La quiete dopo la tempesta*, he explains the intimate connection between pleasure and pain. One sentiment implies the absence of the other, true appreciation of food, drink and sleep only being possible for one who has felt hunger, thirst and fatigue. But returning to his courtly theme, Castiglione, in an unusually frank statement in praise of his own times, writes with pride that his contemporaries are generally superior to their precursors in almost all spheres of human endeavour. This appreciation of the progress of mankind does not prevent him later in the same chapter (II, iii) from praising the 'divine and superhuman intelligences of the past'. Yet even this affirmation of his love of the Classics and of his training as a humanist is balanced by the thought that 'there were, nonetheless, many men of a most vicious kind then to be found'. In those opinions, too, the Mean is visible.

An apology for the diffuseness of the earlier discussion, and a pretty compliment to the Urbino court, lead him naturally back to describe the next day's activities, which begin with a recapitulation by the company, for the benefit of Francesco Maria, of the salient features of the previous evening's debate. It is significant that here Castiglione reinforces his notion of the fallibility of memory by showing that the company disagree even on events and discussions so recently past. The recapitulation, we are told, occupies the daytime, and in the evening, having satisfied Francesco Maria's desire to dine, the courtiers settle into their accustomed places to hear what Federico Fregoso has to say about the appropriateness of the courtier's conduct in various circumstances.

The Renaissance propensity for rule-books is emphasised by the contrasting attitudes of L'Unico Aretino and Federico Fregoso. The former insists that appropriate conduct is a matter of good sense: 'Only a fool would practise fencing when everyone else was intent on listening to music; only a fool would go down a street doing a morris-dance, however great his expertise in such a matter!' (II, vi). But for Fregoso right conduct needs more subtle argument than a general admonition to good sense, and Castiglione once more stresses the fallibility of human judgement, particularly when the individual is (perhaps unconsciously) self-deceptive out of personal motives or private interest. And here again the familiar terms for deception recur: *errori, coperti, velo,* and conversely the need 'for diligent observation' (ibid.). Right conduct consists of discretion and good judgement, and that includes the ability to understand variations in circumstances and to act appropriately. The affectation, condemned the previous evening, is again pilloried by Federico here, for affectation attracts envy or disdain. Here sceptical realism borders on cynicism as he indicts Man's malicious nature, more ready to find fault than to praise, even in cases where faults are absent and praise is due. Envy seems to provide the spur for such wicked judgements, and the courtier must learn to defend himself from envy by such expedients as tempering his virtues with their opposite weaknesses – justifiable pride with modesty, and moderation with a pride in things well done, one virtue helping to put the other into greater relief. The courtier must also weigh carefully the appropriateness of given actions or remarks to the circumstances in which he may variously find himself.

At this point, despite the ponderous authority of Cicero's *De oratore* (ii, lxxv), which gives similar advice, Castiglione has been accused of superficiality in admonishing the courtier not to demean himself, by participating, for instance, in a cattle-rustling foray, nor to exert himself in minor skirmishes unnoticed by his superiors. And when disporting himself athletically, he should not compete with his social inferiors, unless he were to win those contests inevitably and without apparent effort or expertise. Such sentiments might seem to the modern reader, given the inept motives for many sixteenth-century campaigns, to be profoundly sensible, but, to do Castiglione justice, two points must be made. In the first place, these are extremes of the Aristotelean Golden Mean. Aristotle's *Politics* are quoted directly at this stage in the argument as Federico adduces the example of Theodoros, the leading actor who always insisted upon appearing on stage before his fellow-actors, in order to make the maximum impact upon his audience. And the extremes noted above are countered by his other examples of the rodomontades of the man who takes a fortress single-handedly and boastfully, or the expert singer, fencer or dancer who, in public or in private, insists upon foisting his prowess upon his companions. In the second place, Gasparo Pallavicino *is* allowed to put the case for a 'democratic' participation with the lower orders in athletic and other contests. This principle Federico accepts, but on condition that it be made clear that this is not the courtier's profession, that the courtier expects no plaudits for his performance, and that no one knows how much time or effort his 'training' may have cost him.

In less rugged pastimes, discretion should also guide the courtier. In his choice of music, dancing, singing, he should judge the appropriateness of the occasion. Thus a viol accompaniment to poetic recitation is one of music's supreme delights (though it is interesting to note that Castiglione shares the Classical prejudice against the flute, which he dismisses as hardly worthy of consideration). The Urbino court, according to Vespasiano da Bisticci, was furnished with all types of musical instruments and the marvellous wood inlays in the palace which have survived up to the present day reveal the original founder's delight in music. Castiglione himself, to judge from his correspondence with his mother, was an expert on the viol, and had several instruments of his own. One *Elegia* (that of 'Ippolita', see below, p.202) includes this ability as one of his happier accomplishments. He warns, however, that grey-haired, wrinkled and toothless old men should remain dignified and should be chary of playing the viol and singing love songs in the company of women. Their solace from music should be in private practice, or in listening (with appreciation proportionately greater because of their years and experience) to other performers. Federico declares, with a sentiment which echoes centuries of mockery for the 'lover in his dotage', that he does not wish to deprive older courtiers of the pleasure of music, but rather of the ridicule accruing to certain circumstances of performance. But, for both youth and age alike, a certain Mean should be aimed at, young men tempering their natural frivolity (*leggerezza*), old men, without directly aping the young (through make-up, for instance) keeping their old age 'as vital and verdant' as possible. The norm is posited as the *virile età*.

The purpose of these qualifications, Federico proceeds, after some polite badinage, should be to allow the courtier to socialise with the prince, and so to please him that princely favour is won: 'Let him address himself with all his thoughts and mental powers to love and almost adore the prince he serves above every other thing, and let him direct all his desires, behaviour (*costumi*) and attitudes (*modi*) to please him' (II, xviii). The passage is important in its own right and as a forerunner to the courtier's attitude to the prince in Book IV. That such a figure should be adulatory is quickly countered with unswerving logic: adulators are self-interested and love neither their friends nor their prince. 'The courtier should serve his master in those things which are useful and honourable, not in those which bring him damage and shame' (II, xxiii). Yet Castiglione pays his fee to political utility by admitting that, although a man should not commit a treacherous murder, he may kill 10,000 men in a just cause. The essentially unsatisfying nature of his statements here is summed up in Federico's final retreat from controversy. He refuses to answer Pallavicino's question on how to discern real from apparent good action and declines to discuss the matter further, on the grounds that it would require too long a discourse. He leaves 'the whole matter to his hearers' discretion' (*il tutto si rimetta alla discrezion vostra*).

Although Castiglione has been accused of retreats from reality of this kind (cp. Prezzolini's introduction), his very inclusion of Pallavicino's frank question shows that he was aware of the difficulties of the problem and so, by definition, that he was not evading the whole issue. His purpose lies elsewhere than in a metaphysical debate, which is anyway comprehended by the statements of Book IV. Indeed, it is the practicality of carrying out one's master's commands to the letter (even if the orders might lead to inefficient results) which is next debated. The answer given is that results count, and the courtier should expedite matters in the best way possible, taking account of the potential offence to a severe master whose orders were countermanded. (The whipping to death of Licinius Crassus' successful but disobedient engineer is adduced as a salutary example to illustrate his meaning!)

After a brief aside, on snobbishness and favour-currying, Federico gives his advice on the need to dress in a fashion appropriate to given occasions. In a manner typical of so many Italian writers, who attacked the servility implicit in wearing foreign fashions (and their names range from Petrarch to Sacchetti, Equicola to Della Casa), Federico now adversely criticises foreign fashions. He recalls days when less fashionable clothes, however quaint, were at least Italian (and so outward symptoms of liberty), while the introduction of a miscellany of foreign fashions was symptomatic of the inauguration of servitude. All countries whose national dress Italians aped seem to have made war in or on the Peninsula: 'There is now no nation left which has not made us its prey, to such an extent that there is little left to prey upon, and yet they do not leave off preying on even that little' (II, xxvi). The topic is cut short in a manner typical of Castiglione's interlocutors when a controversial subject arises. Critics have suggested that the silence is another mark of Castiglione's lack of commitment and avoidance of main issues. That suggestion may be true incidentally (though he had no need to introduce the issue even in such tenuous form) but it ignores the essential nonchalance or casualness which always characterises Castiglione's style and personality. It is a mark of his admirable sense of proportion and expression. To overemphasise political oppression would have exaggerated one particular aspect of court life in a way inappropriate to the rest of his theme, but to introduce such a topic so casually, lends to it a force more telling because of the less serious subject-matter which surrounds it. Perhaps the casualness with which Castiglione introduces new topics is akin to Ariosto's seemingly fortuitous changes of direction in his narrative, a ploy equally unappreciated until recently (cp. C.P. Brand, *Ariosto*, p.89).

Returning to the point at hand, Federico praises a more austere mode of dress for everyday wear, at all costs avoiding extremes of fashion, and preferring the more sober Spanish fashions to those of France or Germany. And twice he answers reasonably the objection that 'the habit doesn't make the monk' (*l'abito non fa 'l monaco*), agreeing that external appearance was no more than a further attribute (and a minor one) to add to the courtier's many other accomplishments. Not all men may be judged by great achievements in, say, the architectural or literary fields, but all may be judged on their behaviour and attitude. Fashion is simply another concomitant of these last; tastefulness (or lack of it) may add to (or detract from) a man's reputation. Giovanni Della Casa, though not so specific on the subject as Castiglione, was also anxious that his 'pupil' should dress soberly, 'to avoid being accused', he wrote, 'of wearing Ganymede's trousers or Cupid's waistcoat' (*Galateo*, XXVIII). Indeed many of the hints here given on fashion, dress, hair-style, etc., seem to have been taken up later by Della Casa. The apparent superficiality of creating a good first impression is followed, as usual, by a more serious note.

Reputation may also be affected by a man's choice of friends, and friendship forms the subject of Federico's next remarks, which are again introduced with a casualness which belies their profound importance. Pietro Bembo is shown here to be rather sceptical about the possibilities of true friendship: 'There are nowadays very few true friends' (II, xxix). And since his own experiences of friendship have been, he says, very disillusioning, he proposes circumspection, and is reluctant to put his full trust in friendship. The external details of the courtier's clothing, with which Castiglione has been concerned, are now transposed on to a spiritual level. Clothes may superficially cloak the real personality, but how much more devious are the labyrinthine dissimulations of the mind: 'In our minds (*animi*) there are so many hiding-places (*latebre*) and recesses, that it is impossible for human foresight to know the dissimulations which are hidden therein' (II, xxix). Now, in the *Seconda redazione* (p.115), Federico, picking up Cicero's statements in the *De amicitia* (XXIII), and, incidentally, confirming the treatise as one of Castiglione's main sources, accuses Pietro Bembo of being as misanthropic as Timon of Athens! This exaggeration is later eliminated in favour of the milder conclusion, promoted in the edited version, that without friendship man's existence would be less fortunate than that of other animals. Castiglione's statements here echo very closely the *Nicomachean Ethics* and *De amicitia*. Friendship may only exist between men of good will, and true friendship must be strictly limited to a relationship between two persons, he suggests, for it is easier to make two musical instruments harmonise rather than three. To widen friendship to embrace even a third person is dangerous. At the same time, one's relationship with one's fellows should be friendly in the broader sense of affable, courteous and sympathetic. The stress laid upon the quality of goodness necessary for true friendship echoes what Aristotle had noted in the *Nicomachean Ethics* (VIII, iii), and what Cicero had repeated in his *De amicitia* (XVIII). And the Aristotelean Mean is again propounded: against, on the one hand, Bembo's diffidence, and, on the other, a general acceptance of all friendly men as friends, is posited the mean of true friendship, between men who can and do trust each other 'without any deception' (*senza inganno alcuno*) (II, xxx) and who maintain their trust for a lifetime.

The topic will be taken up again in Book III (cp. below, p.136) and the *cordialissimo amore* mentioned earlier by Bembo will recur as a major theme during the arguments of Book IV, but here it might be useful to stress the notion of true friendship and its importance for Castiglione. The *Cortegiano* is concerned for most of its length with externals and façades – not necessarily all of them having wicked associations, but evidently difficult to approach closely or to penetrate. The historical period was one in which intrigue and deceit were the order of the day. Castiglione recognised the essential need felt by the good man for a friend and confidant. The wicked could find contentment in untrustworthy associations 'which were not friendships' (*l'amicizia de' mali non è amicizia*) (II, xxx). To mistrust one's fellows (while maintaining an affable relationship) makes good sense in a society full of intrigue; to mistrust all men all the time brings melancholy, isolation and a black cynicism. That disturbs the harmonious make-up so necessary for the Aristotelean tranquillity at which, as will become evident in Book IV, the author is aiming. From a personal and spiritual point of view, then, as well as for the more practical considerations of having a trustworthy adviser and confidant, 'the perfect friendship' is essential. Castiglione takes this requirement to be self-evident (*con ragioni evidentissime*) and refuses, in the next chapter (xxxi), 'having talked enough of this', to elaborate on the exact 'conversation' between friends; his courtier has enough qualifications by now to find himself at ease in most situations, be they jocund or serious.

We have noted that Castiglione's ideas on friendship could have been culled from a variety of sources, notably the homonymous treatise of Cicero. Leonbattista Alberti's *Della famiglia* also contains similar preoccupations (cp. ibid., Book II), while Plutarch's advice on how to discern an adulator from a true friend must have been well known to our author. If anything, Castiglione's attitude is more akin to the 'decadent' period in which Plutarch was writing when dissimulation might have been more current and more profitable, rather than to the austerer Roman Republican period when Cicero, in both *De officiis* and *De amicitia*, saw friendship not as a diplomatic necessity, but as an ornament to sociability. Cicero used epithets like *praestantior amabilius, copulatius*, and praised the statement of Pythagoras, that friendship should create 'one from many' (*unus ex pluribus*) (*De officiis*, I, xvii). Castiglione's warning, implicit in Bembo's words (II, xxix), reflects his desperate times: 'even the most cordial of friends, who have loved each other for many years, finally deceive each other somehow'. Did Castiglione ever know, one wonders, that his kinsman and 'best friend', Cesare Gonzaga, had once tried to usurp his own diplomatic post under the Gonzaga? A century later, Niccolò Strozzi has such a utilitarian attitude to friendship that his advice may nowadays seem almost depraved; he suggests that one way of getting to know who your true enemies are is to feign enmity with your best friend, concerting the plot with him, so that your enemies in turn may believe that he, too, is your enemy. The purpose of the plot is to 'make them trust him' (*acciò...possino...fidarsi di lui*) so that he may betray them. The Byzantine machinations conclude thus: 'and he can deceive them and draw them out for his own and your benefit and, at need, [you may] inflict unitedly upon them mortal blows' (*et egli poi ingannarli et tirarli fuora a benefizio vostro et suo et, bisognando, darli unitamente colpi mortali*) (op. cit., p.25).

The 'jocund' aspect of friendship mentioned earlier introduces a very brief consideration of games (dismissed swiftly in the *Seconda redazione*, p.117, with the statement: 'I am not worried whether the courtier has knowledge of these things or not'). In the final version, that brusque conclusion is omitted, but stress is laid on the relative frivolity of games which require too much time and preparation, particularly chess, for the too exiguous practical (or even social) reward they produce. Joseph Mazzeo, perhaps wrongly, picks out Castiglione's discouragement of skill at chess as being an indication of his desire not to emphasise any one particular virtue or quality in his courtier (and thus disturb what Mazzeo considers the delicate balance or harmony of the parts). In fact, from a social point of view, chess (unless his master were a keen player) would not be the ideal game to ensure that the courtier would be on hand to seize the opportunities which fortune might offer. Chess, indeed, later forms the subject of one of his witty and possibly satirical tales.

For once, the excision of a statement leads to a sharp break in the artistry of the book. Chapter xxxi ends, in the *Seconda redazione*, p.117, with the remark that games are trivial compared with the other social attributes which may gain favour for the courtier. That led naturally to the following chapter on the need to prepare one's reputation well in advance of one's arrival at a court if such favour were to be protected against the vagaries of fortune. This is omitted in the final edition, where chapter xxxii opens (illogically now) with the adversative *ma*, and, immediately following, states that fortune may be inimical to the courtier's aspirations to grace and favour. Castiglione's excision indicates two interesting preoccupations: in the first place, he is anxious to remove a statement which might seem too extreme; in the second, he is so keen to proceed with what he must know is one of the most important aspects of the present Book that he completely neglects the artistic nexus. Fortune *seems* to be the main theme of the following chapters: no matter how qualified the courtier may be, there are often apparently illogical reasons why his master may not find him to be a pleasing servant or companion. The *real* subject, however, is the difficulty of judging what is true amid a welter of false opinion, rumour, first impressions and external façade.

We have already noted that one of the characteristics of true friendship was that it should be '*senza inganno alcuno*'. The importance of true discernment is emphasised in the next chapters which discuss wittily, and illustrate with *novelle* the weight of first impressions and popular esteem. Even here, incidentally, we may see the operation of the Golden Mean: it is important to send ahead of oneself a good reputation, rather than no reputation at all. And the recipient of such information must weigh it well and come to a reasoned judgement on its speciousness or, conversely, on its potential, hidden virtue. Without such judgement a false reputation for virtue may deceive as profoundly as no reputation at all may mislead. Thus a poem reputed to be by Sannazaro may later be judged less than mediocre when discovered to be the composition of someone less illustrious.

(An interesting indication of Sannazaro's rise to favour by 1524, is the substitution of his name in the final version for the name of Pontano in the *Seconda redazione*.) Further, a known wine may be judged to be from different regions if the drinker is persuasively convinced, 'so firmly anchored in your mind was that false opinion which, however, had been created by another's words' (II, xxxv).

Although the subject is cloaked in the usual urbane badinage, the chapters which follow are designed largely to reinforce in a casual way the dangers involved when one misjudges appearances. Even in the brief aside in II, xxxvii, praising the merits of French and Spanish courtiers, the author is keen to urge the imitation of the *gravità riposata* of the Spaniard; Italians who thought they could imitate the manners, especially the quickness, of the French, usually deceived themselves into a ridiculous aping of superficiality. The concept of *deception* (or *false opinion*) recurs very frequently (in chapter xl, the words *inganno* and *ingannare* occur eight times in seventeen of Maier's lines). Federico Fregoso agrees that a man should show himself off to his best advantage, and certain artificious embellishments (Caesar's laurel crown, for instance, hid his baldness) are legitimate, but prudence and discretion are needed as guiding criteria, just as moderation is necessary in eating, drinking and other activities which Federico passes over quickly as being too obvious to detail (II, xxxviii). The outcome and conclusion of Federico's advice is expressed in chapter xli, namely that 'the greatest security for the courtier's life and daily conversation with his fellows, is always to govern himself with a certain honourable mediocrity' (*onesta mediocrità*) (the Aristotelean Mean again). He will thus avoid that which is to be avoided at all costs – the envy of his fellows.

The rest of Book II is almost entirely taken up with an examination of humour and witticisms, a discussion sparked off in a conversational way by Federico's closing remark that the courtier 'apart from what has been said should be able to entertain his hearers, and with pleasantries and witticisms induce them discreetly to smiles and laughter, so that, without offence/boredom (*fastidio*) or satiety, he may continually delight them' (ibid.). Critics have argued that Cardinal Bibbiena is now given the task of presiding over fully fifty-three chapters which come close to offending, boring or sating his reader. Yet some of Castiglione's jokes are timeless, and one suspects that such adverse criticism has stemmed from humourless critics

(Prezzolini, for instance) or from those who would not like their tastes in humour to be revealed and so diminish their academic dignity. Bibbiena's initial remarks on *facezie* reflect not only the interest which the Renaissance took in such mental agility, but also the humanists' derivation of their subject-matter from the ancients. Thus the introductory remarks on humour are almost identical to the tips given by Cicero in his *De oratore* (cp. ibid., II, lvii), and the Aristotelean view, that humour lies in the manifestation of the incongruous, is also stated. Apart from the references to Cicero, the author's preoccupation with humour has other parallels in Quintilian's *Institutio oratoria* and Pontano's *De sermone*, and in fashionable contemporary collections such as Poggio Bracciolini's witty stories, still printed in popular editions today. Hence Castiglione needed little justification for the inclusion of such a long discourse on wit and humour, and, as will be seen, he had other motives for these chapters. Nor does he neglect his traditional concerns: the propounding of the Golden Mean and the need to use the new attribute (humour) to make his courtier more acceptable to his fellows and his prince.

The fact that Federico urges moderation in the telling of humorous tales (avoiding open insults such as those against given persons) leads Francesco Maria della Rovere to draw the implication that, despite the naturally humorous inclination of, say, the Tuscans, it is also possible for humour to be managed by art. This is the point in the book where Castiglione universalises the Golden Mean: 'These rules [of moderation], Sir, are so universal that they are appropriate and advantageous to anything' (II, xliii). Federico then makes the Ciceronian distinction between a natural talent for story-telling and the witty ripostes of clever men, who hardly need to think about the appropriateness of their reply. The statement, unconvincing in the Ciceronian original (*De oratore*, II, liv) (and equally unconvincingly reproduced in the *Seconda redazione*) undergoes a fascinating change in the final version. Here Bembo is introduced as a mediator between art and nature, as it were, pointing out that good and bad concepts may spring to the humorist's mind, but 'judgement and art polish and correct them, selecting the good aspects and rejecting the bad' (II, xliii). There is another change from earlier versions of the *Cortegiano*, which may reflect its author's growing appreciation of Tuscan wit, and may also reveal a growing feeling of Italianness (*italianità*). Whereas in the *Seconda redazione* the Spaniards are upheld as the most acute exploiters of their natural gift, in the final version it is the Tuscans who are declared to be quicker-witted than any others.

It is evidently important for the courtier to have this added qualification. Under normal circumstances no one is likely to be more welcome than a witty and amusing (but discreet) companion, and to have such easy access to his master's ear would be one of Castiglione's main aims. It has a practical function, therefore. It also follows Classical precedent, as Cian's edition has fully documented, and continues Castiglione's aim to do as Plato, Aristotle and Cicero did in their treatises. Yet the section, I believe, has ambitions beyond these obvious ends. Two aims in particular seem so well concealed by the artist's *sprezzatura* and *grazia* that critics' emphasis on the so-called triviality of the stories seems to have distracted attention from those aspects. In the first place, inclusion of so many contemporary references and so many Italian regions gives the chapters an air of *italianità* akin to the Florentine atmosphere evoked by Boccaccio. Later, Matteo Bandello (1485–1561) would be inspired to elaborate many of Castiglione's *novelle* in his own lively evocation of the courts and society of the period. There is a hint that Castiglione was consciously writing with this aim in mind when Federico praises Bibbiena's method of illustrating his theme 'by the example of so many singular minds, and great men, princes, kings and popes' (II, lxxxiv). The second aspect may be even more important from Castiglione's viewpoint. It is the old question of *inganno*, deception, and, implicitly, the need to see through the lustrous façade to the reality beneath. When the *facezie* have finished, and just before the discussion of the practical joke, Bibbiena remarks that there are many other sources of humour, but whatever the type of humour, 'The main thing is to deceive opinion (*ingannar la opinione*) and give unexpected replies (*rispondere altramente che quello che aspetta l'auditore*). To have grace, the witticism must be seasoned with that deception (*inganno*) or dissimulation (*dissimulare*) or practical joking (*beffare*)' (II, lxxxiii). It is true that here, for the moment at least, there is no need for the usual *warnings* about deception, yet the concept is kept casually before the reader, even in this innocent guise of jokes and tricks. That innocuous quality is emphasised in Bibbiena's exposition on practical jokes in chapter lxxxv: 'The practical joke seems to me nothing more than a friendly deception (*inganno amichevole*) in things which give no offence, or at least very little offence.'

It has been implied above that the witty stories also involved an important concept of *italianità*. Rather as Boccaccio's *Decameron* reflected the bustling new commercial Florence which was rising from its medieval past, so Castiglione's stories, which show a remarkable lack of class-distinction for one who allegedly exalts nobility, reflect in cross-section the world of the High Renaissance, and in particular of the regions of Italy. No less than thirty-seven Italian localities are named as settings for stories or as points of origin for their protagonists. (They include Acqua Pendente, Alessandria, Aquila, Aquino, Bergamo, Brescia, Bologna, Cagli, Castellina, Cervia, Cesena, Ferrara, Florence, Foligno, Forlì, Genoa, Loreto, Lucca, Milan, Modena, Montefiore (Pesaro), Naples, Orvieto, Paglia (Rome), Pavia, Pianella (Abruzzi), Pistoia, Potenza, Prato, Rome, Sarzana, Siena, Treviso, Urbino, Venice, Verona, Volterra.) And different towns have an individuality and local colour lent by a well-known tavern (The *Montefiore*) or a street (The *'Banchi'* in Rome). Further, the localities are peopled with the famous, the infamous, the rogues and heroes of the period or of the recent past: Cosimo the Elder and Lorenzo de' Medici, Ludovico *il Moro*, the Popes – Alexander VI ('Pope by force – *vi!*'), Julius II, Leo X, Nicholas V, Pius III – the Gonzaga and Este dynasties, the Duke of Calabria, Djem (1459–95), the important Muslim prisoner of Popes Innocent VIII and Alexander VI – a current conversation piece in Castiglione's youth. The nicknames of actors and buffoons recur: Berto, Strascino, Fedra, Meliolo. Regional features, such as the semi-comprehensible Bergamasque dialect, help to lend further local colour. Local customs are also described – the Marriage of city and sea in Venice, the Roman Carnival, the Stations of the Cross during Lent in Rome.

Historical events which affected the regions, such as the Pazzi conspiracy, the Florentines' war against Pisa, and generally, the internecine strife and ever-changing alliances of the final years of the fifteenth century are also hinted at or evoked in the mention of a personage associated with such events. And the whole is set against a historical backcloth dominated by the greater French and Spanish dynasties. So the rulers of Spain or France occur at key intervals to tie down to a historical campaign or treaty a particular anecdote or incident, while the discoveries in the Americas and Africa widen the scope to embrace the world and the future. And, apart from such regional details, the exchange and storage of such anecdotes may be compared with the glossaries and common-place books of the time, which kept alive cultural as much as national unifying elements. Certainly the great humour of Boccaccio is recalled and praised many times – as Bembo and his followers recalled his language, to similar 'nationalistic' ends when compiling their rules of grammar and style.

Ludovico Canossa and Bernardo Bibbiena are singled out as being the best qualified to discuss humour. Both were well known during their lifetime as wits. Bibbiena in particular had written the comedy *La Calandria*, the play for which, in 1513, Castiglione had composed the prologue, and he tells a hilarious story against himself in chapter lxxxvii. In typical vein he begins his discourse with a witty reference, stemming from Federico's words that he would now rest and refresh himself beneath the shade of Bibbiena's tree: 'not much shade from this tree!' replies the bald Bibbiena. The therapeutic function of humorous recreation and the peculiarly human attribute of being an *'animal risibile'* are stressed in Bibbiena's introductory remarks, though the exact analysis of what laughter is and how it works is declared to be impossible (as Democritus himself would have found!). Castiglione does, however, break down types of humour under three general headings: urbane narration (*urbana e piacevole narrazione continuata*), quick-witted ripostes (*subita e arguta prontezza*) and the practical joke (*burla*) (II, xlviii). Inside this general framework, examples are given of the double-entendre (xlvii); impersonation (l); regional and other satire (lii); 'shaggy-dog' stories (lv); puns and *bons mots* (lviii); the traditional witty, and so forgivable, insult or excuse (*il dire onestamente villania*) (lxi); and, finally, irony or sarcasm (lxviii). Boccaccio is held up as the supreme example of urbane narration. In particular his story of Belcolore (*Decameron*, VIII, ii) is singled out for praise.

At given intervals during the telling of the stories, Castiglione allows himself to digress in order to urge caution or moderation. Thus Roberto da Bari is praised for his ability as an impressionist or impersonator, but a clear distinction is drawn between his skill (as an amateur and a gentleman) and the skill of the professional stage performer (with whom the courtier should not vie). And just to remind his audience that bad taste must be avoided, he devotes chapter lix to the type of wit which may prove cruel, by attacking, for instance, physical deformities (Pulci's noseless giant is adduced as an example, though in the final edition the *attribution* to Pulci, found in the *Seconda redazione*, is lacking). In another admonition against bad taste, Bibbiena warns that obscenity, however clever, should not be used in stories told in the company of ladies (and typically the misogynist, Gasparo Pallavicino is thus allowed to say that he's known women whose language had caused him to blush!).

To give individual examples of the jokes here would inevitably lead to a loss of flavour in the retelling, but attention could profitably be drawn to the regional satire of Bembo's anti-Florentinism, or to the tale of the Brescian peasant, whose first sight of a slide-trombone player leads him to think that the musician was thrusting two feet of trumpet-pipe down his throat at every note (II, liii). Two splendid 'shaggy-dog' stories are outstanding: the first (II, lv), picked out and used by Rabelais, describes the fur-traders shouting frustratingly frozen words across the thick ice of the Dnieper, the second tells of the chess-playing monkey who, in the presence of the King of Portugal, twice beats its embarrassed master. One *novella* of an anti-clerical and Boccaccesque type describes the Prior (II, lxi) who uses the parable of the five talents in order to justify to his accusing superior his siring five infants by five nuns. That case of *dire onestamente villania* is later flatteringly imitated by Bandello (*Novelle*, III, 56). Puns and plays on words include the poor pedagogue who had no bed (*letto*), so poor was he: '*E come po egli esser dotto se non ha letto?*' (II, lviii); (which might be freely translated, 'How can he be a professor if he hasn't even a chair?') or the new [block] 'flooring' (*mattonato*), which could be obtained by planing down the Bishop of Potenza 'a born block-head if ever there was one! (*matto nato*)'. Some of the stories are timeless, and, in some cases, are adapted from very ancient Classical sources – Plutarch's merchants shouted across a similarly frozen river. An interesting exception since it again 'writes out' Pontano is that of the careless peasant carrying a pack on his shoulders, and barging into Cato, who asks whether he had anything else on his shoulders apart from the packing case. In the *Seconda redazione* the remark is attributed to Pontano; in the final version, Cicero's story (from *De oratore*, II, lxix) is more closely followed, and Cato is made the protagonist.

The Book concludes with a discussion of the practical joke, the *burla*, which is defined, as the English expression declares, as verbal wit in action, its sources similar to the sources of the *facezia*. But there are two main types of *burla* illustrated – the first being a deliberate (but, of course, harmless) piece of amusing deception, the second, the construction of a playful trap into which the victim of the joke falls spontaneously. An example of the first comes in the tale of the two citizens from Prato and Pistoia, who, in a darkened inn (the *Paglia*) cleverly convince their companion, a second Pistoiese, that he has lost his sight. In the second case, Bibbiena, in a story narrated against himself, tells how he was trapped by a clever stable-hand when, one Carnival time in Rome he had tried to play a practical joke on an apparently timorous priest. Unknown to Bibbiena, the 'priest' was also masquerading, offering himself as trembling bait to entrap the lively Bibbiena. The shower of rotten eggs which rewards their subsequent grotesque progress on Bibbiena's horse hurts the future Cardinal's pride more than it does the person of the sturdy stable-hand. Boccaccio is again lauded, this time as the pleasing inventor of some of the best *burle* and his Calandrino stories find a particular mention. The customary warning against excesses in practical joking (especially in jokes against women) brings Bibbiena's discourse to a close and the evening almost to its conclusion – but not quite.

Ottaviano Fregoso explains why society has cast woman in the role she has, why she needs the protection mentioned by Bibbiena. The theme is to be picked up in a later important discussion, in Book III, xxxvii in particular where Bibbiena explains that chastity and con-tinence required of women is society's way of ensuring legitimate dynastic succession (*certezza dei figlioli*) (II, xci). Now, although this and other less complimentary remarks find little sympathy with the Duchess, it must be noted that Fregoso does not impose upon the company the negative misogyny of Gasparo Pallavicino. It is left to Pallavicino to mention those stories from the *Decameron* in which Boccaccio allows the unfaithful wife to triumph over a gullible or cruel husband. And when Bibbiena hedges, trying to qualify the justice or otherwise of the individual cases, Pallavicino says that love may excuse the unfaithful wife (Beatrice and Egano, for instance, in *Decameron*, VII, 7) 'and this you must admit in men as in women' (II, xciv). Bibbiena interrupts to suggest that true love must be defined in more spiritual terms. The lover should not be *principally* concerned with the woman's body, but should rather strive to win over her soul in order that she may reciprocate with love. The alter-native is the temporary satisfaction 'of enjoying her and possessing her against her will, for in such a case I would seem to be master of a dead body' (ibid.). The discussion here contrasts with that of courtly love (Book III) or spiritual love (Book IV) which is to follow. Pallavicino argues back that if the lover masters the woman's body he may also conquer her heart, and the wife of Filipello in Boccaccio's story prefers the caresses of Ricciardo and so gives him her love. Rather weakly, Bibbiena retorts that 'Boccaccio, like Pallavicino, was, wrongly, the enemy of womankind' (II, xcv). After further banter and a 'Bacchant' attack by the ladies on Pallavicino, Emilia Pia charges Giuliano de' Medici to defend the rights of women. He pro-poses, then, to describe the qualities of the gentlewoman (*una donna di palazzo*) in the same way as the company had been discussing the qualities of the courtier. The company breaks up with the understanding that this will be the topic for discussion on the morrow.

At one point in chapter xciv the debate seemed likely to swerve on to the subject of love. Indeed, in the *Seconda redazione*, Bibbiena positively states 'But I would not like to leave the first proposition [practical jokes]...and begin to talk about love' (p.177). This statement changes in the final version to: 'I don't want to go outside the first proposition [practical jokes] and enter into such a difficult enterprise as would be a defence of woman against your views' (II, xcvi). As will become clear, Castiglione wished to reserve the discussion of love for the culminating point of the treatise, in the second half of Book IV. But, at this point, it is important to stress that the crux reached at the end of Book II involves the need to distinguish true from false love. The man who wins 'love' by lavish gifts, for instance, can never be certain that he is truly loved in return, since the woman may simply love his generous gifts. Furthermore the Boccaccesque lovers who win 'love' by means of practical jokes ('which could perhaps be more properly called betrayals (*tradimenti*) than pranks (*burle*)' – ibid.) often use deliberate deception. Can such love be genuine? To discern *proprio e vero amore* is a most important requirement, deferred from this point of Book II to Bembo's intervention in Book IV.

## 5. Book Three of *The Courtier*

The whole of Book III is concerned with the theme, announced on the previous evening, of the formation of the gentlewoman, *la donna di palazzo*. The topic introduces the centuries-old debate on the relative superiority or inferiority of women, with its natural protagonists, the misogynist, Gasparo Pallavicino and the more reasonable feminist, Giuliano de' Medici. They are able to debate the question with their by now characteristic prejudices, and hence with stylistic verisimilitude. The discussion will recall not only Classical debates found as early as Plato and Aristotle, but also medieval debates on love, the ambivalent attitude to womankind found in Boccaccio and his contemporaries, and, finally, the numerous essays on the subject published between the opening of the fifteenth century and the close of the sixteenth. Castiglione's dialogue echoes many of those treatises, and, in turn, his opinions are evoked by the many authors of similar books which followed the publication of the *Cortegiano*.

The few critical items treating of this vast topic which have been published in modern times serve largely to indicate the dimensions of the problem and the lack of anything approaching a definitive, or even adequate, treatment of the subject. We can simply hope to highlight what we consider new emphases laid by Castiglione on certain aspects of the problem. Thus, for example, his lack of interest in parts of the traditional debate, which are reproduced by him for the sake of form and completeness, leads him to become at times brusquely dismissive in attitude. This last, surprisingly enough, is particularly true in the case of courtly love, with which Castiglione is evidently not greatly concerned. On the other hand, he *is* interested in the civilising role of women, and he *is* living at a period when women may potentially be a dominant force in the political sphere (his list of famous women will include such contemporary figures). The debate, however, also allows him to illustrate in passing many aspects of behaviour characteristic of the rest of the book. He is able to posit more examples of the Golden Mean, and he has marvellous opportunities to show the dividing lines between sincerity and deception and between truth and falsehood.

The survey of the position of women in society during the Middle Ages carried out by Conor Fahy shows that, broadly speaking, there were two clearly defined attitudes to the *querelle des femmes*. On the one hand, there were general warnings on the untrustworthiness (or general unworthiness) of women, faults which were satirised, for instance, in the second part of the *Roman de la Rose* (c. 1280). On the other hand, women found defenders in writers such as Antonio Pucci (c. 1300–80), whose work, *Il contrasto delle donne*, was moderate in tone, though he, like many of his successors, including Castiglione two centuries later, insisted upon the essential need for female chastity. Contemporaneously, Petrarch and Boccaccio, despite their eulogies of great women of the past (which were to find echoes until the end of the sixteenth century), dismissed the pleasures of family bliss because the accompanying responsibilities were destructive of the tranquillity so necessary for the academic life. Thus Petrarch in his *De remediis utriusque fortunae* and Boccaccio in his *Corbaccio* still retain something of the medieval asceticism which rejected the notion of marriage in favour of higher callings, suggesting that fame and immortality were better obtainable through virtue and learning than through the propagation of children. Boccaccio's views in the *Corbaccio* are generally acknowledged to be the result of some personal psychological crisis, for there is no denying his exaltation of the 'eternal feminine' and his appreciation of the clever, beautiful and vivacious women visible throughout his *Decameron*. Nor can one ignore the eulogies of Laura and of famous women of the past so frequently found in Petrarch's *Trionfi* and elsewhere.

Coluccio Salutati, by contrast, positively emphasised the social importance of marriage and deliberately opposed Petrarch's views on celibacy, no doubt concerned, because of his civic responsibilities as Chancellor, to keep the population of Florence growing at a steady rate. But ten years after Salutati's death, and at a time when marriages were usually more matters of expediency than affection (as Castiglione's was initially to be), the *De re uxoria* (1416) of Francesco Barbaro (1395–1454) shows humanity and concern for women and for the institution of marriage. Significantly, Barbaro was a pupil of Guarino, and spent much time studying in Venice with both Guarino and Vergerio. In his treatise he underlined the joys of marriage, the advantages for the children of a stable relationship between their parents and the sanction of the institution by the Church. Automatically the treatise added respect for the woman's position, responsible as she particularly was for the early upbringing of the children and the inculcating of a good moral basis for their education. Further, Barbaro insisted that she should receive sympathy and encouragement from her husband and should not live a life of seclusion, in medieval purdah, so to speak. Poggio Bracciolini was impressed enough by the content of the treatise to write congratulating Guarino on his pupil's success.

There followed a spate of works which reflected a general improvement, at least in literary terms, in the status of women. San Bernardino's *Prediche*, perhaps more sincerely, contained very pro-feminist views of family life and inveighed against unfaithful husbands (cp. op. cit., XIX). A similar appreciation of the importance of marriage in the life of the citizen is to be seen in Matteo Palmieri's *Della vita civile*, particularly Book IV, which is eloquent on the subject. But there were writers who preferred women to occupy a more depressed position in society. To Alberti the family was certainly an important unit, but his *famiglia* has more of the undertones of 'clan' (or some would say a mafia 'family'). In his scheme for its survival and the improvement of its status, his women may be useful for the purpose of procreating children (preferably male and as prolifically as possible) and they certainly provide companionship for life for their husband, but their contribution, as intelligent individuals to family life, is strictly limited. Indeed the husband instructs his wife in Book III of the *Della famiglia* as if she lacked any initiative of her own.

Alberti's tough line may have been dictated by his hard practicality, where later works conveyed a more gentle, perhaps more fashionable viewpoint. Thus many treatises during the fifteenth century reflected the influence of Boccaccio's *De claris mulieribus*, regarded very much as a source-book for exemplars of great women (and Castiglione, too, will make good use of them). But it was probably the increasing importance of women in court society which stimulated most of the treatises on the superiority or inferiority of women vis-à-vis men. Such was that of Vespasiano da Bisticci (written after 1480) on the virtues of women, the *Libro delle lode et commendatione delle donne*. Works of this kind seem important as reflections of the increasing emergence of illustrious 'liberated' women, such as Isabella and Beatrice d'Este. In this lies their significance, for it is doubtful whether their exaggerated praise implies much intellectual conviction. The topic seemed as much a fashionable point of debate as a serious defence of women's dignity.

It is probably true that women at Italian courts led fuller and more cultured lives than their contemporaries elsewhere. But that relative emancipation was certainly exaggerated by Jacob Burckhardt in his fine work, when, talking of the equality of the sexes, he can say: 'There was no question of "woman's rights" or "female emancipation" because the thing itself was simply a matter of course' (op. cit., p.241). His acceptance of their social equality with men has led to a tradition which could now well bear a little more investigation. Even Cian quoted his authority as late as 1948 (ed. cit., pp. 310–12), and in his 1974 reprint of *The Elizabethan Renaissance*, A.L.Rowse continued that old idea (his book is dedicated in part to Burckhardt) of the 'freedom accorded to women that so much struck outside observers – at the top of society, something like equality' (ibid., p.16). The original opinion, be it noted, was that of a nineteenth-century Swiss male.

It seems undeniable that some outstanding noble women had an enormous influence upon the social life of the Italian Renaissance, but their influence, for fully fifty years after Castiglione's death, seems to have been limited in almost all cases to the informality of private discussion and advice. Their position, after 1500, seems compounded of a blend of the glamorous influence of the modern Hollywood film-star and the luxurious comfort of the wives of rich Indian businessmen or politicians. Both categories are more emancipated or more influential, certainly more comfortably-off, than their less prosperous immediate consœurs, and, on the Indian subcontinent (and in Ceylon), women have reached, for those societies, unbelievable heights of political power. Yet the vast majority of Indian high-caste wives and the hosts of budding starlets are completely reliant upon their men-folk and upon the influence (and purse-strings) of directors and producers.

A few Italian women in the Renaissance, Vittoria Colonna (1492–1547) being the supreme example, did achieve a fame in the literary or artistic world equal to some of the lesser male geniuses contemporary with them. Vittoria Colonna, it should be added, was born into one of the most important families in Rome, and married one of the most powerful political and military figures of the period. Significantly, when her husband died, she retired to a convent. Later, another very sympathetic figure, Veronica Franco (1546–91) seems to have made good use of her more natural attributes, as well as of her literary erudition, in achieving her reputation as a poet-courtesan. There were other figures of literary importance, such as Gaspara Stampa (1523–54) and Veronica Gambara (1485–1550). There were powerful women in the political and social sphere, Lucrezia Borgia, Elisabetta Gonzaga, Isabella and Beatrice d'Este, for example. They were immortalised by their own achievements as well as by contemporary writers, notably by Ariosto (cp. *Orlando furioso*, XLII, 93).

This may be an appropriate place to refer to the survey of Ariosto's treatment of the *querelle* done by C. P. Brand (op. cit., pp. 116–20). Ariosto's attitude is certainly that of a liberal-minded individual. An argument such as that of Bradamante (who has physically demonstrated her superiority over rival male paladins) claiming her right to equal treatment with men, is akin to those which have cropped up several times during our present decade of woman's struggle for freedom and equality in Britain and America. Yet, reading between Ariosto's lines, we can see that the potential of man for wrecking a woman's life was far greater than any harm which might come to a man through woman. The innocent Ginevra may be legally burnt at the stake on suspicion of adultery 'because of Scotland's harsh laws' (*Orlando furioso*, XI, 4); the trusting Olimpia, who loses father, brother, home, possessions, everything in order to marry Bireno (ibid., X), is positively betrayed by her husband. And though, in this last case, it may be love's power, rather than the faithlessness of men, which is being illustrated, the fact remains that the Birenos of the Renaissance could go on their merry way unscathed. What could the Olimpias, unqualified and unprotected, expect to do in that tough world? They could wait for an Orlando, perhaps, to rescue them? Then, Ariosto tells us, let the rescuing knight be a chaste paladin (and one shortly to be certified insane!) such as Orlando, rather than an uninhibited rapist, such as Ruggiero (shortly to become the fictional progenitor of the oldest feudal ruling house in Italy!) only too willing to take advantage of a damsel in distress, particularly if, like Angelica, she wore no clothes.

The cultural situation in early sixteenth-century Italy, particularly where women were concerned, may be profitably compared with the position in the thirteenth and fourteenth centuries. It was during the fourteenth century that the Italian city-states became more settled after the relative anarchy of the previous two hundred years. Personal survival became less dependent upon individual military prowess, or upon the prowess of single families (rich enough, for instance, to buy for themselves *ballistae* and other weapons from the city's war-surplus stores). Corporate defence was now more important, and, relieved of the military burden, individuals in rich centres like Bologna and Florence, where political and commercial virtues increased in importance, could indulge their more refined tastes and culture. The old chivalric values were transmuted, inspired now not by a call to arms or the capture of a city, but by the call of love and the capture of a lady's heart. It was to the traditions of the troubadour and of the Celtic exaltation of knight errants fighting for love, and not, as Roland had done in the earlier *Chanson de geste*, for King, Country or Christianity, that the refined spirits of the age looked for cultural guidance. For Dante and his contemporaries, the lady inspired her man to higher moral virtue, and 'love and the noble heart were one and the same'. We have already seen a hint of that same refinement in the lady's witty reply to the knight whose sole accomplishments are in the military field (above, p.74) and who is therefore an inappropriate ornament of the sixteenth-century court.

By the end of the fifteenth century, internal squabbles between the individual city-states within the peninsula were swallowed up in the wider conflict between the great European powers. As far as the chivalrous tradition was concerned this had two major effects. In the first place, the importance of the individual combatant was of minimal importance compared with the need for well-disciplined formation fighting. Secondly, the military status of the high-born knight was considerably reduced by the ability of the ignoblest foot-soldier to bring down the noblest of paladins with mechanical gadgets *and* by the acceptance of the convention that the foot-soldier could do this with impunity (medieval chivalric custom would have punished such an outrage). And yet, despite the greater potential for oppression which the European powers had, court civilisation in Italy was relatively settled, and, within that environment, further refinements of culture could develop. Castiglione's insistence upon the central role of women in this development links his views with the tradition joining the fourteenth-century stilnovist poets and the courtly epic of Ariosto. And the views coincide happily with the refinements of the imitative school of lyric poetry which was so strongly dependent upon its fourteenth-century roots and which Bembo's efforts had done so much to publicise.

I shall return to this aspect, but, to give a more rounded account of the *querelle* between feminists and anti-feminists, which may seem more realistic than that of Burckhardt – Swiss, male, nineteenth-century – or that of our contemporary British emancipated woman, I turn to the assessment of the position of women in the Renaissance provided by Conor Fahy's 'Early Renaissance Treatises on Women'. The appendix to that essay provides a wide-ranging catalogue of treatises illustrating the age-old dispute; to these researches I am here indebted for the documentation of the following examples of three such works.

Bartolomeo Gogio's *De laudibus mulierum*, dated about 1487, is a positive attempt to demonstrate the superiority of women (and possibly thus flatter his patroness, Eleonora of Aragon, wife of Ercole I d'Este). His arguments to show the superiority of women smack of the medieval theological method: Adam, for instance, was created outside the Garden of Eden, Eve was formed from his rib within those more perfect precincts and hence had a nobler place of origin. Gogio suggests that women are superior to men in physical beauty, and, quoting Aristotle, that physical softness implies correspondingly greater mental robustness – a tag which he finds confirmed in Quintilian's *Institutio* and which we can see Castiglione using in III, xiii. In procreation Gogio denies that the woman's role is wholly passive. In his second Book he then proceeds to show how he considers the discovery of letters, laws and arts to have been the responsibility of women. Eulogies of the Virgin Mary and of Eve help complete his picture of women as paragons of virtue. His arguments in favour of Eve are noteworthy and liberal in that Eve's offer of the apple 'opened the eyes of the Intellect to man' (ibid., p.36), this, and not the ignorance of the blissful, being, Gogio suggests, man's natural (and preferable) state. The strong pro-feminist viewpoint shown in the treatise is typical of the time, and probably reflects a fashionable debating trend rather than a practical attempt to influence public opinion.

A more realistic assessment of the position of women may be gleaned from the next text analysed by Fahy, Mario Equicola's *De mulieribus*, which is datable to 1501. The first half of Equicola's brief work describes the theoretic equality of women with men, in philosophical, psychological, medical and theological terms. But, although Equicola notes that, in theory, women are the equal of men, yet 'natural freedom is denied to women, either by law or by social custom' (ibid., p.38). His language becomes emotionally charged: 'their freedom is extinguished, abolished, extirpated . . . the girl is kept at home, where she rots with nothing to do (*ocio marcescit*), allowed to have no mental concepts outside needle and thread . . . as soon as she has gone beyond the years of puberty she is handed over to the will of a man' and 'as the vanquished yield to their victors, so the wife's mind yields to the conventions of men' (ibid., pp.38–9). Equicola sees the reason for the manifest inequality of the sexes inherent in the influence of custom and upbringing. He suggests that other societies have had more liberal regimes for their womenfolk, and implies that change is potentially possible for his own era. Finally he adduces Classical, mythological or Biblical figures to illustrate greatness in women, and he includes three women of his own time, including Isabella d'Este. His method and his exemplars are similar to those of Boccaccio in the *De claris mulieribus*, but his trite theoretic opening and the tired list of exemplars could have inspired in his contemporary gentlewomen little confidence or hope of a sudden release from their plight, however liberal his own intentions.

Equicola cut short his *De mulieribus* possibly because he knew of the composition by Agostino Strozzi of a work which later circulated in Mantua under the title *Defensione de le donne*. Although the textual tradition of the treatise is still undetermined, it does serve as a contemporary account of the subject. It is in the final section of his article that Fahy analyses the controversial text and one of his conclusions links the work of Equicola and Strozzi in a gloomy summary of the current situation: 'Like Equicola, the author believes that in other times and in other societies, women have played a very different role to that to which contemporary society condemns them' (ibid., p.44). Environment and convention, then, have conditioned that acceptance of woman's role in society, but the treatise also implies, inconsistently for such a 'defence of womanhood', that women are physically, and so, it argues, intellectually, inferior to men and that 'nature, through her laws and ordinances, has disposed that they be subjected to and placed beneath men' (*la natura, per sua legge et ordine, ha disposto, che li siano soggette e sottoposte*) (ibid., p.46). With defenders like this, the Renaissance gentlewoman needed no enemies! The list of names which concludes the treatise is similar to other lists of great women, following the tradition after Boccaccio's *De claris mulieribus*.

It would not be appropriate to close this brief discussion without a mention of some of the many other treatises, treated more fully by Conor Fahy which occupied the minds of *letterati* throughout the rest of the century, including scholars like Sperone Speroni (in his *Della dignità delle donne*), Stefano Guazzo, Ortensio Lando, and Agnolo Firenzuola (particularly the *Epistola in lode delle donne*). The traditional defence of women was also present in a work which Castiglione might have known, G. F. Capella's *Della eccellenza et dignità delle donne*, published in 1525, and continues until Tasso's more formal *Discorso della virtù feminile et donnesca* of 1582. It would also appear that after about 1530 the practical aspect of the question is lost, as the idea of women's superiority is applied more and more to their inspiratory influence on the life and work of men. The debate is further continued in less obviously didactic form, in the epic and satires of Ariosto and in the lyric tradition of the Petrarchists. Nor can the topic be isolated from such works as Paolo Lorenzetti discusses in his treatise on beauty and love in the sixteenth century. Conor Fahy lists forty-one pro-feminist essays of this kind in the appendix to his article.

We have already seen the many, if sporadic, references to the civilising influence of the ladies at the Urbino court, in particular to the virtues which, in the Duchess Elisabetta, for instance, could ensure the continuation of the court as a centre for civilised living. A further extension of their qualities and power may be seen in the *Cortegiano* in the way the ladies are allowed to abbreviate tiresome or unpleasant arguments. On another level, Castiglione had seen, at first hand, the effect upon Ludovico Sforza of his cultured wife, Beatrice d'Este (and the subsequent premature cultural disintegration of the Milanese court after her death and prior to the French invasion), and, closer to home, the equally civilising effect upon the Gonzaga court of Isabella d'Este. The eulogy of womankind reaches a peak in chapter lii, where they are considered the motive for all the world's most gracious and pleasurable actions. But apart from these more universal aspects, there are subtle passages of appreciation of woman's role in society. There is a definite bias towards the gentle world which Castiglione seems to have experienced during the brief period of his marriage, and I believe, perhaps naively, that Castiglione's feminism is something more than conventional gallantry (though he includes this, too). In the fiercely competitive world he knew, it must have seemed clear to his sensitive soul that women initiated fewer wars and were less likely to cut their rivals' throats than were his male colleagues. And, he implies, the man who makes a bad marriage has to endure nowhere near so disastrous an existence as the woman married to a bad husband – shades of Equicola there.

The opening of Book III contains a lengthy compliment to the Urbino court, in effect an adaptation of a legend about Pythagoras, taken from Aulus Gellius' *Noctes atticae*. The compliment is an extension of the eulogy noted above, and an elaboration of one found in germ in the *Seconda redazione* (p.183). The extended paean of praise replaces at this point the obituaries and recollections featured at the beginning of the earlier version (ibid.), which are now reshuffled to appear in the definitive Book IV. Nowhere, perhaps, is the rewriting of the *Cortegiano* so clearly in evidence. The tears and the laudatory remarks are deferred from the '*terza sera*' of the *Seconda redazione* to the '*quarta sera*' of the definitive Book IV, while the themes of political virtue and Platonic love, which appeared unsystematically at this point in the *Seconda redazione*, are given fuller treatment in the later version.

As promised on the previous day, and despite mild objections from Gasparo that the company might do better to discuss, instead, the practices of foreign courts, the question of formulating the rules for the perfect *donna di palazzo* is taken up by Giuliano de' Medici. But immediately before this, Cesare Gonzaga counters Gasparo's objections by emphasising the beneficial and civilising role of women at courts. Without women to lend adornment and splendour to a court there can be no happiness; no courtier can be graceful, amiable (or even bold); no pleasurable deed of chivalry is possible; no courtly conversation is complete without the participation and presence of women. The old chivalric ideal is thus revived at the outset of the debate. It is interesting to see that Bartolomeo Gogio's treatise, circulating in manuscript form at the turn of the fifteenth century (cp. Conor Fahy, art. cit., p.33) contained similar statements on the need for woman's presence in society. Gogio had concluded: 'What celebration or triumph was ever complete without the presence of woman?' (ibid., p.34).

So now Giuliano takes up his task with a will, hoping, he smilingly says, to keep his perfect woman, as Pygmalion was allowed to keep the animated statue of Galatea! Broadly speaking, Giuliano's court-lady will require the spiritual qualities which the perfect courtier needs, though, physically, she will not have to be so robust or well exercised! Indeed, it is suggested, she will need to be as gentle and feminine as her male counterpart is masculine and strong. But physical beauty is more necessary for the woman, and she needs to be more circumspect in her behaviour and attitudes, in order to avoid even the rumour of being unvirtuous or blameworthy, particularly since she has fewer possibilities to defend herself from calumny. This important theme will be taken up at greater length in later chapters of the *Cortegiano*. Giuliano takes for granted that the ideal *donna di palazzo* will have the 'virtues of mind (prudence, magnanimity, temperance, etc.) in common with the courtier' (III, v), and he passes over these qualities after the briefest mention. Castiglione probably considered it a finer compliment to women to assume that they had those qualities, though it is true that high-born ladies seemed to have enjoyed an educational equality with their male peers. It may be recalled that Leonardo Bruni's treatise on education was composed for the instruction of Battista Malatesta, and that in theory the schools of Guarino and Vittorino gave similar education to both boys and girls. From that education could have come some of those virtues.

More significantly, when Giuliano suggests that she should also, if married, have the good qualities of a loving mother and efficient housekeeper, these domestic aspects are very rapidly reviewed, indeed 'left aside' in a Ciceronian *praeteritio*, so that her more social graces may be elaborated. Later we are told that 'you do not wish . . . managing home, children and family to be her principal professions' (III, vii). Gasparo meets no contradiction from Giuliano in that statement, and this is a strong indication that Castiglione deliberately wants to pass over the purely domestic aspects of the woman's life in order to see her as the hub of social gatherings, in itself an acknowledgement of a dignity which rises above the mechanics of bearing children and keeping house. And from the opening encouragement for her to participate in high social gatherings, the Aristotelean Mean is stated in language recalling Horace's injunction to moderation (cp. *Satires*, I, i, 106–7): 'She needs to adhere to a certain difficult equilibrium (*mediocrità difficile*), composed, as it were, of contraries, and to reach certain precise limits without going beyond them' (III, v). Thus, for example, she must not, in order to appear good and honest, shun company and conversation which might seem a little audacious, in case people think either that she is a prude, or, worse, that she wishes to hide similar traits in herself. And if we consider the original source of the Horatian quotation, we find that Horace is there equating the Mean not only with a reasonable way of life, but also as a pointer to truth and right.

It is possible to see in Giuliano's next piece of advice, despite its apparent superficiality, two further important key topics. His words combine a hint of that avoidance of calumny which recurs so often, with a practical aspect of the gentlewoman's political role: her ability to influence her male companions, who were certainly not so likely to be influenced by boring chatter. More specifically, then, he cautions against idle and malicious gossip, particularly that which concerns other women. We shall see that this has important repercussions in the debate on truth and falsehood, for few things hide the truth more than false rumour, which is akin to envy in its intangibility. Empty chatter, too, Giuliano suggests, should be avoided, and, in order not to bore or offend the companion she is speaking with, the lady should be as widely read as she may, and recognise the status of her companion. If the reader thinks that this is asking too much (particularly in the way of humility) from the *donna di palazzo*, it is worth recalling that many of the courtier's attributes and accomplishments so far developed have as one of their incidental, but important purposes, the amusement of the *donna di palazzo*. Giuliano's final piece of advice in this chapter is that affectation must be avoided, particularly the affectation of pretending to know what she does not know. And again, in his words we can discern the plea for sincerity and frankness characteristic of Castiglione's method.

Gasparo Pallavicino justifiably objects that Giuliano has been generalising too much, and, after some brief badinage (Aretino regrets the disappearance of mixed nude wrestling and Cesare Gonzaga says that he has seen women engaged in nearly all the physical exercises which usually characterise the knight!) Giuliano particularises. And while some of his remarks will inevitably seem trivial (and certainly annoying to modern defenders of women's liberation), his overall conclusions must be seen as liberal for their time. The badinage about women wrestlers is also a sly dig at one of Plato's less practical suggestions. Classical, too, in its origins is the admonition for the gentlewoman to maintain her gracefulness by not playing certain musical instruments particularly drums, pipes or trumpets. If we reflect upon that thought now, how interesting it seems that, four and a half centuries later, examples of female pipers, drummers and trumpeters are so rare as to be regarded as newsworthy curiosities. The Golden Mean is further illustrated, too, by the suggestion that when invited to dance, the lady must not appear over-anxious, 'allowing herself to be persuaded', aiming at a mean between timidity and impudence.

The Classical notion of the artlessness of art is also introduced with regard to the physical beauty of the *donna di palazzo*, a quality more essential to her than to her male counterpart. Nature's gifts may, then, have to be helped, to enhance her appearance, and all this with the least possible sign of artifice. The *Cortegiano* does not expatiate on this topic, which was, however, a very popular subject in contemporary handbooks on toiletries and female dress (cp. T.F.Crane, *Italian Social Customs*, p.201). This may be an indication (akin to the swift dismissal of 'courtly love' which follows shortly) that Castiglione was not so concerned, after all, simply with the refined superficialities of his contemporary society. Furthermore, his words contrast, for their mildness and discretion, with the later more explicit advice of other gallant writers, such as Alessandro Piccolomini or Agnolo Firenzuola.

There follows a piece of advice which might have inspired Giuseppe Toffanin to suggest that Castiglione was creating a bourgeois ideal of womanhood, 'a woman who must be clever in art and culture, in order, not to create, but to appreciate what man creates, to spur man on with her admiration' (op. cit., p.145). The thought is one which accords with Fahy's suggestion of the inspiratory role of women in the second half of the century. Castiglione advises that, although as a woman she cannot be expected to carry out the harder physical exercises of the courtier, she should be well-versed enough in the skills and merits of such enterprises to appreciate them in others. That there *were* possibly women who did carry out such physical activities is in part illustrated in one of Castiglione's own letters to Ippolita Fioramonda, whom he congratulates on being 'skilled in the use of arms' (Serassi, I, p.169).

Finally, in this section, her character is rounded and her reputation maintained, we are told, by the cultivation of the cardinal virtues, though these may have no immediate application to her ability for social conversation. The reader is entitled here to wonder, along with Gasparo, why Giuliano does not offer to such paragons the government of cities and the formulation of ordinances (while men could stay in the kitchen or busy themselves spinning!) Giuliano declares that women could well govern cities, and he adduces that part of Plato's *Republic*, where, 'despite his misogyny, Plato entrusts the city's government to women, leaving all the other, martial, offices to men' (III, x). At this point it should be made clear that in his later *Laws*, Plato is much more severe against women. Cian points out here that Castiglione (and Renaissance scholars generally) were unaware of the chronology of Plato's work and the consequent development of his thought after the *Republic* and up to the *Laws*. There women are considered very definitely the inferior sex, and his law-givers are required to give a compensatory education to the 'weaker' sex in order to bring them up to the level of the men.

The cut and thrust of the debate at this point reveal its Ciceronian qualities, those qualities, for which Vergerio argued in the *De ingenuis moribus*, which bring out the true discernment of the question – unlike the Platonic dialogue, which tended to be a monologue answered by occasional one-word comments from interlocutors who were told what questions to ask. Yet Castiglione makes full use of arguments from Plato and Aristotle. A good instance of this comes in

Gasparo's objection that Giuliano has praised womankind excessively, and, despite the presence of so many distinguished women at the Urbino court, he points to the contention of wise men throughout the ages that women are less perfect creatures than men. The general drift of his arguments is similar to that of Plato and Aristotle; his method, his choice of rhetoric, is that of Cicero. It is a particularly neat point of style, then, that Giuliano should counter Gasparo's objections with a beautifully argued piece of Aristotelean logic, to prove that men are neither better nor worse than women (III, xii). This abstract argument (for which Castiglione half-apologises) and the scholastic reasoning which makes its appearance a little later in the chapter (and by which Pallavicino is usually worsted) interest largely because they testify to the presence, even at this comparatively late date, of scholastic subtleties in Renaissance discussion.

Earlier it was briefly noted that Agostino Strozzi had commented upon the relative physical weakness of women. In his so-called *Defensione* he had suggested that, since women's bodies were weaker, their physical perceptions must also be less effective; the information fed by the senses to their minds would be impaired, and intellectually, therefore, women must be inferior to men! Castiglione is in favour of intellectual equality. Indeed he allows Giuliano to emphasise that, though accident may make men physically stronger, strength, as an end in itself, is not particularly esteemed, even among men themselves, whereas mental agility is equal in either sex. That chapter (xviii) is full of appreciation for women's more excellent qualities, and when, at the end of it, Niccolò Frigio fulfils the role of antagonist, his arguments, by contrast, will have none of the warmth or indeed the originality of the ideas put forward by Giuliano. But, in order to complete the anti-feminist arguments, he is allowed to adduce the trite notion (which we saw turned to women's advantage in Gogio's treatise) that it was a woman, Eve, who caused man's fall from Grace and brought death into the world. That charge is quickly answered by Giuliano, albeit with apparent reluctance 'to bring holy matters into our foolish arguments'. Now, the rebuttal itself is a simple matter – indeed, Frigio's objections and Giuliano's reply would be tiresomely trite if they did not also introduce another important subject for consideration; as will be seen, Castiglione is, with his usual subtlety, steering the conversation into an important digression – on religion.

Giuliano, then, goes on to talk of the superiority of the Virgin Mary, and the many holy women martyrs, not to mention the saintly nuns who live unsung in convents (and here one is reminded of Castiglione's affection for his cloistered sister). As Cian has pointed out, Giuliano's declarations are appropriate to his 'future' status as cardinal and brother to Leo X, and his anti-monastic attitude would add further verisimilitude to his character here; he was well known among his contemporaries for those views. Here the contrast which he now points between the unpretentious religion of the modest nuns and the wickedness of hypocritical priests helps to put the virtue of the former into greater relief. Castiglione's polemic against the degenerate clergy is extensive, running to some four hundred words in chapter xx before he is 'cut short' by Emilia Pia, on the grounds that the subject is distasteful. The 'abrupt' end to the anti-clerical polemic here has seemed to some commentators to be typical of Castiglione's avoidance of the distasteful. To counter that myth it must be stated that he allows his speaker to enumerate many, if not all, of the contemporary faults of the less honourable clergy, and only cuts him short when the list of faults is exhausted. His polemic is as forthright as the letter, written during the winter of 1527–8, in which he was to attack Valdés. Further, the polemic was present in the *Seconda redazione* (pp.243–5), a fact which shows that, even before he was in a position of diplomatic power, he was not afraid to voice these almost puritanical opinions about the corrupt clergy. And so, to counter the charges of non-commitment so frequently levelled against him, it might be worthwhile to see some of the epithets and descriptions he here uses.

Such men as he describes are 'hypocrites (*ippocriti*)...accursed (*maledetti*)...they forget, or take little care for, Christ's teaching' – and, in particular, ignore the need, expressed in *Matthew* VI, for concealing penance or fasting or asceticism. And moreover, their life is one great act with which 'they deceive the simple' (*gabbano i semplici*); they falsify testaments (*falsar testamenti*), put enmity (and sometimes poison) between man and wife, a theme to be celebrated in Castiglione's examination of marital relationships in the debate which follows. They use enchantments (*incanti*) and magic spells (*malie*), and all manner of confidence tricks (*ribalderia*). They teach '*Si non caste tamen caute*' (Be cautious if you can't be chaste), and so persuade their fellows that a hidden sin is easily pardoned. Secrecy and a 'veil of sanctity' (*un velo di santità*) allow them 'to contaminate the minds of chaste women, sow the seeds of hatred among brothers, rule states... behead, imprison and exile their fellows, be ministers of crime (*ministri della scelerità*) and the repositories of the plunder (*quasi depositari delle rubarie*) extorted by princes'. Other priests may be vain and fashion-conscious, pretentious in their well-cut clothes, and deliberately striking studied reverential attitudes. Such men as these are 'wicked and criminal (*malvagi e scelerati*), alien not only to religion, but to all good morals' (III, xx). Powerful words! and certainly the Inquisition was later to think that these remarks were 'committed' statements. When the *Cortegiano* was expurgated by Antonio Ciccarelli for the 1584 edition, Giuliano's polemic was abbreviated and references to the clergy disappeared from the text.

Thus, although Emilia's interruption seems to bring Giuliano's attack to an abrupt end, it is difficult to see what else could have been added to that list of vices. Here her intervention may be seen as timely, as well as abrupt, and Giuliano, returning to what has become a eulogy, declares that women are naturally capable of the same qualities (*virtù*) as men. His statements and his list of great women of Classical antiquity are traditional to the theme. But stylistic subtlety is again in evidence at this point in the dispute, for, with typical casualness, Castiglione allows his misogynist, Gasparo, to interject a seemingly frivolous joke about the husband who preferred to take poison than to endure the continuous nagging of his wife. That humorous aside becomes a serious question tinged with some of the tragedy noted in Equicola's treatise, when Giuliano says that 'there is no displeasure which a wife can cause her husband as irremediable as those which husbands inflict upon their wives, who are thus obedient to their men out of fear if not out of love' (III, xxv). The author's support of the feminist viewpoint is nowhere stronger. Gasparo's allegation, that women usually hate their husbands, he answers with the evidence of history and experience which shows that almost invariably women love their husbands more than their husbands love them.

Castiglione here adduces what he evidently considered an outstanding example of wifely devotion, the story of Camma, which he takes from Plutarch's essay on the virtues of women. As will be seen, he is keeping the names of illustrious contemporary women for a more important place in the debate, yet it is surprising that here his example is so unconvincing. Perhaps his failure to produce outstanding exemplars of contemporary female virtue may be a further indication that Burckhardt's opinions on the status of Renaissance women were optimistic. Thus, apart from Plutarch's famous anecdote about Camma, Giuliano is reduced to deriving his example of wifely devotion from a Pisan tale which is little more than a piece of gossip (xxvii). The debate becomes tedious as Frigio seizes upon his lack of evidence while Giuliano, in turn, replies with fervour but little substance. Nor is the situation relieved by his offering an exhaustive and exhausting list of great women who had benefited civilisation – individually (such as Sappho) or collectively (such as the Trojan women or the Sabine brides). Again the names are traditional in discussions of the kind, and again follow in the Boccaccesque pattern of the *De claris mulieribus*. Some interest is lent to the long list by a piece of historical intuition later to be taken up by Vico (1668–1744) and exploited by Foscolo (1778–1827), namely that the fame of such women has made their stories into fables, and themselves, particularly for some great benefit towards mankind, into goddesses (and here he adduces examples like Pallas Athene and Ceres). When, in reply, Gasparo can only adduce the treachery of the Roman girl, Tarpeia, her solitary example, placed beside such a weight of female virtue, can only bring humiliating defeat for the misogynist.

Castiglione must have realised that he had been over-eloquent in his feminist's defence, and apologises through Giuliano 'fearing that the discourse by now may be too tedious'. But Emilia Pia insists that he continue for a little while longer, and her injunction, added to a further provocation by Gasparo, makes Giuliano prolong his discussion. At first glance the reader may think that his words come close to repeating yet another list of famous women, but Castiglione has cleverly contrived this new catalogue. The barrage of famous names which counters Gasparo's taunts ends with the mention of Countess Matilda Canossa. Stylistically, this allows the list of great women to be brought up to date, for the Countess was said to be a distant ancestor of Ludovico Canossa and thus her name may draw the debate away from Classical heroines to modern times, and to the company present at Urbino.

The interest here now lies in the number of contemporary or near-contemporary names which find mention at this, the high-point, so to speak, of a pyramid of great names. The Montefeltro, Este and Gonzaga dynasties find particular mention, but then, broadening his scope, Giuliano adds the names of famous queens, such as Anne of France, and Isabella of Castille and Spain. She merits a particularly long and fascinating eulogy for her wisdom and abilities in helping to unify Spain and her persistence in holding the kingdom together. That eulogy is far more elaborate in the final edition than in the

*Seconda redazione* where references to her, although equally eulogistic, are scattered more sporadically throughout the book. The
effect of gathering such material together in Book III, xxxv, is to lend
far more importance to this great Spanish ruler, whose virtues, we
are told, included prudence, justice, liberality, mercy and strength of
mind. Isabella's great achievement, it is emphasised, was to unite Spain
so diplomatically that her reforms occasioned no resentment on the
part of the Spanish nobility.

Her presence at this point in the discussion widens the debate to
European proportions. It is also a subtle means of flattering her
grandson, Charles V, Castiglione's host at the time of rewriting the
*Cortegiano*, and her example serves as a good instance both of diplomatic skill and of the successful reconciliation of many opposing
forces. Could Castiglione have seen a similar role for Charles V in the
wider European, rather than Iberian theatre? There may be a further
subtlety of purpose here, for if a 'weak' woman may accomplish
so much, in a country divided as Spain was before Isabella's advent,
how much more practicable should it be for men to emulate that
example in an Italy and a Europe divided by political and religious
interests.

Italy is presented as the cradle of European civilisation, through the
introduction of the Italian dynasties. These also provide the speaker
with exemplars, notably the marchioness Isabella d'Este, whose
virtues Castiglione knew at first hand, and, significantly, her sister
Beatrice, whose influence upon her husband, Ludovico *il Moro* had
helped to convert Milan into the cultural Mecca of Europe, and whose
death, in 1497, seems to have contributed to the spiritual desolation of
the formerly magnificent centre. Giuliano appeals to his audience to
consider the value and merits of the women that they knew personally, 'who, for the most part, are not inferior to their fathers, brothers
and husbands' (III, xxxvi). And if there are no longer great Empresses,
like Cleopatra, there are no longer great conquerors like Alexander.

The mention of Cleopatra and other female rulers (Semiramis, for
one) inevitably introduces the concept of dissolute life-styles.
Although balance is achieved by the introduction of male libertinism,
the chapter ends with an unusually long statement by Gasparo, which
perhaps reflects a strongly held personal view of Castiglione, so
lengthily and emphatically is it asserted, that even if men are promis-
cuous, their actions do not bring the same disruption to society that
an unchaste wife may bring. Fifty years previously, Enea Silvio
Piccolomini (1405–64) had warned, perhaps symbolically, that no

one at court could be trusted, not even one's own children. More specifically the *Cortegiano* seems concerned at this point with the family unit as being the fundamental stabilising element in society. The argument is one which will recur in Castiglione's cursory dismissal of the frivolities of courtly love in chapter lxii of the present Book. His concern seems to have been to prevent further instances of deceit or distrust in an age when it was already difficult enough to believe and trust even in one's best friend. A few years later Castiglione's worst fears would be realised. The unholy alliance of *Cavaliere servente* and Platonic love were to become fashionable excuses for adultery, until, with the final decadence of this combination of chivalric and Platonic ideals, the vogue of *cicisbeismo*, attacked so fiercely by Giuseppe Parini (1729–99) and his contemporaries, was to prove the final ruin of the Italian nobility. Without chastity in a wife, 'the children would be of uncertain paternity and that bond which holds every person because of his blood, and because each one naturally loves that which he has produced, will be dissolved' (III, xxxvii).

While it is true that Gasparo is allowed to state this point of view as a part of his anti-feminist argument (and Giuliano, their defender, is quick to agree with his final conclusions), Castiglione's eye for logic and justice introduces powerful arguments to attack similarly adulterous tendencies in men. Giuliano, quick to agree with Gasparo's conclusions, then, is equally quick to wonder at the illogicality of blaming women for promiscuity, since the same tendency in men is treated lightly and at times even praised, while women cannot be punished enough 'except by a shameful death or perpetual infamy'. Yet if men were equally temperate, the problem would be non-existent. In view of this popular prejudice, then, Giuliano suggests the harshest possible punishment for those who slander the good name of women. And once more *truth* is introduced as a leading criterion for behaviour: 'Every noble knight should be obliged always to defend, with arms where necessary, the truth, particularly when he knows that a woman has been falsely accused of dishonourable conduct' (III, xxxviii). And the strength of Castiglione's statement here becomes more apparent when one recalls that in other matters of etiquette, he advocates the use of arms only in the last resort. The chivalric tradition implicit in the defence of a woman's good name is also closer to the surface here. Gasparo does concede that women, forced by society's code of morals and shame to maintain their virtue and chastity, are praiseworthy, and he goes further, in agreeing that their false calumniators deserve the harshest punishment.

The argument has been brought round again to the topic of truth and falsehood. Indeed Cesare Gonzaga, picking up Giuliano's earlier remark, claims 'the office of an honourable knight, to defend truth' (III, xl). The chapters which follow are among the most cunningly wrought of Castiglione's book – most of them carefully rewritten since the earlier *Seconda redazione*. His purpose seems to have been subtly to show how he equated the concepts of love and truth, an idea given fullest expression in the chapters following chapter lvii. I believe that the discussion has important repercussions for the speech of Bembo in Book IV, and some closer attention to the text here may help in our later appraisal of that speech. For so long that discourse, on love, has been treated as a piece of fashionable Platonism, when it may be one of the most useful pieces of advice proffered in the *Cortegiano*. Yet, as we shall see, Castiglione is nothing if not undogmatic. His major preoccupation continues to seem the exaltation of women, and only by the repetition of notions of truth and falseness in the most diverse contexts is his lesson, on the discernment of truth from falsehood, put across to his readers.

The chapters which follow continue to exalt the position of women, and generally show the illogicality of the misogynist's viewpoint. Perhaps here particular mention could be made of chapter xlii, where the notion of falsehood is again introduced in the potential for slander, for instance, by men who boast of their 'conquests'. For men to slander women by boasting, untruthfully, that they have seduced them, is the vilest sort of villany, and if a woman had perhaps allowed herself to be seduced 'overcome as she was, by false blandishments (*false lusinghe*) feigned tears (*lacrime finte*), continual pleas, lamentations, guile (*arti*), cunning traps and perjury (*insidie e periuri*)' (III, xlii), then to boast of one's conquest would be perfidious ingratitude. The whole of the chapter, indeed the whole of this part of the discussion is punctuated by vocabulary which implies deceit, lying and cunning, and by the emphasis laid on the need for their opposites. Earlier Alexander and Scipio had been posited as examples of sexual continence on several famous occasions. Castiglione is eager to let his reader see beneath this apparently specious argument and suggests through his present mouthpiece, Cesare Gonzaga, that the particular examples quoted by Pallavicino were militarily expedient. Alexander had refrained from insulting the Persian women out of respect for King Darius, while Scipio (if the story be true anyway) won over the hearts and minds of a conquered people by his continence and liberality, 'a stratagem which was worth another army to him' (III, xliv).

It makes an amusing if not irresistible digression here to note one of the examples of chastity which Cesare adduces, and to record the attitude of generations of Italian critics to the episode, which concerns a woman who slept with her lover every night for six months without losing her virginity. Maier's footnote (ed. cit., p.399) describes the practice as 'indicative of sadistic and degenerate eroticism'. His comment reflects a whole tradition of similar remarks on this particular anecdote, including G. A. Volpi's criticism of the Inquisition (who understandably allowed this example of chastity to remain) for their failure to censor it. 'Reason,' he wrote, 'demanded its correction and expurgation at this point.' And even Cian, supporting Volpi, with uncharacteristic indignation, quotes St Matthew in defence of sexual intercourse.

Finally, to end on a typically nonchalant and more amusing note, which takes away some of the asperity of the latter stages of the debate, Cesare quotes the continence of Xenocrates (as related by Valerius Maximus) who could not be sexually aroused, even during a night with a prostitute. Cesare implies that this was senility, not continence, and suggests that, had Xenocrates abstained from wine, he would have shown greater self-control. And though the anecdote seems nonchalant and amusing, it is a further example of Castiglione's search for the truth which lies behind appearance, or, here, accepted tradition. In a similarly casual way his next remarks, while apparently providing a further eulogy of women's self-control, in fact simultaneously continue the polemic against the corruption of contemporary society. Thus Cesare contrasts with the normal self-control of women a variety of actions: the treacherous chatelain who is bribed to betray his master's trust and hand over his fortress to an enemy, adventurers who travel 'over land and sea, killing and pillaging, simply to acquire money, prelates who sell goods belonging to the church, lawyers who falsify testimonies and perjure themselves for profit, doctors who poison their sick patients for the same motive' (III, xlvi). By contrast many contemporary women had chosen to die protecting their *onestà*.

The next chapter is a fascinating epitome of the courting techniques of men, and the wiles they use to snare their female prey. Most of the techniques Castiglione has extracted from Ovid's *Ars amatoria*: gifts, money, tears of desperation, dances, tournaments, serenades, bribery of maidservants, arrangements with parents or relatives and a host of other means useful in breaking down a woman's defences: 'Books have been ingeniously composed and every care applied to teach ways in which women are to be deceived' (*di che modo in questo s'abbiano ad ingannar le donne*) (III, l). Once more it is noticeable that the notion of deceit (*inganno*) is adduced, almost as a warning. Against such an armory of weapons, no wonder that 'these simple doves' (*queste semplici colombe*) sometimes fall for the charms or threats of men. For any such lapses they may be forgiven and if they remain unmoved, they are to be admired as miraculous (*miracolose*). The exaggerated eulogy is to be countered later in the Book by Pallavicino's statement of its opposite, and the 'simple doves' are to become, in his equally exaggerated statement, 'bloodthirsty wild animals'.

But for the moment what could have become a tedious round of stroke and counter-stroke, as Gasparo begins to put his contrary views, is cut short by Ottaviano Fregoso, on the grounds that Gasparo cannot win the uneven contest. And then follow a series of important reflections by Cesare Gonzaga on the civilising influence of women. The whole passage, compared with the original version of the *Seconda redazione* (cp. ibid., p.276), is rewritten with great care: 'Who can doubt that, without women, no contentment or satisfaction may ever be felt in this life of ours, which, without them, would be uncivilised (*rustica*) and lacking in any sweetness, rougher than the life of beasts on the mountainside' (III, li). Their spiritual comforts are impossible to gauge, and they provide stimuli to creative thought and courageous action and unparalleled inspiration for their menfolk; in short: 'Do you not see that the motive for every gracious and pleasurable action (*esercizio*) in this world is attributable to none other than women' (III, lii). In a more obvious piece of lip-service by Castiglione to the chivalric, and even stilnovist tradition, women are also seen as the inspiration for deeds of courage.

There follows next a notable divergence from the early version, where a list of no less than fifteen Italian 'love' poets (ranging from Petrarch to Castiglione's friend Falcone) was produced to show the inspiration lent by women. Only Petrarch's name survives the editing process of 1524 and the following period. But there is one significant example retained in both draft and final edition. It is the example of the *Song of Solomon*, in which Castiglione sees, however misguidedly, an allegorical representation of Solomon's mystic experiences of divine love: 'Solomon, desired to write mystically things of a most high and divine nature, and in order to cover them with a graceful veil, imagined an ardently affectionate dialogue between a lover and his lady, since it seemed to him that he could find on earth no more appropriate or close a parallel to things divine than love for woman' (III, lii). The words implying *feigning* and *veiling* are qualified with adjectives not present in the earlier debate in this foreshadowing of the lover's kiss (cp. below). That brief hint of allegory may well have been retained deliberately from the previous draft to point the way to Castiglione's own overall allegorical purpose – to show the dangers of judging by external appearances. This very important topic is to crop up in Bembo's discourse on love in Book IV, but for the moment, Federico Fregoso leads the conversation back to current court convention, with an enquiry which brings Giuliano de' Medici to give a disquisition on the refined code of gallantry which accompanies formal courtly love.

The topic was evidently an important one at the time, and much space is devoted to it in this section of the *Cortegiano*. The unusual aspect of Castiglione's treatment will be the lack of enthusiasm for the fashion (indeed the positive opposition to it where married women are concerned). The feigning and deceit implicit in courtly love of this fashionable kind are also good vehicles for his advice about perceiving the truth beneath the surface veil. However, the subject was, and was to become, an influential movement for Italy and perhaps merits a little closer attention now. The fashion, which developed into the peculiarly Italian phenomenon of *cicisbeismo*, was ridiculed by foreign travellers and satirists (native and foreign) until the end of the eighteenth century and, in its other forms, until much later. Even now it afflicts some Italian dictionary-makers with inferiority complexes in their attempts to find a non-Italian etymology for the term (cp. Zingarelli, *Dizionario* 1959 and 1971). Luigi Valmaggi's excellent study traces the origin of *cicisbeo*, the word, not the fashion, perhaps to a contemporary, Francesco Berni (1497–1535). Then it was used in a derogatory sense, as 'love-sick'. Yet Carlo Goldoni (1707–93) confesses in his *Mémoires* that by the time he put on stage his *Cavaliere e la dama*, he could not call the play *La Cicisbéature* since that title would have given advance irritation to the 'society of gallants' which would make up his audience (ibid., II, 4). Parini, and even Vittorio Alfieri (1749–1803), were to attribute the decay of the nobility to this fashion, and, as Valmaggi illustrates, their voices were only the most illustrious of a whole group of intelligent critics of the phenomenon during the seventeenth and eighteenth centuries. Hence it is heartening to see Castiglione, some two and a half centuries before Parini's *Giorno*, maintaining a sensible and socially responsible point of view in the face of a fashionable fatuity which was to prove unstoppable. And just as he can adapt his life and work to the equally indestructible social system of the court, so he can adapt its greatest ineptitude, gallant, courtly love, to his several purposes, as a closer examination of the text at this point may now illustrate.

Giuliano's first statement sets the tone, and the import of his words should not now surprise us: 'Women must be taught to recognise those who *simulate* love and those who are *truly* in love.' And Federico hammers the point home, when he urges Giuliano to proceed and 'Teach them which are the most certain and sure signs for discerning false from true love' (*l'amor falso dal vero*) (III, liv). Giuliano warns his ideal *donna di palazzo* against being too ready to believe that she is loved; at the same time she should not reject off-hand any propositions or praises, in case this is taken as an invitation to further blandishments. Giuliano evidently has little enthusiasm for a discussion of courtly love: the lady must take her fashionable beau as she finds him, replying with displeasure to any importunity, but treating with kindness the sensitive soul who becomes too serious, in which case she should lead the conversation round to other channels. If the lover persists in serious avowals of this fashionable rite, then she should 'take it all as a joke' (*pigliarà il tutto come per burla*) (III, liv) and let him know that she considers his attentive remarks 'as having been made to honour her, rather than because they're true' (*ciò se le dica più presto per onorarla che perché così sia*).

Giuliano's indifference to the fashionable phenomenon is striking, and he stresses in the next chapter that it is of this fashion that 'I have spoken, not of one who *loves*, but of one who entertains with amorous talk (*ragionamenti amorosi*)' (III, lv), and he coins the aphorism: '*chi ama assai parla poco*' (great love needs few words). The sentiment is one which runs directly counter to the courtly-love ideal. Its important position here may well indicate further Castiglione's indifference to the pretext for discussion at this point, as well as his advocacy of the married state, confirmed by Giuliano's refusal to allow the courtly game to operate for decently married women: 'I believe that love, in your sense of the word (*come voi ora intendete*), should be restricted to women who are not married', and who may, therefore, be legitimately courted in a serious sense.

As for the unhappily married woman, Giuliano will admit that hatred of her husband may induce her to love another, but he wishes to restrict her emotions to spiritual love, and this conditional on her not allowing her lover to perceive it. The only demonstrations of love he will allow, then, are those which eventually lead to marriage. Yet despite this exaltation of the marriage knot, Castiglione shows himself to be well aware of the incompatibility of some couples and, in his longer treatment of the subject in the *Seconda redazione*, had made allowance for divorce, a sentiment toned down in the final edition, but still present in Federico Fregoso's eloquent speech against loveless marriages (III, lvi). Again the distinction is drawn between 'true love' (*amor vero*), which leads to matrimony, and a facile *appearance* of love, 'moved by the thought that the woman is easy to conquer, but not easy [truly] to love' (*mosso da opinion di facilità, non d'amore*) (III, lvii).

Attention should be drawn to a further important connection between the remarks of the two main speakers here in Book III (on what Castiglione evidently sees as the frivolities of a courtly game) and the conclusions of the final Book. There, in Book IV, iv, it is Fregoso's brother, Ottaviano who, questioning the whole purpose of the model courtier outlined by the company up to that point, says that, if the courtier's main purpose were simply to consist in the superficialities of behaviour (he lists, for example, dancing, singing, merry-making (*festeggiar*) and playing) then these would be 'frivolities and vanities' (*leggerezze e vanità*). Further, he admits that such activities weaken (*effeminar*) the mind, corrupt the young and reduce them to a life of lasciviousness. Now, these are almost identical to the conclusions which Gasparo Pallavicino reached in those *rejected* paragraphs of the earlier redaction which treated of the frivolity of courtly love. In the *Seconda redazione* Gasparo questions the inept qualifications acquired, in order to entertain the ladies, by the model courtier: '*a che servano, altro che a vanità e leggierezze?*' (ibid., p.280). But perhaps the most tellingly important notion common in both versions is contained in the phrase: 'and the effect of this is to reduce the name "Italian" to opprobrium (*abbrobrio*) and there are but a few [of us] who have the courage to undergo any risk at all, let alone the risk of death' (IV, iv). If we look for this information in the *Seconda redazione*, we find a different, and perhaps more 'fashionable', attitude, and the strenuousness of the pro-feminist viewpoint is attenuated there by misogynist arguments which seem much lengthier and harsher. In the earlier version, using identical, if less Tuscanised, terminology, Castiglione had allowed Gasparo to put the blame for that opprobrium (*obrobrio*) on women, in whose service men wasted their talents and time: '*E di tutto questo sono cause le donne*' (ibid., p.280).

Several conclusions may be drawn from Castiglione's final placing of this indictment, not at the conclusion of a fashionable and light-hearted debate on women (in which misogyny is given freer rein) but at the beginning of the serious philosophical, political and moral discussion which treats as mere frivolity what has been said in the whole of the rest of the book up to that point. Firstly, on a superficial level, the abandoning, in the final edition, of the fiercer aspects of Gasparo's misogyny may indicate a change of attitude towards women on Castiglione's part. This is of little relative importance. Secondly, his deliberate retention of the earlier phraseology and his attribution of Italian weakness not merely to the cicisbeism which fifty years later was to ruin Italian society, but to the whole of this foppish court-training, is a strong indication that he is well aware, and wants to *show* that he is well aware, of the defects and faults of the very system he *seems* to be wanting to perpetuate. Why, then, having arrived at such a conclusion, continue with the rest of Book IV? The answer lies in Castiglione's practical, hard-headed appraisal of the situation. There was *no* alternative but to use the system which was sending down ever-stronger roots as the century wore on, and which, we now know, needed, fully two and a half centuries after Castiglione's death, the fiercest revolution in man's history, to eradicate it.

It is in this light that the reader may better judge what has been said so far on the topic of courtly love. The subject meanders on for many chapters yet, during the course of which a growing lack of enthusiasm seems evident from the deprecating attitude to the fashion which dominates; thus the fashionable lover is said to dissipate his love, if he courts more than one woman, by the diversity and consequent dilution of his affection (III, lxii). There are notable apophthegms and well-worn conceits dating back to Petrarch and tying this part of the debate into the Petrarchist tradition of love poetry which so bedevilled the intelligentsia of the remainder of the century. For instance, true love, we are told, is often visible only through the expression in the eyes and should not be known to the public at large (III, lxvi). But, Canossa later suggests, public opinion of a man's love for a woman may cause *her* to fall in love with him (shades of the Dantesque '*Amor che a null'amato amar perdona*'), since rumour 'so often seemed to bring messages more truthful and worthy of belief than any letters, words or even an envoy bearing them on the lover's behalf' (*parea quasi che la fama le portasse l'ambasciate...molto più vere e più degne d'esser credute*) (III, lvii). And there may be more than a hint of warning against believing rumour, in those words. Once again speciousness seems under attack, however subtly, and Giuliano disagrees that love should be publicised in this way, since it is dangerous for the lover to be pointed out (*mostrato a dito*) by the public (echoes of Petrarch's first sonnet). Giuliano's advice is to dissimulate one's feelings as much as possible. The argument seems potentially endless, but relief is in sight after Federico Fregoso's suggestion that advice be given, instead, on how to maintain one's lady's affection.

The slight switch in direction allows Castiglione to introduce several features which leaven the discussion. The first is the reintroduction of the Aristotelean Mean of reasonableness. Thus lovers should not press impossible demands with protestations of grief if they are unrequited (for such attitudes are boring!) but they should not show excessive jealousy for rivals (thus giving the possible impression that they are inferior to them!). Rivalry calls up another brief, but important theme, and we are given a glimpse of the ruthlessness of the period, in a 'proverb' which Giuliano quotes with an ironic smile: 'If one's rival is only up to his waist in water, one stretches out a hand and helps him out of danger, but when he's up to his chin, one puts one's foot on his head, rather, and pushes him under' (III, lxx).

Castiglione continues to utilise the major theme to stress the dangers of deception, channelling his discussion to treat of the undermining of rivals' reputations by means of unsavoury rumours (true or false) and deceits (*inganni*). Giuliano reinforces earlier warnings by urging the courtier positively to win his lady's affections through love (the opposite to deceit) and not to use any deception (*inganno alcuno*) against his rivals for this purely honourable end. That type of advice may be one element which has made critics dub the *Cortegiano* a moral work. It may be more reasonable here to take Giuliano's advice at face-value, however tempting it may be to see him equating love with truth, in the sense that love may only be won through sincerity and truth. The section ends with another allusion to the Aristotelean Mean, this time, possibly to relieve what threatens to become monotony, in two humorous psychological examples, akin to those mentioned above of the jealous or boring lover. The courtier who hopes to gain affection by protesting that he's never been loved, often gives his lady the impression that there may be good reason for his unloved state! On the other hand, the man who protests that a rival is the most fortunate man in the world because (despite his lack of talents) women run after him, may provoke his own lady to join the crowd!

The light-hearted quality of the two examples may serve also to disguise the rewriting process. Book III is long and Castiglione spent much care and attention reorganising its contents. It may be that the short time for revision at his disposal, of which he complains in the dedicatory letter, prevented the latter stages from being treated with his normal coherence and elegance. Nevertheless there are still two important ideas to which he needs to allude before the late hour and the need for sleep make the company disperse for the night. The first is that 'one experiences great relief in telling one's passions to a cordial friend (*amico cordiale*) venting them with him, and, at the same time, pleasures are increased by being able to communicate them' (III, lxxiii).

The allusion there to friendship calls to mind other similar references, some of which have already been noted, and reinforces the need for a confidant, whose main qualities will include not only love for his friend, but also the frankness necessary to correct his errors. The sentiments expressed harmonise with what he writes in Book II, chapter xxx and following, on the perfect friendship, though here the topic may seem, at first glance, to be unconnected with those former notions. And the second important idea which is essential to the continuity of the book is the Aristotelean summing up by Ottaviano Fregoso of the final arguments of Gasparo Pallavicino (whose language becomes ridiculously violent, 'women' being described as 'beasts thirstier for blood than tigresses!') and of Giuliano's perhaps over-eulogistic view of womankind. He prefers a middle path between the two extremes, and wishes, anyway, to turn the subject back to the topic of the courtier proper. His aim, he says, is not, as Emilia accuses him, to diminish the praise of the *donna di palazzo*, but to explain why 'apart from the remarks made so far about the courtier, I would desire many other things' (III, lxxvii). Thus Ottaviano prepares the company for the shocks in store for them on the morrow and it is Elisabetta who enjoins upon him the task of detailing his additional requirements of the model courtier.

# 6. Book Four of *The Courtier*

The final Book of the *Cortegiano* contains Castiglione's most important advice, that concerning the political role of the courtier and his
aspirations to a higher level of existence. The latter, in particular, is
exalted in Bembo's paean of praise to what is generally termed
Platonic (or Neoplatonic) love. Certainly the tone of the final
chapters is Platonic, but that should not lead us to assume that the
whole treatise is an idealist tract; on the other hand, to call Castiglione
an Aristotelean would seem to beg many questions and smack of
dogmatism. Yet it is the contention of the present monograph that
Castiglione's work has more of Aristotle's empirical approach than
Plato's idealist theories. Apart from a few distinguished, but so far
uninfluential items on the subject of his Aristoteleanism, Castiglione
criticism has traditionally been idealist, and too often, as Mario Rossi
so patronisingly put it, 'the ingenuousness of [our] good Castiglione
(*del buon Castiglione*) cannot but appear downright moving [or piti-
ful?] (*addirittura commovente*)' (*B. Castiglione*, p.81). Such opinions
are travesties of Castiglione's thought and achievement in the
*Cortegiano*. In order to bring out what seems to us the true meaning
of Castiglione's text, it may be necessary to do some violence to the
artistic unity of Book IV, by analysing its two major sections separately.
The first concerns the political role of the courtier and is largely
Aristotelean in tone. The second concerns Bembo's praise of Divine
love and is usually considered to be Platonic. In order to bring out
Castiglione's true purpose I need to treat the complex debate on
Aristoteleanism and Platonism with a brevity which may seem
impertinence.

Throughout the present chapter we should not forget two fundamental concepts which divided Plato and Aristotle radically. Both
concepts probably made Castiglione incline more to the empirical
Aristotle than to Plato. Firstly, Aristotle rejected Plato's theory of
*forms* (or *ideas*, εἴδη), the theory, that is, that what we might today
call 'abstract concepts' have an existence outside the world of sensa-
tion. The most important reason for that rejection was that the theory
was not practical. It was unable to resolve the problems it had been

created to solve. Aristotle was interested in the changing objects of the world of *becoming*, while Plato was concerned with absolutes: his *ideas* belong to an immutable world of *being*.

The second point is less fundamental to the systems of the two philosophers, but it is important in revealing their differing 'humanity': Aristotle's analysis of creative writing, in the *Poetics*, shows that he took literature seriously, and particularly the literature involved in the tragic theatre, seriously enough to consider it useful for one of his most subtle methods of achieving spiritual tranquillity. The 'catharsis' of emotion which has so often proved a crux for commentators, is probably an example of Aristotle's Golden Mean in operation. Thus, at a tragic play, the audience, through the medium of the spectacle, find those emotions heightened which might have been present in only small measure at its beginning; conversely, exaggerated emotions, which they might have brought with them into the theatre, are released by the spectacle and so minimised. In either case the result could be a more stable emotional balance. Aristotle saw the need for literary studies on practical, then, as well as aesthetic grounds, and as tutor to Alexander the Great he was reputed to have inculcated into the young man a love of literature. Homer's epic was said always to have been kept by Alexander's bedside, and Castiglione accepts that legendary tradition (I, xliii etc.).

These remarks on Aristotle may be compared with one of the most heart-felt statements of the *Cortegiano*: 'the true and principal spiritual embellishment is...the study of letters' (ibid.) and with the remarks which there follow. In Plato's ideal *Republic*, Socrates condemns poetry because, by stimulating men's emotions, the poet risks destroying the rational foundation of the state. Poetry tends the garden of the passions instead of destroying them (*Republic*, x, xxxvii). It is true that poetry may be used (albeit in a very strictly censured form) in the education of the young (ibid., III, ix, 337), but poets, though not treated in unkindly fashion, are dismissed from the state as potentially dangerous disruptives.

Yet despite what have just been called fundamental differences, Aristotle himself had, as a young man, been strongly influenced by Plato. Indeed two of his earliest works, the *Eudemus* and the *Protrepticus*, were Platonist in outlook. Furthermore, almost all of Aristotle's ideas developed in deliberate opposition to those of Plato, who provided him with a starting point for criticism which then built up into a system of its own. Thus, from the beginning, Platonism and Aristoteleanism were inextricably bound up together, and yet in many respects opposed. The 'resolution' of the conflict between Platonists and Aristoteleans, which was first attempted by the Alexandrian Neoplatonists of the fourth century and later taken up by the Renaissance Platonists, is important for my theme and will be dealt with in due course. For the moment my concern is with the development of Aristotelean philosophy in the period immediately preceding publication of the *Cortegiano*. In particular, attention will be paid to the work of Pietro Pomponazzi (1462–1525), another Mantuan, well known among his contemporaries for his views (Bandello includes him as a character in his *Novelle*, IV, xxxviii) and the most creative Aristotelean thinker of his generation. His work would certainly have been debated in Castiglione's presence. Further familiarity with Aristoteleanism may be indicated by the inclusion in the *Cortegiano* of Paolo Nicola Vernia (d.1499). This scholar, who taught Pomponazzi at Padua, figures in one of the witty stories told in Book II, where he is referred to, familiarly, by the diminutive *Nicoletto*, just as Pomponazzi in Bandello's novella is called *Peretto*.

I have already noted that the educational methods which Vittorino practised in Mantua reflected Greek notions of the healthy mind in a healthy body. Padua, Vittorino's University town, and Bologna (as well as Pavia and Ferrara) were, by the end of the fifteenth and beginning of the sixteenth centuries, the bulwarks of Aristoteleanism. Further south, Plato's philosophy was in greater vogue, even though, it must be said, at Florence the *Nicomachean Ethics* were still the main topic of the public lectures of John Argyropoulos (c. 1410–91), significantly himself an ex-professor from Padua. Aristoteleanism had weathered the medieval storms raised by the ecclesiastical authorities, who had twice banned the teaching of Aristotle at Paris (in 1210 and 1231), and St Thomas Aquinas (c. 1226–74) had, of course, encouraged translations of Aristotle and adapted Aristotelean philosophy to reconcile it with Christian doctrine. By 1300, Aristoteleanism (though not its more openly materialistic off-shoot, Averroism) was acceptable at influential centres such as Paris and Oxford, and it gradually became dominant in the Italian Universities, initially in medicine rather than in theology (which continued to be the preserve of the religious orders).

When the humanists began to turn their attention to Greek studies in the first quarter of the fifteenth century, Aristotle, as well as Plato, began to find new translators, among them Leonardo Bruni, who revised translations of the *Nicomachean Ethics* and the *Politics*. All the time attempts were being made to reconcile the current Platonism with Aristoteleanism. Marsilio Ficino describes Giovanni Pico (1463–1493), whose family were *Conti di Mirandola e di Concordia*, as the 'Duke of Concord' for his ability as a reconciler of the two systems, and Argyropoulos and Poliziano were equally active in attempts at harmonisation. Yet in Lombardy a less adulterated Aristoteleanism was taught at the Universities of Padua and Bologna, initially in the broad tradition of the Schoolmen, but, by the end of the fifteenth century, by more enlightened teachers. Ermolao Barbaro (1453–93), for instance, saw the disadvantages of working with medieval Latin translations of Aristotle, and tried to encourage the publication of the original Greek texts, as well as the production of more accurate and up-to-date translations. Two years after this Venetian humanist's death, the Aldine Press began to produce its classic five-volume Aristotle (between 1495 and 1498), and in 1497 Niccolò Leonico Tomeo (1456–1531) was appointed in Padua to lecture on the original Greek texts. Significantly, Tomeo was a great friend of Bembo and Navagero, and he figures in Book II, lxxi, as the author of a *bon mot* attacking a tyrant's false reputation for liberality.

The greatest exponent of Aristoteleanism in the northern Universities was Pietro Pomponazzi, a student and later professor at the University of Padua. Astonishingly, the historian Paolo Giovio (1483–1552) tells us that Pomponazzi had no Greek; what he lacked perhaps in this direction, he made up for in the brilliance of his expositions, and in the courage with which he put forward views more typical of the Enlightenment than of an era about to plunge even deeper into the darkness of Inquisition and Counter-Reformation. Pomponazzi's finest work is his *De immortalitate animae*, the conclusion of which, a brilliantly logical derivation from Aristotle's theory of soul, effectively shows that neither soul nor intellect may survive the body. And having, for his own purposes at least, demonstrated the mortality of the human soul, Pomponazzi compensates with a positivism or secularism worthy of the nineteenth century, namely that, since eternity, promised by Christianity, was now removed from man's programme in life, some other purpose or reward should be sought. His answer is the Aristotelean one, that virtue is its own reward: 'The essential prize of virtue is virtue itself, which makes man happy' (*De immortalitate*, XIV), while failure to achieve virtue brings its opposite: 'the penalty of the vicious man is vice itself, than which nothing can be more wretched, more unhappy' (ibid.). And virtue may be arrived at by pursuing the particularly human quality of mind which Pomponazzi calls the *intellectus practicus.* Although Man, as was generally accepted, is placed in the cosmic hierarchy 'between Gods and beasts' (*medius inter Deos et bestias*) (ibid., IX), he does possess this peculiarly human attribute, for he shares his factitive or utilitarian intellect (*intellectus factitivus*) with the beasts, while his highest, or speculative, intellect (*intellectus speculativus*) enables him to approach God (or the *Gods*, Pomponazzi might have preferred). Man's practical intellect is used in moral action, and he performs his duty by following it.

Pomponazzi saved his life and preserved his philosophy by careful statements to the effect that, while, as a philosopher, he could argue that the soul was mortal, as a Christian he fully accepted its immortality. In fact, however, the clergy in Venice succeeded in having his book publicly burnt and Pomponazzi himself declared a heretic by Doge and Patriarch. A copy was sent to his patron, Pietro Bembo, with a view to taking proceedings against him for heresy. Bembo found no such faults in the book; Pope Leo X was indifferent to any prosecution and Pomponazzi was free to write a defence of his views in 1517, the *Apologia Petri Pomponazzi Mantuani*, and, in 1519, the *Defensorium*. When one reflects on the Italians who were suppressed and martyred after Pomponazzi's death for their expression of free thought, it seems miraculous that, as late as 1525, he was allowed to profess and write what he did.

In the northern universities, at least, Aristoteleanism was strong, and accessible to those who wished to assimilate its more practical truths. But while virtue might bring its own reward in the relatively peaceful world of Pomponazzi's lecture theatre, in order for virtue to survive at all, the world outside had to be rendered tranquil. Castiglione would undoubtedly know of Pomponazzi's philosophical ideas, just as, later, he knew of the theories of Leone Ebreo (1465–1535?) on love, even though Leone's book itself was not published until 1535, seven years after Castiglione's death. The oral tradition of social gatherings of the type described in the *Cortegiano* would ensure the transmission of current philosophical theory (and confuse the source material for scholars like Cian who sought the originators of some of Castiglione's ideas). However, to the down-to-earth logic of Pomponazzi, Castiglione would have to add the practical experience of the man whose principal accomplishment for the past quarter of a century had been to survive in as congenial a way as possible at the courts of Italy and Spain. Furthermore, as will become clear in Bembo's discourse on love, while Castiglione implies that virtue *is* its own reward, he replaces the starkness of Pomponazzi's Aristotelean conclusions on the mortality of the soul, with Aristotle's own aspirations to immortality: 'as far as lies within our power, make ourselves immortal, do everything we can to live in accordance with the best that is in us' (cp. below, p.182). And with that notion, Castiglione will combine the Pauline advice to the Corinthians, in an amalgam of doctrines which effectively reconciles Platonism, Aristoteleanism and Christianity. But before reaching those heights, he has to talk about the more political aspect of his potential pupil.

Four-fifths of the treatise are over before Ottaviano makes, then, the somewhat surprising statement, introduced in a typically casual subordinate clause, that the company has not yet discussed the *purpose* of the courtier's training: 'The purpose of the perfect courtier, about which we have not so far spoken...(*non s'è parlato*)' (IV, v). One result of Ottaviano Fregoso's intervention at that point in Book IV may be to bring up short the reader who might have been amusing himself (as Dr Johnson amused himself) by perusing an elegant if trivial account of Renaissance court entertainment. The effect of the statement and of the brief chapter immediately preceding it may be compared to that surprise element which Dante achieves when he seemingly arouses his reader's sympathy for certain sinners, only to make them reflect how mistaken they are to have such feelings. The defects which afflicted the Italian court and which Castiglione will shortly elaborate, particularly the defects of complacency and self-indulgence, are the very shortcomings into which the company (and perhaps the reader) have been sliding as the book has progressed. This is how Castiglione puts his case: 'It is true that the perfect courtier, as described by Count Ludovico and Messer Federico, may be a good and praiseworthy object. I think, however, that he should not be so in isolation and for his own sake, but rather because of the purpose to which he may be directed. Indeed, if by being noble, graceful, endearing and expert in so many attainments, the courtier produced no other fruit than achieving such accomplishments for their own sake, I would not consider it reasonable, in order to achieve this courtly perfection, for a man to dedicate so much study and toil as is necessary for its acquisition. On the contrary, I would say that many of the qualities which have been attributed to him, such as dancing, merry-making, singing and playing games, were frivolities and trivia, and, in a man of eminence, reasons rather for censure than for praise' (IV, iv). The words might have come from the sceptical preface of a Prezzolini, but they are Castiglione's own words, put into the mouth of Ottaviano Fregoso. He continues in the same vein for the rest of that chapter, insisting that in themselves those trivial accomplishments simply emasculate minds and corrupt the young. He even goes as far as to ascribe the vilification of the name *Italian* to the national preoccupation with such frivolities, the result being that 'the name *Italian* is brought into disrepute and there are few who have the courage even to undergo a risk, much less the courage to die' (ibid.).

Ever since it had circulated in manuscript form, the *Cortegiano* had been most highly valued for the more superficial techniques described in Books I, II and III. Since its publication (until the present day, indeed) many influential writers have adversely criticised its shallowness. Castiglione had succeeded so well in sweetening the pill of his didactic purpose that only the sweetness came eventually to be considered. The huge audience that his book subsequently reached was more intellectually attuned to court fripperies than to the tougher austerity of the *Nicomachean Ethics*, for it is to Aristotle that Castiglione looks for his most important advice, the seriousness of which, as will be shown below, is deliberately stressed in the final rewriting of the book. By then we are informed that the principal aim of the courtier will be to imitate Aristotle in his role as a preceptor for his lord, to so win his lord's favour and confidence that he may offer him uninhibited advice on the best way to govern. And we are told that (however dear to Castiglione personally) the relatively trivial activities which he has dwelt upon at length in the first three Books: 'the music, celebrations, games and other pleasant accomplishments are, as it were, the flowers of courtly education, while to assist and induce one's lord towards a good end and to dissuade him from bad policies, is the true fruit of the courtly existence' (IV, v).

There was a tradition that Aristotle, by imparting his wisdom to Alexander, had helped him to conquer and civilise the whole of the known world – and an appropriate eulogy of Alexander's achievements is to be found in Book IV, xxxvii. By the time the *Cortegiano* was published, the Spanish Emperor, Charles, was the most powerful man in the world, held sway over the barbarian New World, favoured Castiglione at court and kept his treatise (along with the Bible) at his bedside. It would, of course, have been unthinkable for Castiglione to have claimed openly that he was trying to do for Charles V what Aristotle had done for Alexander. In the first place such a declaration would have been immodest and out of character. Secondly, no Emperor, at a time so shortly preceding the Divine Right of Kings, could admit to being deliberately manipulated in his politics and social actions by a guide-book written by his inferior. Yet Castiglione had stated at the beginning of his book that he was following the tradition of Plato, Xenophon and Cicero in their formulation of ideals (*Republic, Cyropaedia* and *De oratore*), his aim being, as we have seen, to create an ideal of courtly behaviour, so that, even if his style falls short of his ambition, his courtier readers 'will have proportionately less trouble in approaching the aims and purposes proposed by the author' (Dedicatory letter, iii). By the end of Fregoso's intervention we find that the book has a dual advisory function. Aristotle, we are told (iv, xlvii), taught Alexander directly, but his precepts were also meant for his pupils to use in their own advice to their lords; Plato both directly advised the Syracusan tyrant, Dionysius i, and, according to a legend followed by Castiglione, trained Dion to advise him and his successor Dionysius ii. So that although Castiglione's book is openly aimed at his courtier-reader, that particular chapter (iv, xlvii) implies that the book is also a master-copy, so to speak, which the prince may consult directly.

In case these notions seem a little far-fetched, a comparison might be introduced here with the version in the *Seconda redazione* (at p.193) where the names of Plato and Aristotle are included very briefly, in a list of six philosopher-advisers: '*come è da credere che facesse Platone a Dione siracusano, Aristotile ad Alexandro*' (as we may believe Plato did to Dion of Syracuse, Aristotle to Alexander). In the definitive edition, the names of Plato and Aristotle are removed from that place to reappear in a new chapter, xlvii, in an extended reference which reflects, in particular, the political influence of Aristotle on Alexander (Plato is included only in a passing reference at the end, introduced by a casual 'Similarly...' (*Per lo medesimo modo*). Further, that new chapter is the longest in the definitive Book iv. The second longest (chapter xxxvi) is also significant from our point of view here, not only because of its length (which seems to imply added importance) but also because of a reference not in the *Seconda redazione*. In the earlier version, Cesare Gonzaga says that Ottaviano, by his learned and legal documentation of the courtier's qualifications had formulated a 'severe philosopher' (*severo filosofo*) with the attributes of a 'magistrate' (*podestà*) or a 'teacher' (*maestro di scola*). In the definitive edition, the roles are separated: the courtier becomes the *maestro di scola*, and the prince becomes the *bon governatore*. The courtier's role as courtier is played down in chapter xlvii: 'And if you do not want to call him "courtier", I am unconcerned' (*E se non vorrete chiamarlo cortegiano, non mi dà noia*). Four lines further on he states: 'One could say that the courtier's purpose was to become the prince's tutor' (*si poria dir che il divenir institutor del principe fosse il fin del cortegiano*). None of these statements were present in the *Seconda redazione* in the form in which they later appear. They are included in the final version for reasons which, it is hoped, will become clear in due course. For the present, suffice it to say that the new references seem to add a more serious political undertone (and an Aristotelean one, rather) to the book.

Speculation will inevitably continue on Castiglione's purpose, not only in writing Book IV, but in compiling the whole treatise. It would be wrong, whatever one's solution to the problem, to declare dogmatically that he had any one purpose in writing. It was, yes, an attempt at recording for posterity the idyll at Urbino; it was a means of fashioning an ideal of courtly behaviour, at the superficial level of Books I–III; and it was an attempt to give a purpose to that perfection of court life, namely to influence one's political master. The *Cortegiano* is also a lesson in Christian stoicism – 'to endure all and be saved' and to achieve the end of an active life, which was a contemplative ideal. Yet, if the rewriting was done, as seems probable, in the light of Aristotelean principles, there may be another logical explanation for the changed tone. Fregoso's remarks may be seen as completing the Aristotelean order of 'causation' by which change or development (in this case of *man* to *courtier*) was effected. The *matter* is the nobleman, the *form* is the species (courtier) by which he is surrounded and which moulds him by its conventions, the *moving cause* (the shaper) is Castiglione (or, fictionally, Fregoso) and the *final cause* is the purpose of the courtier. If a clearer analogy is required the example of a table may suffice. Aristotle's *matter* is the wood, the *form* is the arranging of the wood in a certain manner, the *moving cause* is the carpenter and the *final cause* is its purpose – perhaps to provide a surface at which to eat. It is a theory which runs through Aristotle's work (notably in *Physics*, I), and one which any imitator would be familiar with. Without the *final cause* the courtier's purpose would be unfulfilled, just as the prince's role, without *his* final cause (good government), is not only worthless, but self-contradictory and pernicious for his subjects. Twice in the next few pages, Castiglione re-emphasises the *final cause* of prince and courtier. And it is to this final cause that we must now return.

The exordium of Book IV had been of a more serious tone than those of earlier Books. It began with sad reflections upon the deaths of Gasparo Pallavicino (d. 1511), of the author's cousin, Cesare Gonzaga

(d. 1512), and of Roberto da Bari (d. c. 1513). That elegiac tone blends with nostalgia as Castiglione recalls the other luminaries of the Urbino court, most of them now dispersed and exalted to high rank in state or church. He brings his account 'up to date' (up to 1515) with a reference to the new Duke, Francesco Maria della Rovere, and his Duchess, Eleonora Gonzaga. The change in tone is appropriate to the new seriousness of subject-matter. There are, too, certain subtle changes in the ritual of the evening, changes accurately documented by Wayne Rebhorn in his interesting article. Ottaviano Fregoso, who had, the previous evening, been delegated to open the discussion, had not been seen all day (the courtiers presume he has been meditating hard on his theme for the evening). He is so late arriving that the company have begun their dancing, under the impression that the usual debate was not forthcoming (the normal routine is that the dancing follows discussions), and when he does arrive, his entrance, though casual and almost unnoticed by courtiers 'occupied in their various activities', draws sufficient attention to him to set him in the centre of the stage and at the same time unostentatiously to stress Duchess Elisabetta's request that he fulfil his promise of the previous evening. The dancing is halted and he begins his discourse.

He starts by making a distinction between the virtues, which, it has been agreed, are good in themselves (temperance, fortitude, fitness etc.) since they promote tranquillity of spirit, and other virtues (justice, liberality, generosity) which are good because of the particular purposes which they may achieve. He also condones the perfect courtier as outlined by Canossa and Federico, but only with the proviso that their courtier has a purpose beyond the acquisition of such perfection for its own sake. There follows the paragraph in which he demolishes the previous ideal and declares that the courtier's purpose has not yet been discussed! Artistically this grave omission of the courtier's true role is worked into the fabric of the book with typically graceful casualness, introduced, as it is, in the subordinate clause 'of which we have not so far spoken' (*del quale insino a qui non s'è parlato*), as if, despite the importance of the new theme, Castiglione wished, at least stylistically, to continue without interrupting the flow of the book as a whole. It may be another indication of his anxiety to add seriousness without blatantly relegating the previous discussion to a secondary level of importance. It is artistically noteworthy that the phrase is not present in the *Seconda redazione*, where Castiglione allows Fregoso to say abruptly: 'These gentlemen have not made any mention of the courtier's purpose' (ibid., p.190). Fregoso (cp. above, p.142) has already shown that attention to the courtier's superficial attributes is of relatively little moment to him.

The usefulness, however, of such superficial attributes as a means of ingratiating oneself with one's master is reiterated at the end of Fregoso's polemic. There are countless activities, which, if brought to perfection, produce more useful results for the individual and society than mere 'excellence as a courtier for its own sake' (*tal cortegiania per sé sola*). Nevertheless, if such excellence is directed at a good end, those activities are 'not only not damaging or vain, but most useful and worthy of infinite praise'. Now, whereas in the *Seconda redazione* Castiglione implies that he has *stated* the courtier's purpose (to advise his master): '*quel fine ch'io ho detto*' (ibid., p.191), in the definitive version (IV, iv) he seems to *look forward* to that 'good end': '*quel bon fine che debbono e ch'io intendo*' (that good end which they must [aim at] and which I intend/mean). That change of tense and verb may be fortuitous and irrelevant, but it could have important consequences in my argument. The importance of 'trivia' has already been noted above (pp.55–6). Fregoso now says: 'Praise for good actions consists principally of two elements, the first of which is choosing a truly good purpose to aim at, the second is knowing how to discover opportune and appropriate means (*mezzi opportuni ed atti*) to bring oneself to the proposed good end' (IV, v).

The whole of the *Cortegiano* is a build-up, as it were, to the two climaxes now reached in Book IV, the political advice of Ottaviano Fregoso and the spirituality of Pietro Bembo's discourse. Jacob Burckhardt, arguing for an ideal courtier in a Platonic mould, and speaking particularly of the apparently indefensible and anachronistic requirement of *nobility*, had justified the inclusion of noble birth on the grounds that 'the perfect man – the true courtier – should not be wanting in any conceivable advantage' (op. cit., p.223). Castiglione certainly wanted his courtier to have every possible advantage, not simply to formulate a golden popinjay, but rather that he may have as many *mezzi opportuni ed atti per condursi a questo bon fine desegnato*, and the 'proposed good end' is to be able to advise his master. If by his ability to sing, dance or ride the courtier may put his master in a receptive mood, then this is why such attributes are, to quote Burckhardt in this new context, 'conceivable advantages'. But such abilities may help, not necessarily in the positive fashion implied in the phrase 'put in a receptive mood'. A justifiable reason for the courtier's being able to dance may be that this is the only reason for his being on the spot at a fortuitous moment. Castiglione has been trying to cover all eventualities, and in a world where fortuitous events were very common, the greater the number of means for grasping fortune by the forelock, the better. Machiavelli, by contrast, for all his provisions to take advantage of fortune, may have been too theoretic in his approach to take advantage of his own opportunities.

When Castiglione, through Ottaviano, argues, in *Cortegiano*, IV, viii, that the greatest and most indispensable gift of the ruler is the ability to govern well, he makes his point by contrasting this major virtue with the trivial accomplishments mentioned earlier. An ignorance of government is calamitous, while an ignorance of music, dancing and riding harms no one. But then, in an aside which is telling for my present thesis, Ottaviano goes on to say that courtiers *without* those skills are unable to participate in such activities at the appropriate time (and, one might add, the appropriate time for conveying information or for finding one's master in a good and receptive mood). One recalls that Pope Leo X, as a special honour, used to allow his courtiers to join his hunting party. Where better could one find the Pontiff in a receptive mood than at a carousal after a successful hunt? Castiglione himself was probably closer to Pope Leo, after the invitation to ride with him in 1520, than he was to any of his masters since Guidubaldo.

Ottaviano's aside on the subject of such trivial pursuits runs as follows: 'Ignorance of music, dancing and riding harms no one; nonetheless (*nientedimeno*) the unmusical is shy and dares not sing in the presence of others (*si vergogna né osa cantare in presenzia d'altrui*), or dance, if he doesn't know how, or ride if he cannot sit a horse well' (IV, viii). Niccolò Strozzi, in the *Avvertimenti*, is more direct in his advice on being at the spot to catch the right moment: 'Be assiduous, for often sudden businesses turn up which the prince commits to the first who appears before him, and from these beginnings often spring occasions for great good fortune, (*nascono bene spesso occasioni di gran fortune*) (p.20). Furthermore, in the society in which Castiglione moved, such shortcomings would undoubtedly be regarded as marks of uncouthness. Della Casa's *Galateo* contains a significant passage which echoes the *nientedimeno* of the passage quoted above, in very similar mood: 'Although unpleasantness and uncouthness in one's habits is not punishable by law, for the law regards it as a trivial peccadillo, and assuredly it is not a grave iniquity, nonetheless (*nondimeno*) we see that nature herself chastises us for it with harsh discipline by depriving us, for this reason, of the companionship and the goodwill of men (*consorzio e ... benivolenza degli uomini*)' (*Galateo*,

1). Della Casa is talking rather of the possession of uncouth traits than of the lack of those qualities mentioned by Castiglione, but the lesson is the same, and the final sentence implies the necessity for the company of one's fellow-men, and, in Della Casa's case, too, one's fellow-courtiers.

Although the niceties of social behaviour are emphasised for the political benefits they may effect (by putting the courtier in closer touch with centres of power), Castiglione was only too well aware of the dangers of non-conformity. Since his ideal of happiness seems to have been an Aristotelean ideal, he *needed* society in which to fulfil himself and so was bound, like Della Casa, to attend to the social graces. Yet, with such attention being paid to appearance, superficiality and triviality, the great problem, for both prince and courtier-adviser, was to discern the truth beneath the façade. The courtier's purpose, as we are now told, is to 'so gain the prince's grace and favour by means of the attributes he has acquired through his courtly training, that he may always tell him the truth about what he needs to know, without fear or danger of causing displeasure to his lord'. The advice is similar to Machiavelli's, but Castiglione goes further: 'He should distract him from ignoble paths to set him on the path of virtue, using his own qualities of goodness, quick-wittedness, affability, prudence, culture and other attributes, to demonstrate to his patron the amount of honour and utility which accrues to him from the practices of justice, liberality, magnanimity, mildness of temper and other virtues necessary to a good prince, and, on the other hand, the infamy which derives from the vices opposite to those virtues' (IV, v).

Such views have been seen as naive, for how many courtiers could summon up the courage to contradict or tell the unpleasant truth to autocratic masters? And yet Machiavelli, hardly an ingenuous observer of diplomatic affairs, was also aware of the dangers and problems inherent in discerning truth from falsehood, flattery from affection. His advice on the subject in the *Principe* is aimed at prince, not courtier, but it does not differ substantially from Castiglione's advice to his potential pupils. Machiavelli warns us that this is an important section of his treatise, and that the problem is one against which princes find it difficult to protect themselves 'unless they are most prudent and have excellent discretion' (*Il principe*, XXIII). The only way of combating adulatory courtiers, he suggests, is to allow decent men to feel free to tell their prince the truth. As a check against irreverent use of this privilege, Machiavelli also urges a prudent

choice of wise followers; to this élite the prince may, whenever he
chooses to ask their opinion, grant free leave to tell him the truth.
Ultimately Machiavelli's prince is the supreme judge of the situation.
Both Machiavelli and Castiglione are echoing Aristotle's *Politics* (v,
ix) at the point where he says that adulators tend to enjoy most favour
with their princes, and advises that decent men love their prince and
refrain from sycophantic adulation.

The value of insinuating oneself into the prince's good graces is
hammered home in the next four chapters, with, at times, a bitterness
not normally associated with Castiglione. Guicciardini had noted
that 'the world and its princes are no longer formed as they should be
but as they are' (*Ricordi*, CLXXIX), and he made plans for such a contingency. Fregoso continues his discourse with reflections on 'the
many faults which are to be found in contemporary princes, the major
ones being ignorance and presumption'. Surrounded by lying
adulators, the ignorant mind deceives itself, 'and this, one might say,
was the greatest and most outrageous lie of all', for princes thus
believed that power *for its own sake* was true felicity (ignoring thus
their true *final cause*) and regarded reason and justice as potential
checks on their autocracy. His language here becomes as near
derisive as his Golden Mean will allow. Such princes were worse than
giant carnival figures stuffed with rags and tow, for those great
puppets are at least well-balanced: 'From an ignorance of government spring so many ills, deaths, destructions, conflagrations, ruins,
that it may be called the most fatal disease on the face of the earth'
(v, viii). Castiglione relies for much of his information here on
Plutarch, and, for his examples of good administration, on Classical
exemplars of princes who were well-advised (Epaminondas by
Pythagoras, Agesilaus by Xenophon, Scipio Africanus by Panetius).
It is interesting that in the *Seconda redazione* (at p.194), Plutarch was
himself included as adviser to Trajan, but his name is deleted in the
definitive edition possibly because Castiglione was about to make
such heavy use of his examples and precepts that he might have
seemed too openly plagiaristic and hence unspontaneous (Plutarch is
quoted or paraphrased no less than nineteen times in the course of
the present debate). Yet how feasible was it to tell the truth, to be a
candid preceptor?
    Bandello recognises the difficulty of being frank with one's master,
and in a brief aside in another novella, which recalls Castiglione's idea
of self-preparation for the role of adviser, suggests that the prudent

courtier is one who 'when he is with a prince whom he knows to be
capricious and unlikely to take kindly to reproaches for an unreason-
able action, knows how to adapt himself so that, without losing his
master's favour, he conducts himself in such a way that he may warn
him of his error' (*Novelle*, III, xxxvi). Adulation produced its own
form of untruth, which was not to be confused with the wider field
of deceit (of the type slated in Pulci's *Morgante*, in the character of
Gano) or political fraud on a wider scale (as advocated by Machiavelli
in the *Principe*, XVIII, and the *Discorsi*, II, 13). This theme will return.
But adulation and dissimulation were problems which continued to
grow after the publication of the *Cortegiano*, so that Tasso may contrast his own times with those of Castiglione: 'If the other handbook
[Castiglione's] was written for the age in which it was written, your
book [Tasso's] ought to be highly esteemed in these times when dissimulation is one of the greatest virtues' (*Malpiglio*, p.49). And a
century after the *Cortegiano*'s publication, it is interesting to see
Niccolò Strozzi positively advise his *gentiluomo* that 'the art of
harmonious relationships is knowing how to pretend to be the
opposite of what one actually is, knowing how to imitate the Orc,
as the saying goes, and being both clumsy and astute at the same time'
(op. cit., p.25). Ottaviano Fregoso proceeds next to mention the
opportune and appropriate methods for delivering one's message of
truth, methods which I have suggested are subsumed in the courtier's
more superficial attributes. The great paradox of Fregoso's advice is
that the courtier must be trained in dissimulation and superficiality
in order to gain an approach to his lord and warn him against the
danger of untruth.

The need for truth in these contexts is of immediate, practical
application and use. Elsewhere we shall be introduced to the importance of truth in a more abstract context as the only proper guide for a
well-balanced life and government. In other contemporaries, there
is much evidence of the ruinous effect on court policy of the adulators
deplored by Fregoso. Again Bandello is a notable witness, warning
his readers that if courtiers find their masters being deceived or in
error about something, 'as long as they are not personally affected,
don't imagine that they'll try to set him straight. No! They all bend
to their master's wishes – come good or ill of it. The reason for this is
the cowardice of many courtiers who dare not tell the truth – on the
contrary, if the master says 'Yes', they add their assent, if he says 'No',
they sing the same tune without regard to the good or evil outcome
of what they say' (*Novelle*, II, xxxvii). Bandello lays the blame as

much on princes, whose life-styles are such that they will not have the truth told, and who revere the men who never contradict them. Nevertheless he advises the courtier to take his master on one side and tell him the truth. 'Oh! How much more happy and fortunate would princes be if they had someone to show them freely the damage which follows many things they do, the opinion which the people has of them, the murmurings against them and the terrible government of many ministers who care only about stealing taxes and converting them all to their own use. If princes knew these things, their dominions would be excellently governed' (ibid.). Bandello even adduces the example of Christ, always making enquiries of his disciples and testing the popular mood, as the prince's model in the quest for truth. Benvenuto Cellini (1500–71) also fell victim to the blinkered fashion, despite his hatred of the adulators of courts, for he preferred to tear up (weeping as he did so) those chapters of his autobiography which reflected his true condition of life while serving Cosimo de' Medici: 'But considering how great princes take it badly that a servant of theirs, when making complaints, should give the truth behind his account / motives (*dolendosi dica la verità delle sue ragioni*)…I tore them up and threw them on the fire' (*Trattato dell'Oreficeria*, XII).

To impart frank and truthful instruction in the ways of virtue is the reason why the courtier insinuates himself into the good graces of his prince. He leads his master in 'the austere path of virtue', a path rendered less austere by his own entertaining accomplishments, which make the lesson sweeter, just as doctors sweeten the rim of a glass containing bitter medicine, 'a health-giving deceit' (*inganno salutifero*) for the benefit of their young patients (IV, x).

The treatise now digresses slightly as Gasparo casts doubt upon man's capacity to be taught moral virtue. The complex discussion which follows illustrates well Castiglione's acquaintance with previous philosophical speculations on the subject as he cites Plato, Aristotle and Plutarch to support his case. He finally plumps for the Aristotelean solution that moral virtues are taught and guided. But first he poses two extreme views: on the one hand Gasparo says that virtue is innate and unlearnable (this he illustrates with a Platonic myth), and on the other Ottaviano implies that man may be trained in virtuous skills (he recalls the much inferior art of training hawks). But Nature or God, Gasparo suggests, seem to make men morally virtuous or otherwise, even though men may dissimulate (just as they do to disguise physical defects). Plato's account of the myth of Epimetheus and Prometheus (cp. *Protagoras*) is adduced by Ottaviano's opponent, who is thus led to the conclusion that 'these virtues are granted to men by God. They cannot be learnt but are natural' (IV, xi). By using proofs from Plutarch's *Moralia* and the *Nicomachean Ethics* (the legal folly, for instance of punishing men for their wickedness if the theory of innate virtue and vice were true), Castiglione overcomes this rather deterministic point of view. He compromises, in effect, between the two extremes. The Socratic concept, that our birth is but a sleep and a forgetting, suggests to Ottaviano that man has innate virtues which need awakening with the aid of a tutor and training to perfection. Such training would allow the pupil to choose truth from falsehood, and thus naturally lead to the virtuous choice. Socrates seems repeatedly to have equated virtue with knowledge (which chooses the good) and vice with ignorance (which induces false judgements). Xenophon, (*Memorabilia*, III, ix), and Plato (*Republic*, *passim* and *Laws*, IX, v–viii) report such ideas expressed by Socrates, and Castiglione sums them up in his logical conclusion: 'Men never choose evil under the impression that it is evil, but deceive themselves because of a certain similarity to good' (*s'ingannano per una certa similitudine di bene*) (IV, xiii).

The debate on reality and truth, the extent to which man could trust his senses, was discussed with particular fervour in the fifth century B.C. and has continued to preoccupy philosophers until the present day. Bembo sums up the problem for his contemporaries in the exordium to his *Asolani*, a work which certainly had a relevance for Castiglione here. Bembo sees, among the foremost reasons for lack of tranquillity in life, our inability (through ignorance) to choose between good and wicked desires: 'Hence this ignorance leads us to love things we should avoid, or fail to love things we should pursue...and so we lead a life of travail and error' (*Asolani*, I, i). The solution of both Bembo and Castiglione is to show wherein true judgement lies; ultimately reason, after adequate training, has the job of controlling the lower instincts. The argument is here worth following in some detail since it shows Castiglione's practical and common-sense adaptation of earlier ideas, and also because it leads, conversationally, and almost inadvertently, to later topics for discussion. Certain virtues (a sense of justice, one's conscience, for example) are innate in us, suggests Ottaviano, but without adequate training and direction to the proper end, they are sterile. Such training of what he calls 'the root of these virtues which are potentially innate in our minds' (*la radice di queste virtù potenzialmente ingenite negli animi nostri*) (IV, xiii), needs the twin aids of reason and education. Reason, in particular, 'purifies and cleans the soul, stripping from it the dark veil of ignorance which causes all of man's errors' (ibid.). To the objection that men often knowingly choose the bad, Ottaviano replies that this is because their knowledge is imperfect. Such a rather obvious statement has a secondary purpose – the introduction of self-control and temperance (*continenzia* and *temperanzia*) and their importance in the courtier's and later the prince's upbringing.

The Greeks had distinguished between the naturally abstemious (or passively continent) man (σώφρων) and the man who consciously tempered his desires (ἐγκρατής), and Aristotle had discussed this thoroughly in the *Nicomachean Ethics*, VII, i–ix. So here, Castiglione regards *continenzia* as a worthy virtue, but as inferior to *temperanzia*, since the latter is the control of one's instincts through reason, and forms the necessary prerequisite for the cultivation of other virtues. The importance of temperance in Castiglione's scheme cannot be over-emphasised. It modifies not only excesses of behaviour, but also of inclination. We have seen that Aristotle's notion of moral virtue implied a *via media*, a Golden Mean, between excess and deficiency, between pleasure and pain. The adherence to such a Mean distinguished virtue from vice. Temperance may control other qualities and guide them according to a Mean. Thus wrath, Castiglione says, may be tempered in order to help the virtue of fortitude; hatred may be tempered to righteous outrage in order to assist justice (IV, xviii). That Mean is familiar to anyone who is acquainted with the ethical structure of Dante's *Inferno* and *Purgatorio*. Other virtues, which are later to be elaborated include fortitude, justice ('without which Jove himself could not rule well' – ibid.), magnanimity, prudence ('which guides the others and judges which choice is best'), liberality, munificence, desire for honour, mansuetude, humour, affability and many others. By possessing these virtues himself and inculcating them into his prince, the courtier will help produce the greatest of all virtues, truly a pearl of great price, namely: 'the manner and way of governing and ruling as is proper, which alone would be enough to make man happy and bring back to the world again that Golden Age, which, writers tell us, existed when Saturn ruled' (IV, xviii).

This theme will recur. In the meantime, the topic of practical government (and a pause in Ottaviano's flow!) leads Gasparo to question the relative efficacy of monarchy or republic to bring about this happy state of affairs. Ottaviano, arguing from the hierarchical structure of nature (from the heart which seems to control the body, to the 'king' bee ruling the hive etc.), suggests that the rule of *one* is

best and 'more natural than that of the republic' (IV, xix). The argument was one common in the Middle Ages and in successive political
theorists, including St Thomas Aquinas in his *De regimine principum*.
This idea is to be modified slightly in later chapters, specifically with
the addition of advisory and administrative councils. Yet, in chapter
xxii of his treatise, Castiglione quotes almost literally from the
*Politics* in his praise of a god-like individual who may rule his people.
The fact is that Aristotle laid down no specific formula for ideal
government. Not for him the ideal state of Plato's *Republic*. In Book
II of the *Politics*, he argues that the best state is one in which men are
happiest, and that it may vary in form. His perfect state is the best
state consistent with what is practicable. He was also open-minded
enough to take into account the possibility of one gifted man being
so far superior in virtue to his fellows that he was like a god among
men. But Castiglione was evidently only too well aware of the dangers
of tyranny stifling liberty. He allows Bembo to object cogently to
arguments in favour of monarchy by adducing examples from
nature of more democratic behaviour, as well as by an appeal to the
feeling, which most men have, that they have a certain god-given
liberty which would seem to be denied if subjected to the rule of one.
He would personally prefer a republic to a monarchy (and here we
see the aptness of allowing the Venetian (and republican) Bembo to
speak on this topic.

Bembo's remarks are so reasonable that Castiglione has to work
doubly hard to counter them. He does so in two ways, the second of
which modifies slightly his notion of an autocratic ruler, so as to
accommodate certain safeguards for the subjects' liberty. He begins
with a rather sophistic justification of monarchy which counters the
objection of the potential corruption of a single individual by the
potential stupidity of a group: it is easier to find *one* wise man than
many. Castiglione evidently felt the weakness of his case here and
inserts four safeguards against corruption: the prince will be noble,
instinctively inclined to virtue; he will be mindful of his predecessor's good example; his education will include the best ethical
training; he will implicitly rely for his training on a wise courtier,
'helped by the teachings, education and skill of the courtier' (*aiutato
dagli ammaestramenti e dalla educazione ed arte del cortegiano*) (IV, xxii).
And in a burst of enthusiasm he says that his prince may have so many
virtues that he 'may be called rather demigod than mortal man'; such
a benevolent prince is beloved of God himself.

Yet despite this eulogy, Castiglione still does not seem to have convinced himself of the practicality of his prince. In the next chapter, therefore, Ottaviano gives a subtle twist to this 'Divine Right of Kings', namely that 'nations are committed by God to the guardianship of princes, who must therefore take diligent care of their charge and render their accounts to God, like good bailiffs to their lord' (IV, xxiii). Furthermore the good example of the prince should mould the character of his subjects, he 'must not only be good, but also make others good' (ibid.). The concept is Aristotelean again ('The prince should prepare for this end, and study that he may make his subjects good and law-abiding', *Nicomachean Ethics*, I, xiii, 2). Yet the pyramidical hierarchy in which the prince reflects the best in the state and moulds the state to reflect in turn his own best qualities was an image also popularised by Neoplatonists in Florence, during Lorenzo de' Medici's domination of the city's affairs. Marsilio Ficino was particularly favoured by the Medici because his philosophical system, reflecting a Platonic ideal, helped to apotheosise the figure of the ideal prince. It is curious to see Lorenzo himself, as Maier has observed, poetising about that ideal in his *Rappresentazione di San Giovanni e Paolo*:

> Lo esemplo al popol molto vale
> e quel che fa il signor fanno poi molti
> ché nel signor son tutti gli occhi volti.
> [Example is of prime value to the people and the actions of the
> lord are imitated by many, for all eyes are turned upon the lord.]

Temperance is again underlined as the first requirement of such a man, and the chapter closes with the idea that only through temperance may he achieve the tranquillity necessary to learn the other virtues.

Guicciardini had meditated upon the efficacy of high office as a measurement of a man's qualities and had quoted the apophthegm *Magistratus virum ostendit* (*Ricordi*, CLXIII), in the same way as Castiglione does next. It is the exercise of power which demonstrates the benevolence or tyranny of a prince. The tyrannical ruler who uses power and intimidation merely to maintain himself in office is sowing the seeds of destruction for his own tranquillity. Here, inevitably, there has been drawn a parallel with Machiavelli's advice about the relative merits of being loved or feared. If forced to choose, Machiavelli would advocate that his new prince employ intimidation rather than blandishment (*Il principe*, XVII), and he justifies his advice with his ultra-realistic view of the selfish nature of unreliable subjects who need to be controlled. The only safeguard implied by Machiavelli in that passage is that his prince should avoid the positive hatred of his subjects. It is a notable contrast that Ottaviano now points. Plutarch's grim exemplars (Clearchos, tyrant of Pontus, who, for security, slept locked in a strong-box, and Aristodemos, who slept in a chamber suspended from the ceiling and approachable only by a ladder, which his mother-in-law took away with her each night!) are to be avoided. The prince, in Ottaviano's view, must live a free life, dear to his citizens and 'so ordered that he participates in both active and contemplative life' (*ordinata di modo che participi della attiva e della contemplativa*) (IV, xxiv).

The relative merits of the active and the contemplative life (which Aristotle had resolved to his own satisfaction in the *Nicomachean Ethics*, x, vii–x and *Politics*, VII, ii–iii) had for centuries formed the basis for prolonged discussion. In particular, during the Renaissance, Cristoforo Landino had debated them at length. Lorenzo de' Medici (in the *Altercazione*), Ficino and latterly Sperone Speroni (1500–88) all used the topic as a basis for debate or for poetry. It was a fundamental tenet of Aristotle that his contemplatives participate in the life of the community, channel back their wisdom freely and willingly to their less experienced fellows. The contemplative ideal is the one which Castiglione advocates: 'The purpose of the active life must be the contemplative, as the purpose of war is peace, the respite from travail' (*Il fine della vita attiva deve essere la contemplativa come della guerra la pace, il riposo delle fatiche*) (IV, xxvi). Before this more momentous topic is discussed, we are brought back briefly, with nonchalant aplomb, to the importance of triviality. Gasparo pays Ottaviano a pretty compliment: he has all the qualities of the courtier being described and lacks only the musical and dancing attributes and 'the other qualities of little importance' (*l'altre di poca importanza*) (IV, xxv). Ottaviano's reply, taking Gasparo slightly to task, re-emphasises the practicality of Castiglione's aim in words which recall the earlier discussion: 'None of those attributes are "of little importance". They help in gaining the prince's good graces, which is a prime essential, as we have described, before the courtier may venture to teach him virtue' (ibid.).

The dominant note of the next part of the conversation is that of peace, the aim and object of war, as it was earlier defined. The first duty of the good prince is to ensure that his subjects 'may live at leisure (*in ocio*) and in peace, without danger, and with dignity, and may enjoy in worthy manner that end of all action which must be tranquillity' (IV, xxvii). The sentiments expressed, the examples adduced (of the blood-thirsty Scythians, for instance, refusing to eat with a fellow-national until he had killed an enemy) are all lifted from Aristotle's *Politics* (VII, ii). Righteous bellicosity (to keep one's frontiers peaceful, to punish evil etc.) is justified; war for war's sake is condemned. All virtues are useful, and evidently such virtues as fortitude and perseverance are particularly helpful in the prosecution of a war. What is unusual in Castiglione's thought is his emphasis that in *peace* virtues are even more essential, in order to maintain the spiritual equilibrium between the mad chaos of war and the unchecked ease and luxury of favourable fortune. The Aristotelean Mean is clear, and Aristotle continues to be quoted, at times word for word, in the following discussion on the proper sort of education for the ruler.

Aristotle had explained (*Politics*, VII, xiii) the distinction in man between body and soul, and, in the soul, between irrational intelligence (or instinct) and rational intelligence. Just as the generation of the body comes before the development of the soul, so instinct precedes rational intelligence, and just as the body must be kept fit and healthy to aid the soul in maintaining tranquillity, so instinct must be trained to aid reason. Physical training of an obvious kind takes care of the body, an upbringing (by assuefaction) in good moral habits will control the instinct, and intellectual pursuits will allow the reason to enjoy the highest quality of life.

Castiglione continues chapter xxx by quoting Aristotle's maxim on the need to ensure that children were not, in age, too distant from, or to near to, the age of their parents, thus providing for the maximum aid from father to child and the minimum disrespect from child to father. And the Aristotelean view is now contrasted, in an aside, with the Platonic notion that, in order to produce such '*figlioli ben disposti e belli*' (well-disposed and beautiful offspring), perhaps polygamy would be a good idea. That sly dig is aimed by the misogynist, Gasparo, at the ladies, and Emilia Pia soon puts him in his place. The remarks form part of the elegant causerie of the evening and are congruous with the characters of the interlocutors, but they also, in a casual way, cast a little doubt upon the validity of Plato's *Republic* as a source of instruction, compared with the more empirical *Politics* of Aristotle.

Castiglione is reaching one of the climaxes of Book IV, for just as the inculcation of so many virtues has a practical end, to condition the prince to govern well, so good government has a practical end – the happiness of the nation. Other safeguards are now added against the possibility of an overweening prince. Chapter xxxi proposes the setting up of a consultative council of a proven élite of nobles (*consiglio de' nobili*) who will give the prince their frank and true advice; to this should be added a popular council (*consiglio popolare*) elected by citizens of lower social rank who would communicate public and private requirements to the upper body. Hence, in his ideal state, although ultimate executive responsibility lay with the prince, 'nevertheless others participate. And so their state would have the form of three good governments, kingdom, oligarchy and democracy (*il regno, gli ottimati e 'l popolo*)' (IV, xxxi). Further admonitions include the careful institution of justice through the appointment to the judiciary of men of proven honesty and wisdom. A reverent and pious attitude towards God is another safeguard, indeed a prerequisite, 'for without God's help it is impossible to govern oneself or anyone else' (ibid., xxxii). Castiglione has been compared here with Machiavelli in their respective attitudes to religion. Machiavelli's cynical appraisal of the potential of religion for political ends (cp. *Discorsi*, I, xii) and the ruinous effect which he thought the Roman Church was having on Italy's political state, seems to make Castiglione's views ultra-naive by comparison. Yet, Castiglione quotes, not a Christian writer, but Xenophon (*Cyropaedia*, I, vi, 3) in support of his advice, and, when he elaborates his theme to embrace possible Christian piety, he warns that 'the prince should be truly religious, not superstitious or given to the vanity of incantations and divinations (*né dato alle vanità d'incanti e vaticini*)' (IV, xxxii).

At this point in the discussion, Castiglione has an interesting aside on the role of fortune in human affairs. The whole of the *Cortegiano* may be regarded as a preparation against the vagaries of fortune, a counsel of prudence. The courtier needs to make himself as self-sufficient, as well-qualified and as accomplished as possible in order to counter fortune's blows or grasp the opportunities she offers. Castiglione's attitude is far less polemical than that of his predecessors or contemporaries. He suggests that no matter how 'fortunate' a man may be, there is always the possibility of bad luck attending him. Indeed for the fortunate man, perhaps becoming complacent in a tranquil environment, adverse fortune is often useful to stimulate further providence and virtuous activity, in just the same way as continence, temperance and justice are more than ever essential once peace has been achieved. So here Castiglione allows for the possibility of God's sending adverse fortune even to the virtuous, 'in order not to allow them to fall asleep in prosperity, thus forgetting Him and their human prudence, which often corrects adverse fortune' (*corregge spesso la mala fortuna*) (IV, xxxii).

From the prince's point of view, one counter to the blows of fortune is the prudent cultivation of one's subjects' affection and the avoidance of their hatred. Patriotic feeling and just dealing within the state, Castiglione implies, better than any mercenary army, ensures the security of the ruler. There are echoes here of Machiavelli's hatred of the foreign mercenary bands which proved unreliable for those who hired them, and dangerous for the regions in which they were billeted. Both men thought that the wretched state of Italy was due in large measure to mercenaries. Castiglione looks for motives for their ravages, and concludes that his 'wretched' country 'has been and still is a prey open to foreigners, thanks to bad government and because the land is replete with such riches' (IV, xxxiii).

The notion of wealth introduces a fine example of the Aristotelean mean. Ottaviano points to the benefits for the community if the majority of its citizens are neither too rich nor too poor. The advice comes from Aristotle's *Politics* and is reconfirmed at the close of the chapter: 'It is a most healthy thing universally to maintain the Golden Mean' (*è saluberrima cosa mantenere universalmente la mediocrità*). Such an attitude prevents greed, dissension and chaos. And the tranquillity which theorists from Dante onwards had spoken of as a prerequisite for civilised living, forms the subject matter for Ottaviano's next remarks on the need to prevent *mutazione di stato* and the Ciceronian *desiderio di cose nove* ('revolution'). Many of these precepts are taken from Aristotle (*Politics*, v) and it may be appropriate here to elaborate briefly on that argument.

Aristotle's theory of the development of the individual pre-supposed a tranquil environment in which he could be trained from an early age to participate fully and widely in civic (or national) affairs. If Aristotle's community was to thrive and be happy, it was essential to educate the young to carry on the cyclical process which ensured that when they, in their turn came to govern, they would inculcate in future generations the same virtues. For Aristotle, man's aim in life was to attain happiness. The difficult decision, to para-phrase Guicciardini, was to know what happiness was. On Aristotle's scale of human values, intellectual values were at the highest point, nearest to the divine, and man's highest happiness consisted in his ability to use his intellectual powers to the full in theoretical know-ledge or contemplation (the original Aristotelean term, θεωρία, is synonymous with both). Yet Aristotle insisted that man was a political animal, needed a πόλις or city-state, could not become a mere hermit, if he was to develop his talents to the full, and even the highest contemplatives in Aristotle's scheme shared in the active life of the state by channelling back into political life the higher wisdom attained by their contemplations. Almost paradoxically, therefore, their contemplations become of greater practical value for the progress of state (and of man) than the more obviously 'practical' virtues such as temperance and justice, which are only means to the contemplative end and conducive, in themselves, rather to an unchanging (or static) society.

When Ottaviano Fregoso is urged by Gaspar Pallavicino to describe the virtues which the courtier should attempt to inculcate into his prince, so that, in turn, he might transmit them to his subjects, his conclusion is almost purely Aristotelean: 'Those are the methods by which I would remind the prince to ensure the preservation of his subjects in a tranquil state (*in stato tranquillo*) and the communication to them of the values of spirit, body and fortune (*i beni dell' animo e del corpo e della fortuna*); but the values of body and fortune in order to exercise those spiritual values, the usefulness of which increases in proportion to their magnitude and transcendence (*quanto son maggiori e più eccessivi, tanto son più utili*), a thing which does not happen in the case of the values of body or of fortune' (IV, xxxiv). The contemplative life is the ultimate goal, just as peace is the goal of war, and Castiglione's notion of the *usefulness* of spiritual gifts echoes Aristotle's.

In Castiglione's case it was no longer possible for the independent city-state to provide the leisure and tranquillity essential for the development of the individual. He has to adapt old theories to fit new circumstances. His courtier, in the chaotic situation facing the world during the first quarter of the century had to train himself (in the manner of Aristotle's successive generations) so that he could pass on his virtues to his ruler. The prince, thus conditioned, might be expected to perpetuate the virtuous environment in which leisure and tranquillity may be enjoyed and used for developing the highest, contemplative values, the wise fruits of which may be returned to society.

And when Ottaviano talks of the idyllic world which might be produced by the exercise of the advice given, he may not be expressing simply the naive ideal of a Boiardo (cp. below, p.191). Castiglione's more erudite readers, with their minds attuned to subtle and symbolic allusions to the Classics, might see in the 'golden age which, writers tell us, existed when Saturn reigned' a double or even a three-fold reference. Saturnus (and his earlier Greek counterpart Cronos) was traditionally the *civilising* god; the planet Saturn, in a tradition most gloriously illustrated by Dante (cp. *Paradiso*, XXI), was the planet symbolising *contemplation*; and, finally, from Ennius onwards, Saturnus had been regarded as the *tutelary deity of Latium*, the original bringer of peace and law to ancient Rome. The adjective *saturnius* meant 'Roman', and, more widely 'Latin' during the Classical period, particularly in the writings of Virgil. The most famous allusion, combining nationalism and civilising power in the deity of Saturn would be familiar to any student of the Classics from Virgil's *Aeneid*, VIII, 319, where the bard of Imperial Rome describes, through Evander's mouth, the civilising power of the god on Italy and the golden age of his rule (the *aurea saecula*), followed subsequently by the chaos of war, greed for acquisition and foreign invasions which finally drove Evander from his *patria*. It might be argued that the third allusion here stretches credibility too far, but it may be equally hard to believe that someone with Castiglione's deep grounding in the Classics and an awareness of Italy's abject position did not see, in Virgil's description, a reflection of current problems, particularly in view of the mention, shortly before, of the wretched state of sixteenth-century Italy, plundered by foreigners for her wealth.

It will be remembered that Castiglione had suggested, very subtly, that the perfect courtier achieved perfection in order that 'the prince who shall be worthy to be served by him, however small his state (or status) (*ancor che poco stato avesse*), may, nonetheless, be able to call himself a great lord' (I, i). The idea is now reiterated by Ottaviano when he says that it is not the multitude, but rather the worth, of his subjects which makes the prince great. And, not, one suspects, without a wicked twinkle, he remarks that if all the subjects of the king of France were suddenly, by some Circean spell, changed into beasts, the king's status would, despite such a great number of subjects, be small.

The conversation is continued by Cesare Gonzaga, who makes the telling remark, changed from the version in the *Seconda redazione* (cp. above, p.144), that what Ottaviano is describing is no longer courtier and prince, but rather teacher and governor. He proposes to add to Ottaviano's list of virtues royal splendour and magnificence, which would increase his subjects' reverence for him. He cites the magnificent architectural projects of the ancient Romans, the works of their own contemporaries (Federigo da Montefeltro, Pope Julius etc.), the great achievements of Alexander in founding cities and, according to Plutarch, such grandiose schemes as the projected sculpting of Mount Athos into a human form with a city in its left hand, and, in its right, a cup into which the local rivers flowed. Although such magnificence is evidently acceptable to him, Ottaviano brings it down to more practical or useful examples. The magnanimity of tyrannicides, for instance, deified such men and raised temples in their honour (Theseus and Heracles are cited): 'The benefit of extirpating tyranny is so helpful to the world...' (*tanto giovevole al mondo*) (IV, xxxvii). The practical undertones of the adjective, *giovevole*, are picked up again later when the example of Alexander the Great is adduced as 'helping (*giovasse*) with his victories the nations he conquered'.

The civilising influence of Alexander is developed at length in this chapter, and, in view of what was hinted above about the possibility of Castiglione's playing Aristotle to Charles v's Alexander, it is worth quoting some of the eulogy in detail, '... having invested with so many good customs those barbarous nations which he overcame, making beasts into men...he built so many fine cities in countries poorly inhabited, introducing morals to them...so that men conquered by him were happier than the rest'. The list of Alexander's virtuous achievements continues until the end of the chapter, which ends elliptically with the statement that a thousand other benefits stemming from his victories could be described as helping mankind (and the word is again *giovamento*). It will be recalled that this was the greatest period of Spanish colonial expansion. Apart from their European possessions, Hernando Cortes had, in 1519, the year of Charles' election as Emperor, invaded Mexico, reorganising the country as a Spanish province two years later. Francisco Pizarro's first two expeditions to Peru were made in 1524–5 and 1526–8 (his final 'conquest' being in 1532). There can be no doubt that these discoveries and conquests formed main topics of conversation in the circles in which Castiglione moved, particularly in Toledo and Granada, and as we shall see, they are particularly significant in view of the eulogy of Charles v, 'potentially the greatest Emperor of all time', introduced in the definitive edition for the first time.

Again Castiglione seems to capture current political feeling when he makes Ottaviano propose a new Crusade against Turks and Arabs. The notion is not so naive or overambitious as might seem at first glance. Pope Adrian had been keen on the enterprise, and not without cause, for it was precisely during this period, and the rule of Suleiman I in particular (1520–66), that the Ottoman Empire reached its greatest and, for the West, most dangerous extent. (It will be recalled that in 1529 the Turks just failed to take Vienna.) Possible saviours of Christendom included Henry VIII, Francis I, and last, but most important of all, Charles V of Spain. The eulogy of Charles V was not in earlier drafts of the *Cortegiano* and Castiglione has to return fictionally, in the definitive edition, to 1508 to praise by hindsight the aptitudes of the then eight-year-old Don Carlos, prince of Spain! Even as a child Charles is there said to have shown such potential for all the virtues that 'if, as is thought, the Imperial Crown of Christianity will be his one day, one can believe that he must leave in relative obscurity the renown (*nome*) of many ancient Emperors and equal in fame the most famous that the world has ever known' (IV, xxxviii).

The Aristotelean Golden Mean is underlined as the necessary guide for such princes. (Cian and Maier give full documentation of the Aristotelean sources for these and other remarks here.) Prudence and the choice of the *via media* (*mediocrità*) are essential, despite the difficulties of finding the central 'point of virtue, set at the mid-point of two extremes, faulty (*viciosi*) because they are either excessive (*l'uno per lo troppo*) or defective (*l'altro per lo poco*)' (IV, xl). The subject has evidently changed radically from the portrait of a perfect courtier to that of ideal emperor. And just as we were warned that the trivia of society were not to be despised if they were means to an end, so now Ottaviano warns that the prince requires all the advantages he can possibly have, and no accomplishment is too slight for him to master if success will attend his learning it.

Ottaviano acknowledges that there could be no greater or more proper eulogy of a prince than to call him 'a good governor' (*bon governatore*). By now the political message of the *Cortegiano* is virtually complete. There remain a few remarks about the more domestic concerns of the prince, who should rule his subjects rather as though they comprised a vast family. In fact, with an aside which betrays his adherence to the Aristotelean ideal of city-state (πόλις), Castiglione advises 'that the city be all united and harmonious (in love and) in friendship, like a private house' (*che la città fosse tutta unita e concorde in amicizia come una casa privata*) (IV, xli). The *Seconda redazione* ends the political discourses entirely at this point. Ottaviano is then called away from the discussion in the early version, having made an almost brutal and (for him) most uncharacteristic judgement against women, a statement considerably abbreviated and toned down in the definitive edition. Yet Castiglione wants to underline two further political points (not in the *Seconda redazione*): first, the possible identity of his future world saviour, and second, the identification of his courtly adviser with an Aristotle *redivivus*. Naturally, Castiglione does not put his points so baldly.

First, Frigio wonders whether what has been described is not an impossible ideal, 'like Plato's *Republic*, and whether we are ever to see its like, except perhaps in heaven' (IV, xlii). Ottaviano's reply is sophistic and may reflect Plato's own words, that 'Possibilities, even though difficult, one can hope, may yet come about' (cp. *Republic*, VI, xii). The possibilities of salvation may lie in the hands of the European rulers noted earlier, though even in Italy (despite necessarily limited powers) there were princes such as Federigo Gonzaga, who might make up in virtue what they lacked in political dominion. Federigo Gonzaga was only seven at the fictional time of composition, and this is evidently a means for retrospective eulogy. From this viewpoint the remarks made in praise of his qualities are unlikely and exaggerated, yet one must acknowledge Castiglione's realistic assessment of the situation. The salvation of the world (and so the peaceful restoration of order in Italy) must be imposed from a great power source (certainly outside Italy), since only men of the calibre of Francis I, Charles V or Henry VIII are capable of aiming at the 'highest rank of perfect prince' (*supremo grado di perfetto principe*), while, in Italy, there were many young princes of promise, 'though they are not about to have such power' (*benché non siano per aver tanta potenzia*) (IV, xlii). That may be the most realistic political statement from an Italian in the first quarter of the century. It is further proof of his more serious intentions in the *definitive* edition that the *Seconda redazione* limits its potential saviours to Francesco Maria della Rovere and the infant Federigo Gonzaga! There Federigo, in a parallel story from Plutarch on the young Alexander's brilliance, is seen as a potential new Alexander. The definitive edition views the situation much more realistically, excises the anecdote, and reserves for Alexander a position of much greater significance, as will become clear.

In the meanwhile, Giuliano de' Medici voices some doubts arising from Ottaviano's general description of the courtier's attributes. The courtier is far superior to his female counterpart; he seems to be set even above his prince; if his purpose is attainable (which Giuliano doubts), he can no longer be termed a mere courtier; if the courtier is to produce by his advice an excellent prince, he must be equally excellent; finally, what happens when the age of courtier and prince is so disparate that the *young* courtier would be unlikely to influence the old prince, while the *old* courtier would be hard put to it to carry out the courtly activities apparently requiring youthful agility. Ottaviano grants the reasonableness of some of the objections, but answers all, subtly and well, countering Giuliano's sophistry with down-to-earth empirical examples. Most important is that concluding statement, '*e se non vorrete chiamarlo cortegiano, non mi dà noia*' (and if you don't want to call him *courtier* I am unconcerned) (IV, xlvii). Indeed Plato and Aristotle 'acted as courtiers' (*fecero l'opere della cortegiania*).

Already in earlier drafts of the book, Plato and Aristotle are linked together briefly, but nowhere in the *Seconda redazione* does Aristotle get the attention he now receives. Plato, by contrast, as had happened earlier (cp. above, p.144) is dealt with in an aside at the beginning of the chapter, and as an example of the courtier whose prince is so intractable that ultimately he has to leave his service. The kernel of the discussion concerns Aristotle's relationship with Alexander the Great. The earlier eulogy of Alexander's civilising power is reiterated in more or less the same terms: 'made the world one country and all men as one people...living in friendship and concord under a single form of government and a single legal code...brought men from their ferine state to that of human beings, etc.' Ottaviano reaches a pitch of fervour only to be equalled by Bembo in his discourse on love, and all these marvels are ascribed to the influence of the 'courtier', Aristotle – 'and of all these Aristotle was the initiator in Alexander, by his use of the methods of the good courtier' (*di queste cose in Alessandro fu autore Aristotele, usando i modi di bon cortegiano*) (IV, xlvii). The fervour of Ottaviano's eulogy is toned down, and he is brought to earth, by Gasparo Pallavicino's amusing interruption as he wonders at the ability of Plato and Aristotle as dancers or musicians. On this minor note the important discussion ends.

There is a vast body of critical literature surrounding the topic of Platonism in the Renaissance and here I can do little more than trace its development and examine one aspect, the Platonic attitude to love, which is of particular relevance to the final section of the *Cortegiano*. It has already been observed that, from the beginning, Platonism and Aristoteleanism were inextricably intermingled, if often opposed, systems of thought. In the so-called Neoplatonic school of philosophy which sprang up in Alexandria six centuries after Plato's death, there were those who attempted a revival of and an elaboration of Plato's philosophical system, and, at the same time, a reconciliation with the new Christian theology, already by that time a force to be reckoned with. Indeed, it is significant that while one Neoplatonist, Synesius of Cyrene (c. 370–413), eventually became Bishop of Ptolemais (one of his hymns is present in our *Hymns Ancient and Modern*), another, Proclus of Byzantium (c. 411–485), evolved a philosophical system which embraced several of the ancient philosophies and vindicated the rights of paganism over Christian theology. Plotinus (born c. 205) and his follower Porphyry (233–c. 301) were the leading exponents of the Neoplatonic school (and Marsilio Ficino, in his maturity, was to translate and comment on the *Enneads* of Plotinus).

With some variations, the early conflict of views on paganism and Christianity, along with the further clash between Aristoteleans and Platonists, is to be carried over into the Italian Renaissance, when reconciliation of the systems again became a paramount issue. A major factor which alienated the Renaissance Platonist from completely accepting Aristoteleanism was its apparently materialistic basis, and the consequent absence in its system of an afterlife or an anthropomorphic creator. Plato seemed to have gone out of his way to 'prove' those concepts. It may well be symptomatic of the Platonists' preoccupations, as well as the negative pressures from Aristoteleans like Pomponazzi, that the Lateran Council of 1513 came to the extraordinary decision to make the Immortality of the Soul part of official church dogma. One resolution to the conflict may be seen in Castiglione's treatment of Divine love at the conclusion of Book IV.

The long symbiosis of Aristoteleanism and Platonism, the tradition of oral teaching and the acceptance of medieval syntheses of the two philosophies in the Schoolmen's theology mean that, although the broad distinction between the two remains, it is unscientific to be dogmatic about the 'conflict' during the Renaissance. Pomponazzi used Plato, and quoted directly from him, when he was useful to bolster his thesis, just as Ficino used Aristotle. Indeed Ficino has been the object of philosophical attack for the manner in which he garbled earlier systems of philosophies, accepted ancient forgeries and misinterpretations (and Ferdinand Schevill has a particularly scathing attack on Ficino, in *The Medici*, p.157). Plato had been known and well-loved throughout the Middle Ages, Aristotle was popular during the Renaissance, and old distinctions that Aristotle dominated medieval theology, while Plato supplied the Renaissance with its philosophical bases, have now been rejected. Apart from information about Plato available in the Latin Classics, the Middle Ages had other sources: Augustine was imbued with Platonic thought, indeed maintained that Plato's philosophy did not run counter to Christian theology and that 'he came nearer to Truth than any one of the entire set of ancient philosophers' (*Civitas Dei*, viii, 9). Apuleius' writings, especially his *De Platone et eius dogmate* and his *De deo Socratis*, were also effective in keeping alive and, to some extent, popularising the Platonic tradition. The *De consolatione* of Boethius is also steeped in Platonism, and Aquinas, for all the use he made of Aristotle, was equally well acquainted with those earlier writers and their Platonic notions. Yet, significantly, the Aristoteleans were suspect to Petrarch, who was averse to the philosophy for two main reasons. Firstly, Aristotle seemed over-concerned with what is human and temporal, instead of with the divine and eternal and had an enormous (and, in Petrarch's view, misguided) following. Secondly, Petrarch could only know Aristotle in the medieval Latin translations, particularly that of the *Nicomachean Ethics*, made about 1250 under the direction of Robert Grosseteste, Bishop of Lincoln. The standard of Latin in such translations was, by his own criteria, atrocious, and its unpalatable style prevented him from effectively comprehending Aristotle's purpose. But he did have Latin texts of the much more accessible (and congenial) *Timaeus* and *Phaedo* of Plato. Hence, in his *Trionfo della fama* (III, 4), it is natural for him to assign to Plato, whom, in the *De ignorantia*, he calls *princeps philosophiae*, a position above Aristotle. His reverence for Plato is further evidenced by his boasted possession of 'sixteen or more of Plato's books at home' (ibid.), which were tantalisingly unreadable for him because he had no Greek. Petrarch's influence, particularly in the sphere of the love lyric, was to be supreme in the Renaissance. His popularity (cp. *Cortegiano*, III, lii, where he alone is selected as representative *par excellence* of the love lyricist) owed a lot to the happy coincidence of his love themes and the vogue for Platonic philosophy. Bembo's unique awareness of the advantages for the 'new' vernacular of blending the linguistic and artistic supremacy of Petrarch with the popularity of Neoplatonic love themes increased the favour of both trends.

Plato's poetic prose was given further boosts by the translation of his *Republic* by Manuel Chrysoloras after 1397. Seven years later, Leonardo Bruni translated the *Phaedo* (1404–5), noting at the same time its resemblance to Christian theological thinking. The interest of the humanist scholars doing work on the text of Plato was not only literary and stylistic (and in this respect, the beautiful prose of Plato would contrast with the arid lecture-note-style of Aristotle) but they were also appreciative of the artistic and imaginative facets of his dialogues. At the same time they found him compatible with Christianity. To this 'Western' humanist interest in Plato was added the enthusiasm for Platonism which derived from Byzantine scholars, for whom Plato had long provided an acceptable philosophical system. In particular Gemistus Pletho (c. 1355–1450), for whom Platonism was a living reality, visited Italy in 1438–9 and converted many with his enthusiastic advocacy of what to him was a familiar and well-loved discipline. John Argyropoulos at Florence was another of these Byzantine scholars, as was Cardinal Bessarion (1403–72), a stout defender of Plato against the Aristotelians. Indeed, the anti-Platonic and anti-Aristotelean polemics which perturbed the intellectual climate of the mid-fifteenth century may be summed up in the anti-Platonic criticism of the *Comparatio philosophorum Aristotelis et Platonis* of George of Trebizond (1395–1484) and in Bessarion's reply, *In calumniatorem Platonis*.

Platonism was given its most important Italian impetus by the work of Marsilio Ficino. The process of his 'conversion' to Platonism may seem far removed from the experimental science of the centuries which followed. Yet his enthusiasm for the new philosophy was undoubtedly boosted by the discovery of manuscripts which seemed to confirm, practically, as it were, the theories which he had put forward as a young man. In 1454, having completed his studies at Florence and Pisa, he composed the essay *De laudibus medicinae*, in which he based his thought on received ideas to sketch out a theory of the necessary equilibrium, for the contented man, between body and soul. For the next eight years he continued to philosophise on current ideas and to perfect his knowledge of Greek. He was particularly eager to trace a possible continuity of thought between the ancient philosophies and the Christian tradition (he quotes St Augustine as a relevant precursor on the subject). By 1462, his impressive scholarship had convinced Cosimo de' Medici to finance his leisure, accommodate him in a villa, at Careggi, and provide him with an important new group of Greek manuscripts recently acquired for the Medici in Macedonia, and reputedly the work of Zoroaster, Orpheus, Hermes Trismegistus and Pythagoras.

The new material seemed to be the missing link in what Ficino called the *pia filosofia*, man's mystic search to understand his position in the universe, a tradition which had led to Christianity. From that point on, his output was even more prodigious, and his influence increased enormously. The five years, 1464–9, saw the appearance of his translations from Plato and the organisation of the Academy at Careggi, modelled on the Greek, Platonic, Academy. There, informal discussions were held among a circle of selected friends, including men of the calibre of Lorenzo de' Medici, Leonbattista Alberti, Luigi Pulci, Pico della Mirandola, Cristoforo Landino, Angelo Poliziano, Michelangelo Buonarroti (1475–1564) and many other, lesser, geniuses. The cross-pollination of Platonic philosophical notions with literary and artistic currents led to such compositions as Poliziano's *Stanze per la giostra* or Lorenzo's *Altercazione*, the exposition in verse of the Platonic doctrine of happiness, or to the themes of many of Michelangelo's sonnets or the idealisation of the human form painted or sculpted by him and his successors. The list is endless. In Florence, and the tendency was to spread throughout Italy and Europe, there was virtually no intellectual or artistic field unaffected by Platonic philosophy. Ficino went on from strength to strength, composing his *Theologia platonica*, begun in 1469, to demonstrate his favourite theory that Plato's philosophy provided relevant intellectual support for Christian theology.

It would be inappropriate to proceed with these brief remarks without also mentioning the Platonists' exaltation of the dignity of man. Ficino considered man as the ruler of nature and exalted his almost divine attributes 'He is like a God (*utique Deus*) on the earth' (*Theologia platonica*, XVI). Man's universality and greatness are evident to Ficino from his actions, his thought and his aspirations to reach God. Those notions are beautifully expressed in Giovanni Pico della Mirandola's *Oratio de hominis dignitate*, another of the influential texts of the Renaissance. Pico's opening remarks reflect his pre-occupation with the reconciling of past philosophies and Christianity, the blending of religion and philosophical truth. He then proceeds to show how man was created by God and placed in the world, where through the use of his free-will he might degenerate as a brute or regenerate as an angel. Pico's aspirations are clear, and reflect, *in nuce* Ficino's view: 'Our mind should be invaded by a kind of sacred ambition not to be contented with mediocrity, but to aspire to higher things, to force ourselves to attain them with all our energy from the moment we are able' (*De dignitate*, p.82). It is man's will which may give him that ability, and we shall find Pietro Bembo expressing similar views in Book IV of the *Cortegiano*. Pico also picks up Empedocles' ideas on the subject of the dual warring nature of man and the universe, and suggests that concord might be brought about by man's outstanding qualities of heart and mind. Leading on from that, he introduces the theme of civil discord, only to emphasise that 'we have grave internal struggles worse than civil wars, which only moral philosophy may sedate and compose if we wish to escape them and obtain that peace which would place us on high amongst the elect of the Lord'. The Renaissance Platonists, despite their frenzied creativity in the arts, aimed rather at a *contemplative* ideal, and, as a corollary, the political and social ideas worked out in Plato's *Republic* and *Laws* find relatively few commentators during this period.

The moral thought of Ficino and his followers was preoccupied with spiritual experience, with the need to ascend to a vision of the Divine, to lead the soul, through the Platonic degrees of knowledge and love, to that vision of God. Man and his soul were, for them, on the borderline between the intelligible and the eternal, and the visible and mortal universe, and his condition in life, according to the Platonists, may be determined by his moral and intellectual choice. The position may not seem very distant from that of Pomponazzi, but Pomponazzi's grim (for the Christian) conclusions are far removed from the aspirations of Pico and Ficino, who could see in Plato's *Phaedo* a 'proof' of the immortality of the soul. For the select few, the aims of the Platonists, to attain to the vision of the Divine, which Bembo is to exalt in Book IV of the *Cortegiano*, may be possible during their lives, but if *all* men were to be potential participants in such a divine vision, then the soul *had* to have an afterlife in order to give 'ordinary' mortals the necessary opportunity. The contemplative ideal is emphasised in the next section of Pico's *Oratio*. Theology was for him supreme in its ability to give peace, and, significantly, he quotes from St John's Gospel and from *Matthew*, xi, 28, 'Come unto me all ye that labour and are heavy laden, and I will give you rest', and the work concludes with an augury for peace, both civic and moral, which links the centuries between Marsilius of Padua (1275– c. 1343) and Castiglione. Although Pico was profoundly influenced by Ficino, notably by the *Theologia platonica*, he was not an exclusive Platonist, preferring what he called a blend of 'the Homeric eloquence of Plato' and the 'theory of Aristotle'. On the other hand, in an exchange of letters with Ermolao Barbaro, he is adversely criticised by Barbaro for not treating Aristoteleanism in its pure form, preferring to add the accretions of centuries of commentaries. But perhaps in Pico's appreciation of the empirical side of Aristoteleanism and his admiration for the poetic heights of which Platonism was capable, one sees something of Castiglione's attitude.

Ficino and his fellow-Platonists have had many tomes dedicated to their lives and work, and here this brief account must suffice. As far as Castiglione was concerned, Ficino's *Commentum* on Plato's *Symposium* was of paramount importance, for it is largely upon this commentary that Castiglione is generally assumed to have based the discourse on love he puts into the mouth of Pietro Bembo in Book IV. The work, which Ficino later translated into Italian and entitled *Dell'amore*, was begun in 1469 and published in 1474. It is true that the commentary lies at the basis of the second part of Book IV of Castiglione's masterpiece, and more specific references will be made to it during my discussion of the text. But what may prove equally interesting is to note those fashionable elements of Ficino's thought which are carried through into the *Asolani* published by Bembo in 1505 and imitated in the *Seconda redazione*, but which Castiglione decides deliberately to excise from his final version. We know that the excisions are deliberate because they are not made in the *Seconda redazione*. Hence in giving now a résumé of Ficino's views on Divine love, it is not my intention to produce a comprehensive or definitive view of those theories, but rather to highlight, by showing what Castiglione later omitted, the different (and perhaps more Christian and stoic) emphasis which Castiglione laid upon the theme. Certainly I hope to show that by omitting more fashionable aspects of the doctrine (the myth of the two Venuses, for instance), Castiglione may have had a more serious aim in mind than is usually suggested.

Ficino himself coined the phrase 'Platonic love' to describe the emotion or experience which forms the subject of his *Commentum*. But his theory of love is derived from several sources, most notably, of course, from Plato (from the *Symposium* and the *Phaedrus*) and from Plotinus' interpretations of Plato. At the same time, Ficino blends with these theories the Christian concept of love as elaborated by St Paul and St Augustine (*charitas* or ἀγαπή), Classical notions of friendship (the *amicitia* of Cicero) as well as interpretations of the courtly love of the poets of the *stil novo*. The commentary takes the form of a meeting of the Platonic Academy at Careggi on 7 November, traditionally the date of Plato's birth and death. There, seven speakers are given the task of discussing in seven *Orationes* the speeches made by characters in Plato's *Symposium*. In view of the impossibility of including all details of the discussions here, I have chosen a series of apophthegmatic statements to represent the main points of Ficino's thesis. Further discussion may be sought through items in the bibliography, and Nesca Robb and P. O. Kristeller may

here be mentioned as having provided particularly valuable information in their critical treatises. Ficino's work is divided formally into
the *Orationes*, which provide my points of reference.

The first *Oratio* treats of the origin and function of love, the most
ancient of the Gods. The created substance or essence of the universe
sprang directly from God's own mind. That substance turns back to
its Creator, with an innate longing for its origins, and is illumined and
shaped by Him in the forms of created objects (heavens, elements,
stars, metals, plants etc.). Those forms are Ficino's equivalent of
Platonic Ideas and were, he observes, given mythological names in
antiquity (Zeus represented heaven, Vulcan, fire etc.) (*Or.* I, ii). The
longing of created matter to turn back to its Creator is love. Orpheus
had confirmed the primary function of love when he placed love at
the heart of chaos, even before the creation of Saturn or Jove (*Or.*
I, i). Love is the desire for beauty (*Or.* I, iii). Love may convince men
with immediacy of the need to pursue the Good, and hence, operates
more quickly than many man-made institutions, such as legal and
philosophical systems, to set man on the path to virtue. Love may be
apprehended only by the mind, eye and ear, and desires only temperate, modest and honourable objects, while physical, sensual
desires are 'madness' (*rabies venerea*) not love (*Or.* I, iii). As a corollary,
corporeal beauty alone is not enough and produces only fleeting
satisfaction, whereas the conjunction of a beautiful soul in a beautiful
body produces 'vehement admiration' (*Or.* I, iii). Love inspires
Goodness because the lover always desires to be worthy of and
respected by his beloved. God (and Goodness) is at the centre of four
circles: Mind, Soul, Nature and Matter, and in all of them Divine
Beauty is diffused (*Or.* II, iii); hence the lover desires not corporeal
beauty, but the divine splendour infused into the beloved object
(*Or.* II, vi). There was a tradition of two Venuses, the first, Venus
Urania, daughter of Celios, the second, daughter of Zeus and Dione.
The first had no mother and is not associated with matter, the second
is concerned with generation. The first contemplates Divine Beauty
and diffuses it into the second, who transmits it to the material world.
The soul has two powers, which correspond to the two Venuses –
powers of contemplation and of generation. Only when *Venus
volgare* usurps the place of *Urania* does evil ensue (*Or.* II, vi). Love
springs from the lover's recognition of some affinity between himself
and his beloved (*Or.* II, ix). Love is the moving and harmonising
force of the universe, and such 'sins' as envy derive from an excessive
love of self, or such 'conflicts' as those between fire and water are

simply the love or desire of water to extend its own coldness by spreading it to fire (*Or.* III, iv). Art and learning are impossible without love. It is essential for love to exist between master and pupil, between pupil and his work and between all learners and truth. All art is an expression of love, since it imposes order on chaos, brings harmony from disparate elements (*Or.* III, iv). By exercising the cardinal virtues, the soul may, in a man's years of discretion, begin to understand its true position in the universe, and aspire to know its Architect (*Or.* IV, iii). Love is the best and most beautiful of things. It desires beauty, and it is endowed with wisdom, strength, foresight, mutual contentment, peace and happiness. There are two daemons in man's soul, the extremes of love being the superior daemon, who stimulates to the eternal love of contemplating Divine Beauty, and the inferior, concerned with the 'occult stimulus' to generate children (*Or.* VI, viii). Profane love is a kind of madness and may be overcome by various means (including alcohol). Divine love is the noblest of the divine *furores*, which awaken and harmonise the soul, through the incantation of poetry, the purification of prayer and sacrifice (*Or.* VII, xiii). And the chapter which eulogises love most (VII, xvi) is full of Classical allusions to the characters of Plato's academy. The concluding chapter is a paean of praise to Socratic love.

Ficino's death in 1499 brought an end to the informal meetings in his villa at Careggi. The role of Academicians passed to the learned men who met in the gardens of the Rucellai family (the *Orti Oricellari*) and Ficino's traditions were continued there, notably by his pupil, Francesco Cattani da Diacceto, whose *Tre libri d'amore* follow Ficino's treatment of Platonic love. The *Asolani*, published by Bembo in 1505, also show strong (if more 'fashionable') Ficinian influences, and echoes of both Cattani and Bembo are present in the *Cortegiano*. Further, as late as 1525, Castiglione was trying to obtain a copy of Leone Ebreo's *Dialoghi d'amore*. In view of the tradition of social discussion of such topics, it is probable that his own discourse also reflects current discussion of Leone's views. For these and other similar treatises, reference will be made to the text of the *Cortegiano*. But before leaving Ficino altogether, it is worth emphasising again his immense influence on succeeding generations, whether or not his philosophy (with its naive acceptance of Zoroaster and Orpheus, for example, as authentic philosophers) was 'impure'. His *De amore* survives in at least nineteen codices in its original form, and nine in its vernacular form, an indication of its early popularity. In the following century the *De amore* ran into twenty editions. Further aspects of his philosophy are described in R. Marcel's study.

Bembo's discourse on love is introduced with the casual grace which usually accompanies important topics. Gasparo Pallavicino begins the new episode with a reminder that, the evening before, they had left the subject of love in abeyance. Since wisdom, so necessary in advising princes, almost invariably comes with age, he continues, is it not incongruous that a courtier of advancing years should, as was suggested the previous evening, fall in love? The debate starts with the positing of the Aristotelean extremes: Ottaviano says that it would be a sad deprivation if the ageing courtier weren't allowed to love; Gasparo counters in his usual misogynous way with the opposite extreme, that to be free of love's perturbations is one perfection more in their perfect courtier. Bembo proposes a *via media*, that the older man, thanks to his acquired wisdom, would not feel the excesses of despair which young lovers usually experience, and can derive an enjoyment from love which the young can almost never experience.

The Duchess next gives Bembo the task of expounding this *felice amore*, and, with some courteous and witty demurrings ('I wouldn't like the ladies to think me old if I defended the right of old men to love!' – (IV, l), Bembo calms his thoughts for a moment in silence. He then explains that he must expatiate on the nature of love itself if he is to maintain his thesis of *felice amore*, and, after a brief acknowledgment to philosophers who have carried the Platonic tradition, Bembo repeats the definition found in Plato's *Symposium* (XXIII), that 'Love is the desire for beauty'. Cian's notes show how Castiglione's sentiments here are word for word repetitions of Ficino's *Dell'amore* (I, iv), and are also found in Francesco Cattani's *Tre libri d'amore* (I, vii), Bembo's *Asolani* (III) and in Mario Equicola's *Di natura d'amore* (II). For further discussion, a reference to Cian's edition may suffice (cp. ibid., p.472).

Desire, then, may be for Good, but it can only arise for things which we *know,* and needs guidance. Man has three ways of obtaining such guiding knowledge, through senses, reason and intellect. Sensual perception is a faculty which we have in common with animals and it produces sensual appetite; rational thought is a characteristic of man, and allows us choice, while the intellect is a quality which man has in common with the angels, and the intellect generates our will. The theory is one common to the Platonists and finds particularly elegant expression in Bembo's *Asolani*, III, xiii, during the Hermit's discourse to Lavinello. Man can be drawn to beauty on any of these three levels, but mere physical possession of a loved object indicates that the lover has been deceived by an overemphasis on the lower level of consciousness. Such love is either fleeting – indeed, may on occasions result in hatred of the beloved (as if the sensual appetite repents and feels resentful at the deception worked upon it by the false judgement of the senses) or it remains unsatisfied, a miserable ever-present craving. Such love is almost exclusively experienced by the young. The irrational passion they have in common with animals, but, in addition, they experience greater (spiritual) disturbances.

It is notable that Castiglione's vocabulary here contains many allusions to the idea that, without *true* knowledge of beauty and love, man's senses lead him astray. Proportionately he seems to devote much more space to that concept than Ficino (cp. *Oratio*, II, vi), who writes on the *Passions of lovers*, or Bembo, who allows Perottino to inveigh against love in his *Asolani*, I, ix, and his Hermit to describe the deceptive nature of the senses in *Asolani*, III (*passim*). Cattani devoted only one line to 'that which the power of perception judges to be good' (cp. Cian, ed. cit., p.472). On the other hand, the older courtier allows his appetites to be directed by reason, and he has none of the resentment and all of the blessings which result from possession of beauty. If the young succeed in attaining this degree of beatitude, they are indeed divine, and even if they fail, they may be excused on the grounds of their youth. If the mature adult is forced by sensual appetite into irrational love, he reduces himself to the same level as unthinking animals (xlix–liv). Castiglione's compassion for the young differs from similar statements made in the *Asolani*, which merely state that 'Those men who despise mortal things are as gods...' (III, xvii). His condemnation of the mature adult, on the other hand, is harsher than Bembo's (cp. ibid.).

As is the case with other major topics, Castiglione allows detractors and sceptics to break in and voice their opposition to the main speaker. Here Morello, the cynic, seizes on a pause in Bembo's discourse to suggest that such beauty is no more than a dream. As for Bembo's point about beauty being naturally good, he had known several wicked but very beautiful women: beauty had made them proud and pride had made them cruel. Giuliano de' Medici reinforces Morello's implication that beauty and goodness are not necessarily concomitants one of the other (lv–lvi). Thus Bembo is led on to a defence of the thesis that beauty and goodness are identifiable, since beauty is, as it were, a circle, with good at its centre. That was an idea which Marsilio Ficino emphasised in his commentary and it seems to have provided Castiglione with his subject here. Ficino's *Oratio*, II, iii, for instance, has as its sub-heading: 'Beauty is the splendour of divine goodness and God is the centre of four circles'.

Rather uncharacteristically, Bembo goes on to state that the ugly are wicked and the beautiful are good, since their inner character influences their external appearance, and if the beautiful are occasionally wicked, the fault usually lies outside themselves (poverty, an importunate lover etc.). Bembo adds a caution that our eyes may wrongly judge beauty, since they are fallible like any other sense organ and deceive us (lix–lx). This statement may be an attempt by Castiglione to add verisimilitude to his account, as may be the lovely analogies from nature (a bird's wing, leaves on a tree etc.) and from man's own creations (ships, buildings etc.), which we know are beautiful *and* good. Yet the tradition was one which Ficino himself had accepted from Plato and Plotinus. His commentary on the latter's *De pulchritudine* states as much: 'Ugliness is a kind of grim face of evil' (ibid., chapter II). As for the notion that beauty is the result of graceful proportions, this is also found in Bembo's *Asolani*, III, vi, where Lavinello declares that 'Beauty is nothing other than a gracefulness (*grazia*) which springs in things from their proportion, appropriateness and harmony'. And Bembo there applies the same criteria to the harmonious soul as to the well-proportioned body, just as Castiglione is to do next. The language with which Castiglione praises the world and its beauty deserves particular comment for its elegance. In turn the beauty of the universe is a fit setting for his placing the microcosm (*picciol mondo*), Man, at its centre. The world is fair and man is a microcosm of the world and our instinct that this beauty is good is a true one. Beauty is the highest sign of the soul's victory over the material.

In chapter lx the discussion is interrupted again, this time by the conversational wit of Cesare Gonzaga. Bembo then adds that the point which Gasparo had made earlier, about the ageing courtier's being able to fall in love, has been answered, and he prepares to withdraw from the debate. He is pressed to continue by the Duchess, anxious to hear more about perfect love. Bembo expounds further on the higher level of love under the guidance of reason (lxi); he attempts a scientific-psychological analysis of the process of love's generation in man, following very closely the ideas of Ficino (cp. *Or.* VI, vi, entitled 'How we are caught by love'). In particular he imitates Ficino's idea of the senses of sight and hearing (as well as thought) being the true pabulum of love, while man's more 'earthy' senses (smell, taste, touch) provoke, not love, but *libido, rabiesque* (cp. *Or.* I, iv). In such a way the courtier and his lady may attain to felicity: 'the desire of both will be most honest and in harmony, and, in consequence, they will achieve great happiness' (IV, lxii). Morello seizes another pause to suggest cynically that to generate a beautiful child in a beautiful woman is effectively 'generating beauty in beauty'.

In chapter lxiv Bembo describes the Platonic kiss, in an attempt to convince his audience that even such apparent sensuality may be sublime, as Solomon had declared in the *Song of Songs*, I, 2: 'let him kiss me with the kisses of his mouth'. This citation may be another verisimilitudinous touch (for Castiglione believed that the song was an allegory of things divine). Yet it is true that many critics here feel that Castiglione is *not* convincing and seems to be simply reflecting a favourite Neoplatonic theory of the age. One influential critic, Nesca Robb, goes as far as to say that *throughout* his discourse on love, Castiglione is unconvincing. This, she implies, was because the discourse was a fashionable addition to complete the gamut of topics favoured by contemporary conversation. Certainly there are unlikely tracts, even though Castiglione did accept them from Neoplatonic tradition, such as the identification of beauty with goodness. Even more unconvincing is the theory that kissing, for the 'rational' lover, is compatible with honest or Platonic love, while it is not so for the sensual lover. That Castiglione felt these sections to be awkward is in part demonstrated by the sophistries which he has to adduce to prove his case, as, for example, in the following argument: 'The rational lover realises that although the mouth is part of the body, nevertheless it is through the mouth that one gives egress to words (which are the interpreters of the soul) as well as to that inner spirit which is itself called soul.' Hence kissing lends delight, not because of any 'dishonourable desire thus aroused' but rather because of the mingling of souls, 'and the kiss may therefore be called a joining of soul rather than of body' (*più presto congiungimento d'anima che di corpo*) (IV, lxiv). The sophistry is lent support by two quotations, one attributed to Plato, the second culled from the *Song of Solomon*, as noted above.

Cian also compares the notion of joining soul to soul with the treatment of the theme in Pontano's *Lepidina*, and Pontano, we know (if only because he was so often deliberately excised from the final edition) was a poet familiar to Castiglione. Justification for the kiss has also been seen as a justification for the unhappily married woman (or even the unmarried woman playing at courtly love) to indulge in what seems, but is not, sensual joy outside marriage. I believe this to be an unlikely explanation for Castiglione's introduction of the theme, even though, subsequently, it may have been used by 'adulterous' lovers as an excuse. I prefer to see the 'lover's kiss' of chapter lxiv as a rare weak point in Castiglione's argument.

Further arguments are advanced to stress the need for spiritual rather than physical love. The awe of the lover in the presence of his beloved is reverence in the presence of divine beauty (iv, lxv). The notion is one not far from the morally uplifting effect of love as witnessed in the *stilnovisti*, and again reflects a passage from Ficino's *Commentum* (*Or.* ii, vi). Spiritual love of the beloved's beauty, for instance, implies that, in the imagination one can continue to enjoy that beauty even in the absence of the loved object, whereas to the 'physical' lover such absences bring pain, sorrow and tears. From such an imaginative contemplation of abstract beauty, the step is made easier for Castiglione to ascend to a higher plane of theorising, as Plato had done in the *Symposium* (xxvii–xxix) and to urge the contemplation of the idea of beauty (again another Ficinian notion). The notion that the imagination was the 'faculty' most appropriate for learning was an ancient one. Perhaps here Castiglione is himself influenced, if not inspired, by that idea to rise artistically from the sensory to the intellectual and spiritual plane. Even so, such contemplation still involves the imagination, which, being fed largely by sensory perception, has fallible corporeal elements which will obscure the ultimate vision of beauty. This is the penultimate step in achieving perfect felicity. By continuing to follow the guidance of the loving principle, the lover may next ascend to a higher intellectual level. There the soul 'not only entirely abandons the senses, but no longer needs the discourse of reason...enjoying that true happiness which is incomprehensible to the senses'. From *Oratio*, vi, xv, onwards, Ficino's commentary, too, had taken on a more specifically mystic character as he talked of theological hierarchies, rising through body, soul, angels and God. The language there becomes more abstract, and the style more arid, smacking rather of Thomist theology. Castiglione now goes beyond what either Bembo or Ficino had written, and his conviction seems stronger. His language is more enthusiastic and less abstract than Ficino's, and the argument rises above the static, fashionable discussion which Bembo had presented in his *Asolani*. Plato had gone little further in his *Symposium*. He concluded that man should proceed from the love of a beautiful form to the perception and love of universal divine beauty. At that point in the Platonic dialogue Alcibiades enters, drunk, and delivers a eulogy of Socrates (whose ugly exterior is, incidentally, said by Alcibiades to conceal such divine attributes, such charm and wisdom!).

Castiglione's language at this point becomes not only mystic, but increasingly more Christian. Biblical quotations liberally besprinkle Bembo's sentences. Dante and Petrarch are cited and Neoplatonic images abound. The love which allows men to contemplate divine beauty was manifested, Bembo continues, in the flames which ensured the immortality of Hercules (an allusion taken from Ovid, *Metamorphoses*, IX, 152), in the burning bush of Moses, the tongues of fire of the Apostles and the blazing chariot of Elijah. And so, in contemplation, we may rise to the sublime dwelling-place, 'wherein abides the heavenly, beloved and true beauty which is hidden in the inner sanctum of God, where profane eyes may not see it; and here we shall find the most blissful goal of our desires, true repose from our labours, an unfailing remedy in our wretchedness, a health-giving medicine in our infirmity and the safest of harbours in the turbulent storms of the tempestuous seas of this life' (IV, lxix). And in the following chapter this '*santissimo Amore*' is panegyrised as the intermediary between earth and heaven, the harmonising power of the universe, the source of true pleasure, 'in short, the beginning and end of all good'. As Bembo invokes such Holy love, there is nothing to distinguish his address from a prayer to the Christian God: 'Deign to hear our prayers, lord, infuse thyself into our hearts, and, with the light of thy most holy fire, illumine our darkness, and like a trusted guide in this blind labyrinth, show us the true path.' Bembo's discourse is almost at an end, his language becomes more and more redolent of the New Testament: 'after our long delirium, grant us the true and well-founded Good'...'the inexhaustible fount of contentment which ever delights and never sates'...'purge our eyes of the darkness of their ignorance with the rays of thy light'...'finally let us die a most happy and vital death, as those ancient Patriarchs died, whose souls thou, through the most ardent virtue of contemplation, snatched from their bodies and united with God'.

Bembo's eulogy is ended, but interesting things are yet to be revealed. The sequence is as follows: Bembo is 'beside himself' (*fuori di sè*) with the vehemence of his invocation. He is brought back to earth when Emilia Pia tugs at the folds of his robe and warns him that he is distracted enough to be in danger of separating his own soul from body because of the thoughts he's been expressing. A general discussion breaks out. The book is within a few moments of its ending, and though Bembo is urged to continue, he considers that he has penetrated as far as is allowable in his analysis of this Divine love: 'perhaps it is not lawful to speak further of this matter' (*non è forse licito parlar più di questa materia*) (IV, lxxi). As part of the subsequent back-chat, Gasparo Pallavicino adds his usual anti-feminist view, in this case that only *men* experienced this Divine love, men such as Plato, Socrates, Plotinus, St Francis, St Stephen and St Paul. Giuliano de' Medici denies Gasparo's allegation, adducing Socrates' statement that all the secrets revealed by him in the *Symposium* (cp. ibid., XXII–XXIX) had been taught him by the priestess Diotima. Giuliano also recalls the Christian women mentioned by him on the previous evening and to their number adds Mary Magdalen, who had loved so strongly that her sins were forgiven her. And there the discussion ends.

With consummate skill Castiglione then concludes his book with a brief lyrical description. He introduces this last with his usual apparent artlessness when the Duchess says that it is so late that any further discussion must be postponed until the following evening. 'You mean until this evening', says Cesare Gonzaga, pointing to the light which was creeping in through the windows. The discussion had taken them through until dawn. The windows are thrown open and they observe the sunrise: 'They saw a beautiful rose-pink dawn already born in the east, and all the stars had disappeared except for the sweet ruler of the sky of Venus, which marks the confines of night and of day' (*Videro già esser nata in oriente una bella aurora di color di rose e tutte le stelle sparite, fuor che la dolce governatrice del ciel di Venere, che della notte e del giorno tiene i confini*). How much more subtle is this introduction of a celestial Venus than the traditional discussion of a mythical Venus Urania (and her counterpart, Venus daughter of Dione) which is usually found in other exponents of these ideas and this philosophy. The dawn chorus begins, and the company disperses. Emilia Pia has the final word of the book as she looks forward to the discussions which are in prospect for the coming evening. With this anticlimactic ending the treatise concludes, as casually as it had begun.

The disquisition on love has generally been regarded as a late addition (at least a late rewriting), inserted perhaps for reasons of contemporary cultural fashion, perhaps to complement Fregoso's discourse and add seriousness. It *was* a later rewriting (as we may see from the *Seconda redazione*), it *does* introduce a fashionable topic, Neoplatonic love, and it certainly adds profundity to what had gone before. But Bembo's discourse must have a more serious intention than these rather superficial suggestions if the *Cortegiano* as a whole is to be granted a serious purpose. The care with which Castiglione went through the earlier drafts, rewriting and rearranging, not simply with the object of greater elegance, means that he must be given credit for a more momentous aim. Only recently has an attempt been made, by Wayne Rebhorn, to see the discourse as a truly integral part of the work of art, providing, Rebhorn suggests, a higher aspiration for the courtier than the closed round of court-life, and the relative trivia of social accomplishments, pointing out the need for truthful vision and allowing the courtier continuing and higher ambitions of self-improvement. One might add that this is in full accord with the Aristotelean principles which Castiglione has consistently enounced throughout the book.

Aristotle's famous conclusion to the *Nicomachean Ethics* was that 'we must not follow those who tell us that as we are men we should have human aspirations, as we are mortal we should have mortal ambitions; on the contrary, we must, as far as lies within our power, make ourselves immortal, do everything we can to live in accordance with the best that is in us'. Before moving on from Aristotle, it would help our future understanding of the case if we briefly recalled here the contrast between Platonic and Aristotelean attitudes to the contemplative philosopher. Both are agreed that this is the highest level which man may achieve; it exalts him to the level of the gods themselves. Plato argued that for the philosopher who had achieved those dizzy heights, having experienced the 'highest form of knowledge' and ascended to 'the vision of Good', to be forced thereafter to indulge in practical activities (particularly the practicalities of government) was a lowering of his felicity. Aristotle had argued that practical activity is undertaken in order to obtain leisure, while philosophical activity is an end in itself, but he takes the virtues associated with practical activities to be both human and acceptable in his scheme of things, and his contemplatives benefit their fellow-men (in a non-compulsory manner) with the aid of their additional wisdom. Nevertheless, one must re-emphasise here the superiority of philosophical activity in Aristotle's scheme of things. To theorise or contemplate (and $\Theta\epsilon\omega\rho\epsilon\hat{\iota}\nu$ in this context is the same concept as 'to contemplate') the philosopher needs only his own intellect (and a minimal amount of sustenance), whereas to exercise one's other virtues one needs one's fellow-men. Thus to practise justice one needs one's fellows to whom to be just, etc. These ideas are certainly contained in Bembo's discourse on love, but Castiglione has an even profounder purpose.

During the informal conversation that concluded Bembo's discourse, the anti-feminist Pallavicino behaves in a predictable way by adducing the names of men who have undergone this divine experience. This casually provides the *Cortegiano*'s reader with the sort of concrete exemplars of divine lovers that Castiglione wants his audience to appreciate as having had the experiences described. Plato, Socrates and Plotinus are passed over quickly. (Fregoso simply says: 'Many men, such as Plato, Socrates and Plotinus and many others.') Much more time and space is devoted to the three specifically Christian mystics, Saints Paul, Stephen and Francis. Of St Paul, for instance, it is said: 'Nothing but the virtue of love was able to sweep the Apostle Paul up to the vision of those secrets which it is not lawful for a man to utter' (*Né altro che virtù d'amor poteva rapire San Paulo apostolo alla visione di quei secreti di che non è licito all'uomo parlare*) (IV, lxxii). The same list of Christian ecstatics includes an allusion to St Stephen, 'who was shown the opened heavens'. Gasparo's allusion to St Paul, and Bembo's earlier statement (*non è forse licito parlar più*) are unacknowledged quotations from the New Testament, in particular II *Corinthians*, XII, 1–5, where Paul writes: 'How that he was caught up into paradise and heard unspeakable words, which it is not lawful for a man to utter.' (The allusion to Stephen is another unacknowledged quotation, from *Acts*, VII, 56). Castiglione seems, much more specifically than his contemporaries, to be equating his Platonic or Neoplatonic love with the message of St Paul. This theme will return; we may now look with profit at the contrasting treatment in the *Seconda redazione*.

To begin with, there are none of those mystic references in the earlier version. Particulars of the love experience (how to assess whether a woman is in love, the power of the eyes as indicators or stimulators of love, how public opinion can cause esteem to grow and produce love, etc.) comprise by far the most extensive part of the discussion there. Bembo is deliberately and specifically introduced as the author of the *Asolani*: 'having written of and expressed so divinely in his *Asolani* the beauty of true beauty and the divinity of love' (*avendo esso nelli suoi Asolani scritto et espresso così divinamente la bellezza della vera bellezza e la divinitate d'amore*) (*Seconda redazione*, p.299). Camillo Palleotto, an interlocutor later excluded from the definitive edition, declares that they all know the *Asolani* ('I believe that there is no one among us who has not read them [the *Asolani*]' (ibid.) and urges Bembo, 'Repeat, then, live, what you have written' (*Dite,*

*adonque voi con la voce viva quello che avete scripto*) (ibid., p.300).
Bembo labours the point by asking 'You would, perhaps, like me to
recite a book here?' (*Vorreste voi forsi ch'io qui vi recitassi un libro?*).
And although Duchess Elisabetta politely says that Bembo has knowledge additional to his book, his brief discourse there *is* a reiteration
of part of the subject-matter of the *Asolani*.

The old Neoplatonist paraphernalia is introduced, particularly the
myth about the two Venuses, Celestial Venus, the superior love, born
of heaven, and *Venere vulgare*, Common or Garden Venus, born of
Zeus and Dione, the first stimulating to heavenly love, the inferior
to corporeal love. The only novelty about the discussion here lies in
the questions which the courtiers put to Bembo at appropriate
moments, though the questions tend to be of a specific nature (How
can one hide a dishonest love affair? etc.), and effectively prevent an
uninterrupted 'universal discourse' of the type we find in the definitive
edition. And though Bembo does praise the 'most holy love which
imparts grace to the world and which I [Bembo] have adored from
my earliest years in a manner different from that of the profane and
sordid masses' (ibid., p.313), nevertheless the effect, even here, is to
make his speech much more of a convention, part of the stock in trade
of the cultivated individual. Only by being presented by Bembo is it
saved from a possible charge of superficial, second-hand *kultur*.
Indeed there is a strong hint that fifty per cent of the discourse is
largely a matter of common sense, for when discussing the theory of
the beautiful being good and the ugly, wicked, Camillo says: 'Indeed
to expatiate a lot in praise of beauty seems superfluous to me, since
everyone knows that there is nothing in the world which is naturally
so pleasing and desirable as beauty and nothing so vexatious as ugliness' (*Ma invero estendersi molto in laude della bellezza parmi superfluo,
perché ognuno sa che al mondo cosa non è che naturalmente sia tanto grata e
desiderabile quanto la bellezza, né tanto molesta quanto la bruttezza*) (ibid.,
p.292). Yet there the discussion continues for many pages.

In the definitive edition Castiglione deliberately extracted the
higher vision of love from the particulars surrounding it, and placed
it in the supreme position in his book, just as the political material was
given a grade of only fractionally less importance. Why did he choose
the notion of Divine love as the culminating point of his book? For
the purpose of argument it will be here assumed (though I consider it
a self-evident truth) that Castiglione had a serious purpose in
rewriting the *Cortegiano*. Rebhorn, in the article cited, suggested that
the emphasis laid in Bembo's discourse on seeing the truth, picks up

and answers what he calls the question of 'deception' with which the courtier's life (and court life generally) is so concerned. Truth is certainly a strong element in the speech.

There are constant allegorical hints for men to seek the true love; deceived (*ingannati*) by an appearance of love, the sensualist experiences only unhappy passion (cp. lii); the senses are deceiving (*fallaci*) (liii); reason must correct the wickedness (*nequicia*) of the senses, etc. Amid the welter of criticism which sees the discourse as fashionable Platonism, Rebhorn's thesis is a pleasure to read. Yet it may not present the whole picture. The earlier part of Book IV has also been concerned with warnings against deceit, untrustworthy adulation and the like, and with specific declarations such as the need for the courtier always to tell his master the truth (cp. above, p.132). Furthermore, although the truth is generally sustained against the deceptiveness of the senses, there are weak points in the argument, such as the equation of goodness with external beauty, or the emphasis laid on the lover's kiss. It could be argued that Castiglione's thesis *is* weak in those instances. But the question of truth may be said to be satisfied by the stage of reason (reached in IV, lxiv), the rational love, in other words, which allows us to discern and choose true from false love. The mysticism of the following important chapters would then be a reinforcement of the argument and little else, and the advice would be concerned not with Aristotle's *final cause* (the perfection of the individual) but with the 'apotheosis' of a further piece of advice to his lord. Truth, Goodness, Beauty, Love are divided, if they are divided at all, by a very thin line at the metaphysical level of the discourse on love, but there would seem to be more to the book's purpose.

Castiglione has been instructing his courtier on means of attaining perfection. Perfection as a courtier, however, is not his *final cause*. It is a means to further ends. In particular he needs perfection in order to approach his master, become his firm favourite and, without fear of the consequences, give candid advice. The giving of advice is, in turn, still not the final cause, though the establishment of a peaceable society through the wise counsel offered to the ruler of that society is certainly a good aim, as is a concomitant of that peaceable society, namely tranquillity for the individual courtier. But the final cause, the ultimate perfection of the courtier, is the contemplative ideal of Aristotle added to the Christian aspiration to a paradise after death, when our souls are joined with God: 'Finally, let us die a most happy and vital death' (*In ultimo moriamo di felicissima e vital morte*) (iv, lxx). Fregoso's polemic in the earlier part of Book iv destroyed the foppish ideal which had been elaborated during the earlier three Books, and propounded, instead, a clever court chancellor, aware of the apparent ineptitude of certain accomplishments, but willing to accept the need for such triviality if it could help the cause of justice and public good; in themselves, these attributes are not incompatible with goodness, discretion and wisdom (cp. iv, xlviii). Bembo's intervention is equally important from the point of view of undermining the earlier triviality, but his advice may even attenuate the seriousness of Fregoso's statements.

The best parallel for the situation is the advice of St Paul in I *Corinthians*, which enjoins upon his flock certain worthy precepts, only to attenuate their relative importance in the conclusion to his twelfth chapter. With the exception of Paul's final chapter (which is a practical description of his projected journey to Corinth and a list of visiting preachers) the rest of the *Epistle* is concerned with a rising crescendo in praise of love. Parallels between Bembo's discourse and the letter are striking. When the Duchess urges Bembo to talk about his truly felicitous love, she adds that 'It may be one of the most *important* and *useful* attributes yet assigned to the courtier' (*forse sarà una della più importanti ed utili condicioni che per ancora gli siano attribuite*) (iv, l). 'And yet shew I unto you a more excellent way,' says St Paul (I *Corinthians*, xii) and the whole of chapter thirteen of his letter is relevant to what Bembo has to say. Despite all the advice given by St Paul to the Christian, the man who has not charity (love, ἀγαπή) is 'as sounding brass or a tinkling cymbal'. For the courtier who does not see through superficiality to the purpose of all his behaviour and activity, the attributes he has are no more than '*leggerezze e vanità*' (frivolities and vanity) (iv, iv). And although Bembo's speech, as we have seen, was in the Neoplatonic mould, positing an ideal which need not necessarily be a Christian ideal (which in the secular context of Castiglione's volume and the repressive religious atmosphere of the time could have been regarded by his superiors as blasphemous) it does give to the courtier's and to mankind's existence a purpose beyond the trivia of superficial and fashionable behaviour and even beyond the more important political aspirations mentioned by Ottaviano. It complements the active life of the political adviser with the contemplative ideal of the man who had won his war, and yet it does even more than this, for it puts off childish things and shows the adult higher aspirations.

Only after the shock of Fregoso's intervention had a suitable point been reached for Bembo's more mature advice. And here again Paul has a relevant word to the wise: 'And I, brethren, could not speak unto you as unto spiritual, but as unto carnal, even as unto babes in Christ. I have fed you with milk, and not with meat: for hitherto ye were not able to bear it' (1 *Corinthians*, III). Bembo has moved on from 'the things which young lovers do' (IV, xlix), which, Gasparo says, would bring ridicule upon the head of an Aristotle, to aspire to immortality. St Paul's charity or love, we have seen, may well have been understood by Castiglione as the ideal at which Bembo is aiming in his discourse. Paul says that without love (charity), as he conceives of it, a man is nothing:

Charity suffereth long and is kind; charity envieth not; charity vaunteth not itself, is not puffed up.

Doth not behave itself unseemly, seeketh not her own, is not easily provoked, thinketh no evil;

Rejoiceth not in iniquity, but rejoiceth in the truth;

Beareth all things, believeth all things, hopeth all things, endureth all things.

Charity never faileth.   (1 *Corinthians*, XIII)

All the evidence we have of Castiglione's life and character indicate that those statements applied very strictly to him after his early advance to maturity. His life seems to have been governed by those precepts. St Paul had earlier described his efforts to put over the gospel message: 'I am made all things to all men that I might, by all means save some' (ibid., x), an echo of which is to be found in the notion (stressed by Burckhardt) that the courtier must have every conceivable advantage to put over his image. And St Paul had earlier urged 'Know ye not that they which run in a race run all, but one receiveth the prize? So run, that ye may obtain' (ibid.), an idea similar to one which Castiglione had borne in mind from the outset of his work, though *his* simile is that of archers aiming at a target (Dedicatory letter, iii). If we add to St Paul's advice Aristotle's aspirations to immortality: 'as far as lies within our power, make ourselves immortal, do everything we can to live in accordance with the best that is in us', we have something approaching the ideal which Castiglione set himself and advised for his fellows, and which he might again see confirmed in St Paul: 'So when this corruptible shall have put on incorruption and this mortal shall have put on immortality, then shall be brought to pass the saying that is written, Death is swallowed up in victory' (1 *Corinthians*, xv). Bembo's *'felicissima e vital morte'* is probably a reflection of that Christian notion, but Castiglione's 'happiness' was assured even without a Christian paradise. Paradise for Castiglione, as for Aristotle, would have been an added bonus, just as a cardinalate would have offered him contingent comfort, but he probably needed neither, the perfect example of Aristotle's self-sufficient contemplative. And in the political context of the years following 1527, when the *courtly* advice might have been useless, the courtier's striving can be seen to have a goal which was independent of courtly success.

# Conclusion

In an early and subsequently discarded preface to the *Cortegiano*, Castiglione suggests that, for centuries, there had existed 'this kind of men whom we call "courtiers" (*questa sorte d'uomini che noi chiamiamo 'Cortegiani'*). He goes on to say that 'only recently has a profession been made of this court service, if we can call it that, only recently has it been refined to an art and a discipline' (*da non molto tempo in qua fattasi tra gli uomini professione di questa Cortegiania, per dire così, e riduttasi quasi in arte e disciplina*) (Serassi I, p.193). His conscious, but semi-apologetic use of the term *cortegiania* almost as a neologism (*per così dire*), in the sense of 'professional courtiership', marks a new grasp of the contemporary situation; his consequent codifying of the necessary professional qualifications marks a novel departure from traditional views on the training or education of the individual. In the two hundred years which run between Leonbattista Alberti's *Della famiglia* (1433–40) and the *Avvertimenti necessari per i cortigiani* of Niccolò Strozzi (c. 1640) society's 'gentleman' found it necessary to adapt his qualifications to meet ever-changing political situations. Increasingly, talents are cultivated not to create the ideal of a fifteenth-century *uomo universale*, but to achieve a successful career in what might broadly be termed diplomacy. Whereas Alberti and his early contemporaries, such as Vergerio, Guarino and Vittorino could permit the cultured individual the luxury of self-perfection for its own sake (though even they had their own practical considerations) this was no longer feasible by the end of the century. The many trivial accomplishments detailed by Castiglione could have been, and often had been, ignored with impunity by the universal men of the earlier Renaissance. Castiglione's contemporaries, by contrast, simply could not afford to ignore any possible preparation which might ingratiate them with a patron and so ensure for themselves a relatively safe haven. It was a period when, outside the protective confines of the court, for the sophisticated individual, there existed only chaos and danger. The development is even more striking by the time Tasso composed his dialogue on the court, *Il Malpiglio* (c. 1586). There, adulation and sycophancy are taken for granted as obvious requirements, almost, indeed, as professional qualifications in themselves, and Tasso, aware of this, often comments on the contrast between the tone of his own precepts and those of Castiglione. Just fifty years after Tasso's dialogue, in Niccolò Strozzi's private admonitions, ingratiation and deceptive adulation are essential requirements, while cultural attributes and qualifications are completely ignored in favour of practical and often less scrupulous means of obtaining and maintaining a secure position at court.

Changed attitudes had been largely brought about during the five years between 1494 and 1499 which marked the beginning of foreign domination in the peninsula. When, in 1499, Castiglione witnessed the triumphant entry of the French under Louis XII into Milan, he became aware that the old order had ended. The small court, such as that of Ludovico *il Moro*, was no longer a practical unit without wider coalitions. After 1500, the great powers (and a stricter moral code) increasingly ensured that no upstart minor dynasties could be newly created, as had been possible earlier under the vigorous leadership of families like the Visconti, Sforza, Gonzaga and Montefeltro. At the same time, individuals, such as Castiglione, would, even more than in the previous century, be destined to obscurity (and probably disaster) without the protective power-base which a court could provide. The French invasion, added to the uncertainty following the death of his patron Guidubaldo, stimulated Baldesar to devise contingency plans both for himself and for his fellow-noblemen.

It is Vincenzo Calmeta who remarks in Book II that if you happen to be a gentleman serving at certain courts there is little you can do to change your situation, 'like an unfortunate bird born in a grim valley' (II, xxii). Calmeta is there fulfilling the role of the *advocatus diaboli*. Castiglione refused to believe that view. He has different lessons to impart: men are not birds, imprinted on their environment, and the courtier has to learn those graces and attributes which make him acceptable anywhere, give him the freedom to change his environment as necessary. The notion of freedom in society, for the courtier willing to cultivate his own gifts, runs through the discussion in Book II on whether to obey one's lord in all things. Here reflection upon the bitter experiences of some of the most famous courtiers of the Renaissance is important. The contrast between, say, the invective against court-life of an Aretino, or the irritation felt by a Piccolomini or a Della Casa, and their simultaneous need to belong to such a group, stresses the harshness of the world outside the court. In the compromise effected between independence and security, we can discern greater and more realistic political judgement than in almost any of the contemporary suggestions made in specifically political treatises. Compromise, rather than idealism, is the norm in Castiglione, and to help achieve it he imparts a further lesson – that of stoicism. The physical rigours of the courtly life described by Enea Silvio Piccolomini in his *De curialium miseriis* required more than a fair degree of resignation to one's lot if they were to be endured. Even the minor irritations of the diplomatic society described by Giovanni Della Casa were enough to drive him to distraction and provoke the grumpy, if amusing, advice to his nephew contained in the *Galateo*, the other etiquette book which survives, with the *Cortegiano*, to be read today.

Yet the most splendid minds of the period had, since the early Renaissance, been forced to submit themselves to the pettiness of their master's whims. From the biographies of scholars and statesmen such as Pierpaolo Vergerio, Lorenzo Valla, and Giovanni Pontano, to name but three, the toughness of their endurance may be judged. Among Castiglione's distinguished contemporaries, Michelangelo, Ariosto, Machiavelli, Matteo Bandello, Pietro Aretino and Benvenuto Cellini complain, at times bitterly, about the caprices of their patrons, the wickedness of envious fellow-courtiers or diplomats, the physical discomfort of working conditions or living accommodation, the dangers of insanitary and plague-ridden cities, the perils of campaigning alongside untrustworthy allies in wars for which they had no enthusiasm. Yet all were willing to tolerate personal hardships in order to guarantee their own and their family's safety and avoid the uncivilised insecurity of life outside the court.

The personal discomfort of the individual courtier could not be separated from the tragic overall situation in the peninsula. Tasso's cries for order and peace, in his famous letter to Maurizio Cattaneo of 1592, sum up the attitude of the century and help to explain his own eulogy of the benevolent despot and his particular support for the notion of the Divine Right of Kings: their rights are divine because they are peacemakers. 'If order is the supreme and most intrinsic blessing in the universe, consequently peace-making is one cause of its perfection and hence holds the highest place in the deeds of those who govern the world, and the peacemaker is like God.' A century before those words were written, the fortunate courtier did not have to be so sycophantic. Matteo Maria Boiardo, for instance, regarded his own era, until 1494, at least, as seeing the return of the golden age of chivalry. He concluded that the period between the decay of the medieval feudal system and the rise of his own semi-feudal superiors in contemporary Ferrara was an unwholesome one, characterised as it had been by chaotic internecine struggles in the peninsula. He praised to the heights, then, the disciplined legality of the old feudal system which he considered was making a return during his lifetime: 'Now the evil storm and that winter is over, and the world is flowering with virtue again' (*Orlando innamorato*, II, i). Even the realist Francesco Guicciardini, analysing the final decade of the fifteenth century in his *Storia d'Italia*, shows himself unusually nostalgic about the condition of Italy at that time, characterised, he says, by 'unprecedented prosperity... peace and tranquillity... economic and agricultural progress... profitable trade... magnificent princes... splendid cities... solemn religious attitudes... outstanding intellects and artistic talents and justifiably famous in the eyes of other nations' (*Storia*, I, i). Guicciardini's nostalgia, as he gazes on an Italy broken and ruined by foreign invaders, is understandable, and he surely idealises the picture rather more than one might expect of such a hardheaded pragmatist, but there is no denying the vast change in atmosphere after the inroads of the French. It was dramatically illustrated by Boiardo's poem, which reflects for most of its length an idyllic existence, interrupted in mid-flow by the French expeditionary force bound for Naples in 1494; it was noted with regret in Castiglione's letter to Jacopo Boschetto; it is recorded with pathos by Federico Fregoso in the *Cortegiano* (II, xxvi).

One important consequence of the change was a stricter adherence to dynastic succession. It is hard to believe that, only a century before Louis XII entered Milan, Giangaleazzo Visconti, whose power encompassed most of Italy, had so little thought for dynastic succession that his will divided his possessions equally between his children; or that fifty years later Filippo Maria Visconti had made no provision for a successor, and Milan was thus effectively forced to become a republic. After 1500, however, the combination of foreign influence (which tended to maintain the status quo), and society's stricter moral codes (which ensured that dynastic succession went to legitimate children) meant that there could henceforth be no guarantee of the individual ruler's competence for command. Indeed the successor to a dynasty might be an infant or a lunatic. Under such circumstances, the institution of preceptor to the ruling prince (Castiglione's primary definition of his courtier) was more important than ever before. With few exceptions, if an infant or a lunatic were to rule, it was largely because of the *éminence grise* behind the throne. Mazarin and Richelieu, Wolsey and Thomas Cromwell, Metternich and Bismarck and a hundred other courtiers influenced the course of history more decisively than their regal 'superiors'. Natural selection, after 1500, operated, not for the ruler but for his courtiers. Castiglione anticipated that development with the foresight of genius.

Matteo Bandello issues frequent warnings in his *Novelle* on the precariousness of the courtier's position. He is a valuable witness, for a while an adopted fellow-citizen of Castiglione's and, according to his own account, a personal friend of the latter's family. His tale of Artaxerxes and the seneschal Ariabarzanes allows him to give a long aside on the capricious favours of princes, which better than any data sums up the situation: 'Similarly you will see in the courts of kings and princes a courtier who enjoys his lord's full favour. It may be that the prince can do or say nothing without him, and yet, when the said courtier strives his hardest and tries his utmost to maintain or increase his lord's favour, what happens? The prince's mind changes and is turned towards another, and the person who was previously the first man at court finds himself, in a twinkling, the most abject. Next, there may be another courtier, diligent and solicitous in his service, well-versed in all the practices of courts, a man who takes more thought for his master's affairs than for his own life, but all his attention is in vain, since he is never rewarded and grows old in unrequited service. You may see another, most learned in every and any science, yet at court he dies of hunger, where another, an ignoramus, perhaps, without any virtue, is loaded with riches by his master out of caprice rather than because of merit. That doesn't mean that men of learning and virtue are obnoxious to the prince (for he may favour and exalt many such) but it happens because certain people are not congenial to him, and, as the saying goes, "Their blood is unsuited"' (*Novelle*, I, ii). And in this tale of patience and faith unrewarded, Ariabarzanes is sustained by his courtly training and self-discipline, and his story ends on a note of rejoicing.

Bandello's tale might, with minor variations, be applied to Castiglione's own experiences. His ordeals and anxieties as a courtier fell into two main categories: the trivial tasks, beneath such a man's dignity, which we know from his letters he had to undertake on behalf of his patrons, especially Federigo Gonzaga (who, at the time was half Castiglione's age), and the major diplomatic negotiations where failure meant disaster. Thus we find him writing long and complex racing reports largely aimed at excusing the failure of the Mantuan horses in the Roman *Palio*, or seeing to the repair or adjustment of a harness, buying trinkets and horse-brasses, acquiring cloth

for his men's livery, ordering his own tent, ensuring loans for unworthy masters who rarely repaid them, notable among them,
Francesco Maria della Rovere. On the diplomatic front, among many
nerve-racking trials, was the period 1521-2, when, as we have seen,
he had to struggle hard to obtain ratification of Federigo Gonzaga's
appointment as leader of the papal forces. His task was made more
difficult because of the interregnum between Popes Leo and Adrian,
during which he had to obtain funds for a largely anti-French
campaign from a College of Cardinals which included a formidable
French element in their ranks. In Rome the plague was raging (and
two of Castiglione's servants died as a consequence) but he was
forbidden by Federigo Gonzaga to leave before the election of the
new Pope and the confirmation of his master as papal commander.
When Adrian VI was elected, he seemed willing to provide papal
funds only to finance a crusade against the Turks. Castiglione eventually succeeded in his diplomatic objective though the process took
two horrifying years and was almost undone when Adrian died after
only one year on the papal throne.

Trivial vexations and mental exhaustion of the type noted above
were an everyday experience for Castiglione. They were part of the
compromise, payment for the benefits of belonging to a relatively
stable environment and for the blessings of being reassured of his
family's security back in Mantua. There were always tragically bitter
instances of noblemen who had somehow lost that protection. Perhaps the most outstanding example of such an unfortunate, from the
point of view of Castiglione and his *Cortegiano*, was the friend from
Urbino days, Ottaviano Fregoso. He was captured by the Imperial
troops of Charles V in 1522 and handed over to the Marchese di
Pescara. Notwithstanding the pleas of Castiglione himself and despite
influential letters from the Urbino court, notably from the Duchessa
Elisabetta, whose nephew Fregoso was, he died in captivity two years
later. I believe that Castiglione's eulogy on his old friend's death is
one of the most deeply-felt pieces of writing in the *Cortegiano*. It
occurs in the dedicatory letter to De Silva, which Vittorio Cian dates
to the spring of 1527, perhaps the time of Castiglione's greatest
tribulation. He might there be writing his own epitaph. Here it is in
full:

> Morto è il signor Ottavian Fregoso, omo a' nostri tempi
> rarissimo, magnanimo, religioso, pien di bontà, d'ingegno,
> prudenzia e cortesia e veramente amico d'onore e di virtù e tanto
> degno di laude, che li medesimi inimici suoi furono sempre

constretti a laudarlo; e quelle disgrazie, che esso constantissima-
mente supportò, ben furono bastanti a far fede che la fortuna,
come sempre fu, così è ancor oggidì contraria alla virtù
(Dedicatory letter, i). [Ottaviano Fregoso is dead. This man was
a rare spirit of our time, magnanimous, religious, full of goodness, wisdom, prudence and courtesy, the true friend of honour
and virtue and so worthy of esteem that his very enemies were
forced to praise him always. And those afflictions which he bore
with such great fortitude were enough to testify that fortune is
today, as ever, the opponent of virtue.]

Only the Duchessa Elisabetta receives anything like the praise
which Fregoso is given here. The tribute becomes more personal and
moving when one considers that nine of the other Urbino courtier-
friends had also died in the period 1508–27, and their deaths are duly
recorded in the dedicatory letter, but in Fregoso's particular case,
Castiglione seems to be reflecting on the man's isolation from a protected environment, which, combined with his bad luck, had made
his downfall more wretched. The elegiac tone of Castiglione's fare-
well to his friend is universalised by his introducing that concept of
fortune's adversity. No matter how powerful the monarch, how
clever the philosopher or how brilliant the artist, there could be no
guarantee that ill-luck, in some form or other, might not prevent the
flowering of the individual's talents. Baldesar had experienced enough
tragedy in his life to be keenly aware that man could take nothing for
granted and that the only certainties in life were uncertainty and
death. Francesco Guicciardini beautifully sums up the spirit of the
time when he writes: 'When I consider the number of accidents, the
risks of infirmity, ill-luck and violence to which human life is subject,
when I consider the many concomitants necessary throughout a year
to ensure a good crop, I never cease to be amazed to see an old man or
a fertile season' (*Ricordi*, CLXI). The tragic threats which surrounded
the greatest figures and the greatest works of the Italian Renaissance
were the brevity of life and the uncertainty of privilege and status.
Castiglione knows that his plans may be overwhelmed by the
vagaries of fortune, yet the very opposition of reason to the blindness
of fate and his assertion of human will are, in themselves, some
consolation.

Leaving aside the period of Castiglione's youth and adolescence
(and he himself implied that happiness is hardly appreciable by the
young), we are left with eight years in the service of Guidubaldo and
perhaps five years spent with his wife and family at Mantua, which

have a slight claim to be considered happy. Those few years of happiness were shaded by tragedy: the untimely deaths of his father, of Duke Guidubaldo, of Ippolita and of many friends. Yet in this atmosphere of personal sadness and of 'national' disaster and instability. Castiglione seems tranquil. His handbook has for centuries suggested calm, harmonious perfection, and has been assessed, rightly or wrongly, as presenting an unruffled Platonic ideal of behaviour, akin to Bembo's model of language or Michelangelo's image of beauty. His ideal, however, is only incidentally such. His principal aim is practical and stoic, his main contention that the Delphic μηδὲν ἄγαν is the only tolerable norm. The final discourse, put into Bembo's mouth, with its emphasis upon the virtues of stoic continence and Christian self-denial, lends to the advice given throughout the *Cortegiano* a meaning beyond its apparent superficiality or triviality. 'This is how to make life tolerable', Castiglione is saying in the early part of his book, 'and these activities may also provide essential social advancement, but without the tranquillity which stoic and Christian values produce, then my advice is incomplete.' The book has many facets but all else is incidental to Castiglione's main purpose of creating, in a fiercely, and sometimes bloodily competitive world, an oasis of tranquillity where the beauty of some of man's greatest cultural achievements may be enjoyed. He offered hope. On his pages the sensitive and intelligent individual who did not wish merely to adjourn to a cloister could find a solution to his dilemma and achieve serenity.

# Appendix : The Minor Works

After the splendour of the *Cortegiano*, Castiglione's minor works, the *Rime*, the *Tirsi*, the *Encomium* of Guidubaldo and the Latin *Carmina*, come as an anticlimax. Maier goes as far as to declare that, 'It is enough to accord them only a brief mention, given their rather minimal importance (*piuttosto scarsa importanza*), especially compared with the masterpiece' (ed. cit., p.41). And, indeed, if one stresses the importance of the minor works for the further insight they give us into Castiglione's life and for the information they add to our assessment of his masterpiece, the result is, inevitably, to play down any artistic merit they may have. It is tempting to dismiss his minor works as inferior, but this is not entirely justifiable since much research still remains to be done, even after five centuries, into his unpublished work, research for example on a vernacular *canzoniere*. On the other hand, to praise his vernacular poetry as lavishly as Serassi, or to exalt his Latin compositions as he and Gravina did, is to exaggerate the other extreme. Here, too, some sort of reassessment is necessary, but, regrettably, space permits here only the briefest mention of his *opere minori*.

Apart from his reputation as the author of the *Cortegiano*, Castiglione was regarded by his contemporaries and immediate successors as a major literary figure for his other compositions. It is to be hoped that work will proceed on the task of publishing an adequate edition of these hitherto rare or unpublished minor works. Carlo Dionisotti has given a good indication of the value of such research, if for no other reason because of the further light it may cast upon the rest of his life and achievements. As things stand, the traditional selection of his poetry, ten sonnets and four *canzoni*, published by Serassi and reproduced by Maier, gives the impression of compositions by an unenthusiastic versifier, typical of so many fashionable Renaissance sonneteers. The *Rime* contain few, if any, original thoughts, and their heavy reliance upon direct quotation from Petrarch (without, that is, any notion of dynamic imitation) emphasises how little personal inspiration they contain. Thus, in the 227 lines of the four *canzoni*, there are some sixty more or less direct quotations from Petrarch, which vary in importance from entire lines, lifted whole from his *Canzoniere*, to traditional phrases and conceits. And each of the ten sonnets contains at least five major quotations from Petrarch. Even artistically then, and even taking into account the personal and emotional detachment which was so necessary to the Renaissance sonneteer, Castiglione seems to have been content with uncreative imitation.

The first sonnet may be seen as typical of several and serves as a good example here. The poet requests the traditional recompense of grace (*mercede*) from his lady, while the sight of the burning flame (*fiamma ardente*) in his face, the river (*fiume*) pouring from his eyes, consumed as he is by ice and fire (*or ghiaccio or foco mi consume*) reveal his state. Serassi's comment, 'that the sonnet is splendid (*bellissimo*) and that this is a beautiful and novel way (*vaga e nuova maniera*) of describing the acts of an impassioned lover' provides rather a comment upon the dearth of poetry in the mid-eighteenth century and upon Serassi's over-enthusiastic attitude, which continues in his criticism of the other poems published by him. The lines are, instead, more reminiscent of the satirical use made of such Petrarchism by the anti-Petrarchists, or even by Ariosto in such an episode as that of Sacripante and Angelica (*Orlando furioso*, I).

Carlo Dionisotti has published two further sonnets which reinforce the notion of courtly Petrarchism (*Review*, cit., p.43), as well as the important *Cesare mio, qui sono ove il mar bagna*, which helped to prove that Castiglione was campaigning with Francesco Gonzaga around Naples in 1503. Dionisotti also unearthed the sonnet which Castiglione wrote on the death of his brother, in which personal emotion is typically held in firm literary control, and, finally, the sonnet *Io dico spesso: Amor che dà tal vena* which he called 'a step forward in Italian Renaissance culture' (*una conquista nuova della cultura italiana del Rinascimento*), noting there an objective and dispassionate attitude to love, which is 'not simply deduced from Neoplatonic notions nor yet the mere echo of the Boccaccesque Petrarchism of the *Asolani*' (ibid., p.48). Yet, to judge by Castiglione's indifferent treatment of the fashionable façade of courtly love in Book III of the *Cortegiano*, one is forced to wonder whether he was seriously concerned with following this aspect of court fashion.

Just as, in the *Rime*, he seemed content to plagiarise Petrarch, without expending much mental effort on assimilating and readapting the traditional lyric, so he seems to have wasted little original thought on the language of his dramatic eclogue, the *Tirsi*, composed in cooperation with Cesare Gonzaga, for the Urbino carnival of 1506. The plot is made relevant to the occasion and situation and casts further light upon his attitude to the Urbino court, and more especially upon his own wide reading and erudition, but the language and phraseology resemble some *Gradus ad Parnassum*, rearranged to suit the current festival. Maier's edition documents the multitude of borrowings contained in the fifty-five octaves. Yet, of all the minor works, the *Tirsi* does help to illustrate some aspects of the *Cortegiano*, and it may be worth while to give a few more details here.

We have already noted that, during his time at the court of Ludovico Sforza, Castiglione might easily have been influenced by the cultural traditions of the Medici court, transmitted to Milan by the well-travelled scholars and poets whom Ludovico patronised. Bucolic compositions variously embraced under the head of *Eclogues* had been the fashion in Tuscany for fifty years past. The Neapolitan Sannazaro's *Arcadia* had relied heavily on the literary and linguistic traditions of the Tuscans, and, by its great success, had proved the immense popularity of the pastoral eclogue form. The appearance of the definitive edition of *Arcadia* in 1504 (preceded by earlier unfinished versions and by one pirated edition in Venice in 1502) coincided with a letter of Castiglione's to his mother, asking for his brother Girolamo to forward his copy of Poliziano's *Stanze volgari*, another indication of the cross-pollination of ideas immediately preceding his composition of the *Tirsi*. Further, Poliziano's formal structure of his play *Orfeo* could also have influenced him. The *Orfeo*, significantly, was performed for the first time in Mantua in 1480, while Poliziano was in self-imposed exile there following the Pazzi conspiracy of 1478. And it is also possible that Castiglione might have met Sannazaro when he accompanied Francesco Gonzaga to Rome and Naples in 1503.

The *Tirsi*, then, was a dramatic eclogue composed expressly for the carnival of 1506, had particular relevance for the Urbino court and has been traditionally considered interesting as being the allegorical prelude to another 'idyllic' existence – that of the court described in the *Cortegiano*. The setting is the countryside near Urbino, given a precise location by a mention of the Duchess Elisabetta out walking along the Metauro, the river which flows not far from the city. Action is almost non-existent; three shepherds, Iola, Tirsi and Dameta, and a chorus of shepherds who make a brief intervention, form the characters (Castiglione took the part of Iola and Cesare Gonzaga that of Dameta). Iola begins the performance with a lament on the cruelty of the nymph, Galatea, whom he loves with a hopeless passion. Tirsi arrives on the scene, drawn more immediately by the sound of Iola's song, but attracted also by the fame of the goddess. The Parnassian quality of Iola's song, the physical locality and the presence of this deity (in whom we are to recognise the Duchess), indicate that this is the court of Urbino. Dameta's offer to take Tirsi to the goddess and her court allows him the opportunity to describe the wonders of the place and his eulogy includes an identifiable group of courtiers, including Bembo, Ludovico da Canossa, Morello da Ortona, Giuliano de' Medici, Roberto da Bari and Giacomo di Sansecondo, as well as the Duchess and Emilia Pia. Presiding over this new Arcadia is Duke Guidubaldo, the *buon pastore*.

Bruno Maier's edition of the eclogue painstakingly notes the many debts which the poem owes to its predecessors, and the many echoes which reveal Castiglione's wide reading of the Classics, as well as the recurrence of Petrarchan conceits – antitheses abound, Galatea's beauty is as generic as that of any Petrarchan heroine, Nature and all her creations weep in sympathy with the forlorn Iola and there are many other echoes. The combination of sophisticated literary borrowings and of feigned rusticity leads to some inappropriate conceits such as the use of *latte stretto* to indicate the whiteness of Galatea's breast. Nevertheless the eclogue seems to have won the appreciation of the court and particularly of Pietro Bembo, who was presented with a copy of the play by the Duchess, and who refers to it in a letter as 'Castiglione's' eclogue. Perhaps more important from the point of view of the *Cortegiano* is the light which the eclogue may cast upon his attitude to the court, even in spite of the evident literary formality which is there present. Thus, when Iola hands over Tirsi to Dameta's guidance, he remarks upon the blessings of 'service': 'You know how service is a great boon' (*gran guadagno*). And the reciprocal relationship between master and servant is also hinted at in two *stanze*, the first of which mentions the good government of Guidubaldo (and stresses the need for a peace-maker): 'With us you may hope for eternal peace (*pace eterna*), and expect to shatter the snares and traps (*spezzar le insidie tante*) of wolves, thanks to a good shepherd (*mercé d'un buon pastore*) who governs the prosperous fields and blessed countryside' (*Stanza* 50). The second instance shows the chorus of shepherds, by whom we may understand the courtiers listed earlier, who pray that the 'goddess' may accept their tribute, promising to 'observe her holy ordinances' in the hope that their flocks may be renowned above all others. And in the *Canzonetta* of Iola, there may be more than a hint of Castiglione's awareness of the proximity of the emotions of sadness and joy, a theme which exercises him particularly in *Cortegiano*, II, ii, and of his stoic acceptance of that fact: 'Hence, since my love so offends me (*il mio ben tanto m'offende*), I shun remedies which might attenuate grief, fearing that suffering (*martiri*) and pleasure (*piacer*) are always close neighbours' (*Canzonetta*, ll. 11– 14).

The eulogies of his lord and master are continued in the encomium *Ad Henricum Angliae regem Epistola de vita et gestis Guidubaldi Urbini Ducis*, written after Guidubaldo's death to celebrate his great personal qualities in terms which recall the praise accorded to him in the dedicatory letter of the *Cortegiano*. A reference to the *Epistola* is perhaps contained in a parenthesis of the *Seconda redazione*: 'We have written more extensively of his abilities in some other part (or place)' (*più a llungo in qualche altra parte...*) (p.6). The letter, which was sent to Henry VII, is reproduced by Serassi (op. cit., II, pp.348– 359) and confirms what has been noted about Guidubaldo's personality. Perhaps the most important aspect, in view of Castiglione's apparent admiration for his master's stoicism (cp. above, p.65) is the allusion to that Christian resignation implied in Guidubaldo's final words, murmured to Baldesar just before he died: 'As long as I live this life, the black mud and the misshapen reed bind me around, and the slow-moving marsh and unlovely wave of Cocytus'. And that marvellously apt quotation from Virgil is probably an allusion to his stoic resignation, rather than, as Cian suggests, 'an instinctive reconciliation of things pagan and Christian' (*Un illustre nunzio*, p.195). Of further interest among the expected laudatory remarks is Castiglione's attribution to his dead master of the particular quality of decorum (*illud quod πρέπον Graeci vocant*), which he had seen eulogised in Cicero and which he himself exalts in one of the most important sections of the *Cortegiano* (cp. above, p.77), when he deals with his new concept of *sprezzatura*. Cian, followed by Maier, suggests that the *Epistola* points the way ahead to the rapport between prince and courtier to be elaborated in the future Book IV of the *Cortegiano*, but, if the letter has to be considered in relation to the masterpiece, it is more probably a general indicator of the need for stoicism, self-denial and other qualities, exalted not only in that fourth Book, but also throughout the rest of the work.

Castiglione seems to have been well known during his lifetime as the author of Latin *carmina*. In the long section which Cian devotes to the *Opere minori* in his monograph (a third as long again as his chapter on the *Cortegiano* proper) he provides useful documentation of the fortune of Castiglione's Latin poems, both during his lifetime and posthumously in collections of Latin poetry published during the following two centuries, up to and including Serassi's 'definitive' edition of nineteen *carmina* (two of them spurious) which was published in 1771. The majority of these poems seem typical of Castiglione the humanist, imitating in a fashionable manner the eclogues and elegies of Classical Latin. Serassi's *Adnotationes* are helpful in pinpointing his more obvious borrowings from the Classics, including such figures as Theocritus, Virgil, Lucretius, Propertius and Tibullus. And between them, Cian and Serassi have said more than needs to be said on the subject in this brief account. However, three of the compositions deserve particular mention here. *Alcon*, the eclogue written on the death of his friend, Falcone, and modelled on Virgil's fifth eclogue, is notable for the personal sentiments with which it concludes – feelings of sorrow, the genuineness of which seems confirmed by letters written home at the time of Falcone's death, in which Castiglione expresses a clear and sincere grief that he had lost a beloved companion (cp. Serassi, I, pp.23–24). Falcone's death seems to have been one more step on the road to Christian stoicism, and the distress visible in the final verses may be evidence of a lack of detachment which in later years would be concealed.

*Alcon* is elegiac in tone, and, indeed, might have been more suited for treatment in an elegy, a form which he later favoured, probably because the elegy was more congenial to his temperament than other genres. The laudatory notes of the elegy on the death of Raphael (*De morte Raphaelis pictoris*) and the essentially personal tone of the elegy in which he imagines his wife, Ippolita, writing to him, regretting his absence in Rome, the *Elegia qua fingit Hippolyten suam ad se ipsum scribentem*, are more in keeping with the traditional elegy form. Originally a song of mourning, the elegy was used for other purposes at an early stage in its development. Coleridge's observation that the elegy was the form of poetry natural to the reflective mind seems a fitting comment on the contemplative Castiglione's preference for the genre.

The Latin *Carmina* and the *Elegies* were perhaps the only backward glance in Castiglione's literary production. We may legitimately regard the *Cortegiano* as the forerunner of a hundred similar treatises and as the precept book for three centuries of diplomatic training; the dramatic eclogue, *Tirsi*, foreshadows the popularity of Tasso's *Aminta* and Guarini's *Pastor fido*, which, in their turn were to have such an immense influence on European pastoral poetry. His sonnets and *canzoni* are no better or worse than the vast majority of fashionable compositions which fill the pages of *litterati* throughout Europe for the next two hundred years following his death, and one sonnet, '*Superbi colli e voi sacre ruine*' has a rolling magnificence which overcomes its minor plagiaristic faults and sets it apart. His reply to Valdés is a foretaste of the Counter-Reformation's defence of the Roman Church, prophetic of a thousand similar works.

Serassi's two-volume edition of Castiglione's minor works and letters has provided generations of Italian critics with the raw material for their theorising (not to mention their editions). We have already noted the importance of Castiglione's letters, the usefulness (and some of the grace) of the sonnets which Carlo Dionisotti is still bringing to light. Perhaps in this the year of Castiglione's quincentenary more coordinated efforts may be made to carry out the implications of Serassi's motto of two centuries ago, '*Quidquid sub terra est in apricum proferet aetas*', and finish the work he so lovingly began. In particular it is to be hoped that the edition of the *Epistolario*, announced by G. La Rocca (see Bibliography) as forthcoming from Mondadori's presses under the editorship of Dante Isella, will fill a long-felt need.

ITEMS LISTED HERE have been of particular value in the present study and may provide useful indications for further reading on the specialised subjects they treat. Attention might profitably be drawn to the excellent bibliography appended by Erich Loos to his monograph, and to Ettore Bonora's edition, which contains the most up-to-date Italian bibliography. The *Enciclopedia italiana*, G. Treccani (Milan-Rome) has been used to verify dates. [*G.S.L.I.* = *Giornale Storico della Letteratura Italiana*]

1. *Works by Castiglione*

*Il libro del Cortegiano del Conte Baldesar Castiglione* (Venice 1528)

*Il Cortegiano del Conte Baldassare Castiglione, riveduto e corretto da Antonio Ciccarelli* (Venice 1584)

*Opere volgari e latine del Conte Baldessar Castiglione*, ed. G. A. and G. Volpi (Padua 1733)

*Il libro del Cortegiano del Conte Baldassar Castiglione, colla vita di lui scritta dal Sig. Abate Pierantonio Serassi* (Padua 1766)

*Delle lettere del Conte Baldassar Castiglione, con annotazioni storiche illustrate di Pierantonio Serassi* (Padua 1769/1771)

*Lettere* in *Raccolta di lettere sulla pittura, scultura ed architettura scritte da' più celebri personaggi dei secoli XV, XVI e XVIII*, ed. G. Bottari (Milan 1822)

*La seconda redazione del 'Cortegiano'*, ed. G. Ghinassi (Florence 1968)

*Lettere inedite e rare*, ed. G. Gorni (Milan 1969)

'Due lettere inedite di B.C.', ed. G. Gorni in *Strumenti critici* 7 (1969) 21–3

'Dieci lettere inedite di B.C.', ed. M. L. Doglio in *Lettere italiane* 33 (1971) 515–30

'Sette lettere di B.C.', ed. M. L. Doglio in *Studi in onore di A. Chiari* (Brescia) vol. I, 437–46

Other letters are to be found in the monographs of Julia Cartwright and G. Bongiovanni, in V. Cian, *Nel mondo di B.C.* (Milan 1942) and in G. Comisso's *B.C. Le più belle pagine* (Milan 1929). G. La Rocca indicates less accessible items in his article (see below for this and other references).

There have been many editions of the *Cortegiano*. Those of V. Cian (Florence 1894 and 1947, fourth ed.) and B. Maier (Turin 1964, second ed.) are well annotated and both have full lists of their predecessors in the task. Maier's edition also includes a good selection of Castiglione's minor works. Other editions published this century in Italy are by O. Bacci (Milan 1916), M. Scherillo (Milan 1928), G. Morpurgo (Milan 1932), M. Rigillo (Milan 1936), G. Prezzolini (Milan 1937), M. Luzi (Milan 1941), G. Preti (Turin 1960), C. Cordié (Milan 1960) and E. Bonora (Milan 1976).

Among notable and influential translations of the *Cortegiano*, of particular interest are those of Juan Boscán (Madrid 1534), Sir Thos. Hoby (London 1561), J. Colin (Lyons 1537) and G. Chapuis (Paris 1585).

Recently published English translations include those of C. S. Singleton

(New York 1959), G. Bull (London 1967 and 1976) and reprints of the Hoby translation (London 1928/1976/1978). L. E. Opdycke's translation (New York 1901) includes a good survey of previous editions.

## 2. Works specifically concerned with Castiglione

A. BONADEO, 'The function and purpose of the Courtier' in *Philological Quarterly* 50 (1971) 36–46

G. BONGIOVANNI, *B.C.* (Milan 1929)

G. BULL, 'Introduction' to the Penguin translation (London 1976)

J. CARTWRIGHT, *B.C., the Perfect Courtier. His Life and Letters* (London 1908)

V. CIAN, *La lingua di Baldassare Castiglione* (Florence 1942)
— *Un illustre nunzio pontificio del Rinascimento, B.C.* (Vatican 1951)

C. CORDIÉ, 'B.C.' in *Cultura e Scuola* 32 (1969) 17–24

A. DI BENEDETTO, 'Alcuni aspetti della fortuna del *Cortegiano* nel '500' in *G.S.L.I.* 148 (1971) 1–13

C. DIONISOTTI CASALONE, 'Recensione a *Un illustre nunzio pontificio*' in *G.S.L.I.* 129 (1952) 31–57

P. FLORIANI, 'La genesi del *Cortegiano*' in *Belfagor* 24 (1969) 373–85
— 'Esperienza e cultura nella genesi del *Cortegiano*' in *G.S.L.I.* 166 (1969) 497–529
— 'Idealismo politico del *Cortegiano*' in *Rassegna della Letteratura Italiana* 76 (1976) 43–52
— *Bembo e Castiglione, Studi sul classicismo del '500* (Rome 1976)

G. GHINASSI, 'L'ultimo revisore del *Cortegiano*' in *Studi di filologia italiana* 21 (1963) 217–64
— 'Fasi dell'elaborazione del *Cortegiano*' in *Studi di filologia italiana* 25 (1967) 155–96

J. GUIDI, 'Baldassare Castiglione et le pouvoir politique: du gentilhomme de la cour au nonce pontifical' in *Les Ecrivains et le Pouvoir en Italie à l'Epoque de la Renaissance*, ed. A. Rochon (Paris 1973) 243–78

G. LA ROCCA, 'Studi Castiglioneschi: Nuovi rinvenimenti archivistici di lettere, note e ignote di B.C.' in *G.S.L.I.* 102 (1975) 234–65

E. LOOS, *B. Castigliones 'Libro del Cortegiano', Studien zur Tugendauffassung des Cinquecento* (Frankfurt am Main 1955 – *Analecta Romanica* 1)

B. MAIER, 'B.C.' in *Letteratura Italiana – I Minori*, ed. A. Momigliano (Milan 1961)

W. A. REBHORN, 'Ottaviano's interruption: Book IV and the problem of unity in *Il libro del Cortegiano*' in *Modern Language Notes* 87 (1972) 37–59

M. ROSSI, *B.C. La sua personalità la sua prosa* (Bari 1946)

L. V. RYAN, 'Book IV of Castiglione's *Courtier* – Climax or Afterthought?' in *Studies in the Renaissance* 19 (1972) 156–79

G. TOFFANIN, '*Il Cortegiano* nella trattatistica del '500' (Naples 1961)

J. H. WHITFIELD, 'Introduction' to the reprinted Hoby translation (London 1976/8)

P. ZOCCOLA, 'Di un passo controverso del *Cortegiano*' in *G.S.L.I.* 151 (1974) 97–102

## 3. Medieval and Renaissance Source Material
L. B. ALBERTI, *Opere volgari*, ed. C. Grayson (Bari 1960–73)

P. ARETINO, *De le corti*, ed. G. Battelli (Lanciano 1914)
— *La Cortigiana*, ed. G. Petrocchi (Milan 1971)
SAN BERNARDINO DA SIENA, *Le prediche volgari*, ed. P. Bargellini
    (Milan 1936)
V. BORGHINI, 'Difesa del Boccaccio' in *Manuale della letteratura italiana*,
    ed. A. D'Ancona and O. Bacci (Florence 1918) vol. III 55–8
— *Storia della nobiltà fiorentina*, ed. J. R. Woodhouse (Pisa 1974)
L. BRUNI, *De studiis et litteris*, see under Garin, *L'educazione umanistica
    in Italia.*
V. COLONNA, *Carteggio*, ed. E. Ferrero and G. Müller (Turin 1889)
DOVIZI, Bernardo da Bibbiena (Il Bibbiena), *La Calandria*, ed. P. Fossati
    (Turin 1967)
L. EBREO, *Dialoghi d'amore*, ed. S. Caramella (Bari 1929)
M. FICINO, *Opera omnia* (Turin 1959, facsimile of 1576 ed.)
— *Commentaire sur le Banquet de Platon*, ed. R. Marcel (Paris 1956)
E. GARIN, *L'educazione umanistica in Italia* (Bari 1949) – includes selections
    from Salutati, Bruni, S. Bernardino, Vergerio, Palmieri, Alberti, as
    well as information on Vittorino and Guarino.
N. MACHIAVELLI, *Lettere*, ed. G. Papini (Lanciano 1915)
F. PETRARCA, *Opere*, ed. A. Bufano (Turin 1975) (vol. IV contains the
    *De ignorantia*)
E. S. PICCOLOMINI (PIUS II), *De curialium miseriis*, ed. W. P. Mustard
    (Baltimore 1928)
G. PICO DELLA MIRANDOLA, *De dignitate hominis* etc., ed. E. Garin
    (Florence 1942)
A. POLIZIANO, *Prose volgari inedite. Poesie latine e greche*, ed. I. del Lungo
    (Florence 1867)
P. POMPONAZZI, *Tractatus de immortalitate animae*, ed. G. Morra
    (Bologna 1954)
N. STROZZI, *Avvertimenti necessari per i Cortegiani*, ms. in the *Kunst-
    historisches Institut*, Florence, shortly to appear in print, catalogued
    K 783/17.
*Trattati del Cinquecento sulla donna* and *Trattati d'Amore del Cinquecento*,
    see Zonta.
T. TASSO, *Opere*, ed. B. Maier (Milan 1963–5) (vol. V contains *Il Malpiglio*)
— *Lettere*, ed. C. Guasti (Florence 1854)
P. P. VERGERIO, *De ingenuis moribus*, available in translation – see
    Garin; Woodward.
VESPASIANO DA BISTICCI, *Vite di uomini illustri del secolo XV*, ed.
    P. d'Ancona and E. Aeschlimann (Milan 1951)
G. ZONTA, ed. *Trattati d'Amore del Cinquecento* (Bari 1912)
— *Trattati del Cinquecento sulla donna* (Bari 1913)

4. *Critical works on the cultural background*
H. BARON, *The Crisis of the Early Italian Renaissance* (Princeton 1955/66)
— *From Petrarch to Bruni, studies in Humanistic and Political Literature*
    (Chicago 1968)
C. P. BRAND, *Ludovico Ariosto* (Edinburgh 1974)
J. BURCKHARDT, *The Civilisation of the Renaissance in Italy* (London 1960)

T.F.CRANE, *Italian Social Customs of the Sixteenth Century and their Influence on the Literature of Europe* (New Haven 1920 and 1971)

C.DIONISOTTI CASALONE, *Geografia e Storia della Letteratura Italiana* (Turin 1967)

— *Gli umanisti e il volgare tra Quattrocento e Cinquecento* (Florence 1968)

C.F.FAHY, *The Intellectual Status of Women in Italy in the later Sixteenth Century*, Ph.D. thesis, University of Manchester 1954

— 'Early Renaissance Treatises on Women' in *Italian Studies* 31 (1956) 31–55

E.GARIN, *Scienza e vita civile nel Rinascimento italiano* (Florence 1947)

— *L'educazione umanistica in Italia* (Bari 1949)

— *Il pensiero pedagogico dell'Umanesimo* (Florence 1958)

D.HAY, 'Italy and barbarian Europe' in *Italian Renaissance Studies*, ed. E.F.Jacob (London 1960)

— *The Italian Renaissance in its historical background* (Cambridge 1970)

R.KELSO, *The doctrine of the English Gentleman in the sixteenth century* (Urbana 1929)

— *The doctrine for the Woman of the Renaissance* (Urbana 1956)

A.J.KRAILSHEIMER (ed.) *The Continental Renaissance* (London 1971)

P.O.KRISTELLER (with E.CASSIRER and J.H.RANDALL jnr.), *The Renaissance Philosophy of Man: Petrarca, Valla, Ficino, Pico, Pomponazzi, Vives* (Chicago 1948)

— *The Philosophy of Marsilio Ficino* (New York 1943)

R.MARCEL, *M.Ficin* (Paris 1958)

G.MASSON, *Courtesans of the Italian Renaissance* (London 1975)

G.MATTINGLY, *Renaissance Diplomacy* (London 1955)

J.A.MAZZEO, *Renaissance and Revolution* (London 1967)

B.MIGLIORINI, 'La questione della lingua' in *Questioni e Correnti di Storia Letteraria* (Milan 1949)

N.A.ROBB, *Neoplatonism of the Italian Renaissance* (London 1935 and 1968)

D.J.B.ROBEY, 'P.P.Vergerio, Republican and Civic Virtues in the work of an early humanist' in *Past and Present* 58 (1973) 3–37

A.L.ROWSE, *The Elizabethan Renaissance. The Life of the Society* (London 1971)

L.RUSSO, *N.Machiavelli* (Bari 1957)

M.SANTORO, *Fortuna ragione e prudenza nella civiltà letteraria del '500* (Naples 1967)

F.SCHEVILL, *The Medici* (New York 1960)

P.A.STADTER, *Plutarch's Historical Methods: an analysis of the Mulierum Virtutes* (Cambridge Mass. 1965)

C.TRINKAUS, '*In our image and likeness.' Humanity and Divinity in Italian Humanist Thought* (London 1970)

L.VALMAGGI, *I cicisbei* (Turin 1927)

G.WEISE, *L'ideale eroico nel Rinascimento – diffusione europea e tramonto* (Naples 1965)

W.H.WOODWARD, *Studies in Education during the Age of the Renaissance* (Cambridge 1906)

— *Vittorino da Feltre and other Humanist Educators* (Cambridge 1897)